mother teresa: a life of dedication

Raghu Rai

HARRY N. ABRAMS, INC., PUBLISHERS

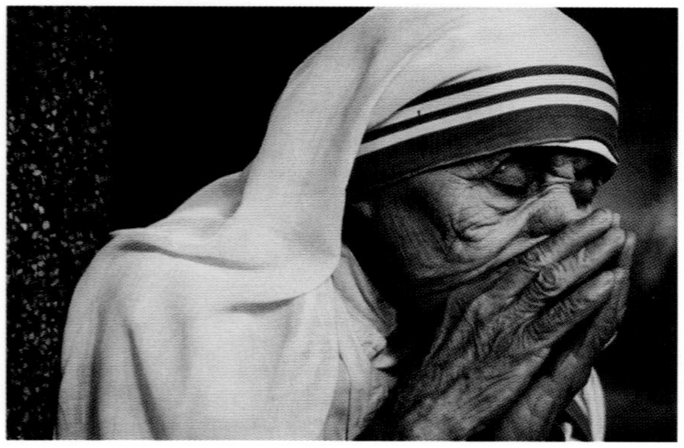

If we pray, we will believe
If we believe, we will love
If we love, we will serve.

—*Mother Teresa*

6 **the equality of prayer:** restoring us to ourselves

MOTHER, THESE PAEANS ARE FOR YOU.

Written in words, painted in photographs, their intensity is slave to moments of transformation; transformation through little marvels you revealed to me in your presence—your solitude, your silence. When was it, Mother, that I first ventured to suggest that I do a book on you?

The years have imploded. Was it in the fall of 1970 when we first met? I cannot remember. There were so many encounters as almost three decades sped by. Each time you were kind enough to see me for a day or two or a week.

I remember your initial reluctance and heard your silent reproaches. "No, not another book!" You were already a Nobel laureate. The Bharat Ratna was yours. The whole world loved you as you had loved it.

What was it about my persistence that finally made you relent, Mother? Had you sensed that I felt the urge to be close to your *sewa* (service) and the spirituality that illuminated your work? I admit to an uncanny feeling of purification, a connectedness in the presence of an energy that flowed from it.

I pleaded, "Yes, Mother! For me, also, it's not just another book. Every time I work on any 'other' project, I strongly feel that I should come back to you." And you answered, "Let me do my prayer and I shall let you know."

These words were your answer, Mother. In my mind, it was as if you were seeking divine acceptance. I sensed this intensely at that moment and said, "Mother, I have said my prayer and the answer is yes."

"Okay, we will do it," you responded. Almost immediately this touched the core of my very being. I saw clearly, for the first time, that you not only believed in the power of prayer, but also that you had an egalitarian sense about prayers. Yours were not above anyone else's.

After all, we are all equal in the eyes of our Divine Maker.

Mother, I remember you for this moment, not through words or through my camera but through your hands. Each time I met you, I would prepare myself mentally, physically, and spiritually. I still feel the energy flowing through your tender hands.

Those hands with which you held other hands as you did mine, your eyes looking deep into me, every time you restored me to myself.

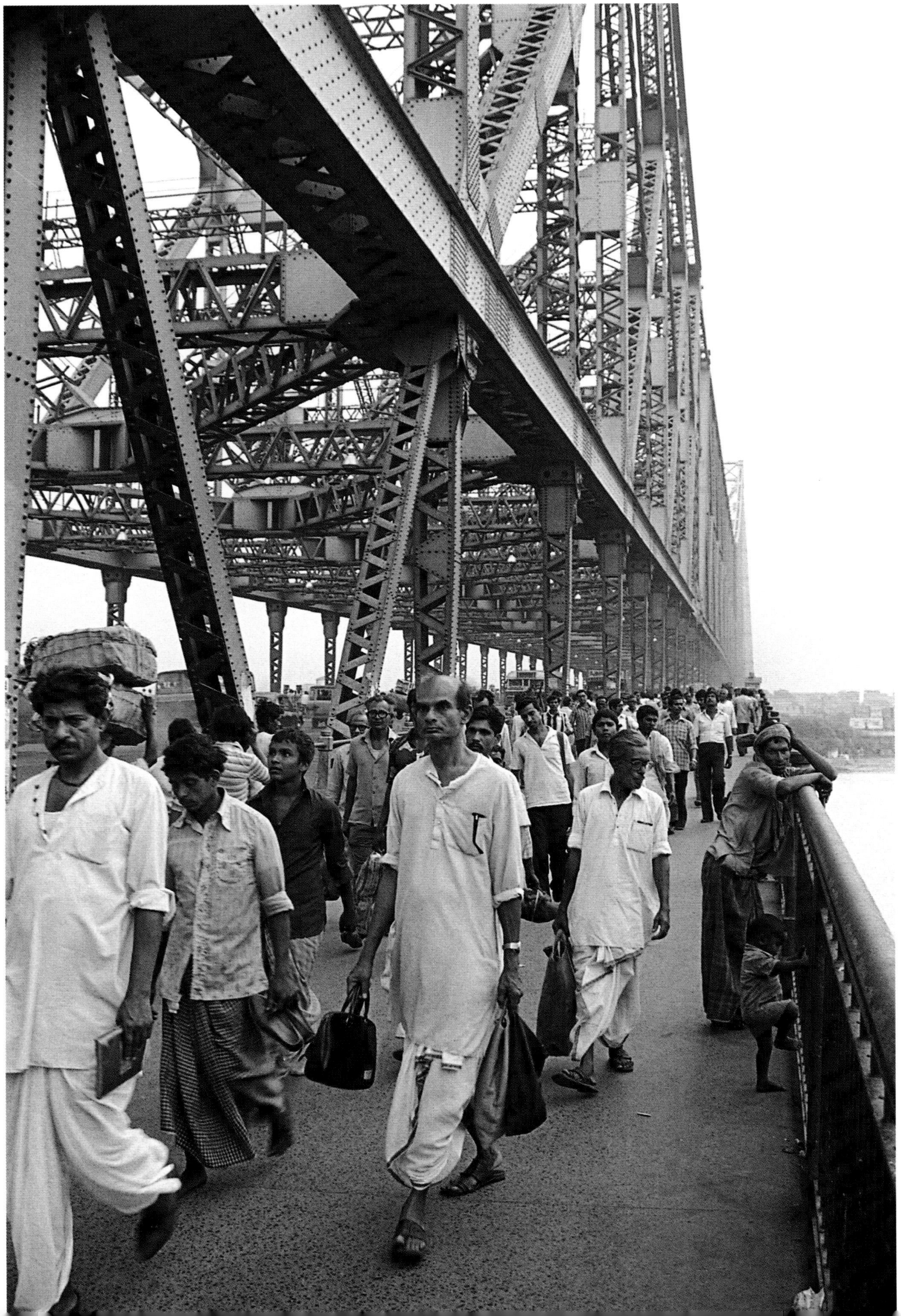

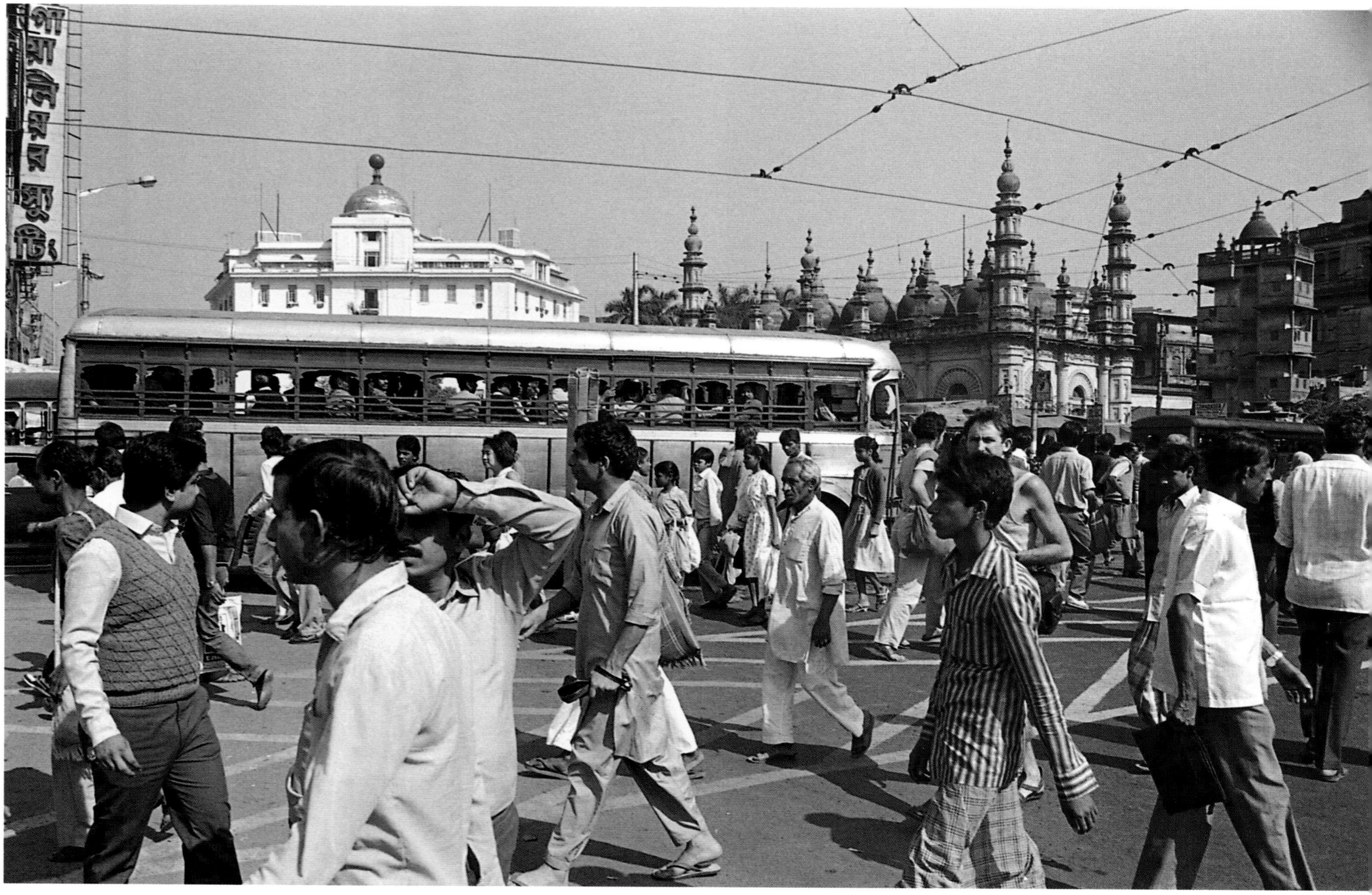

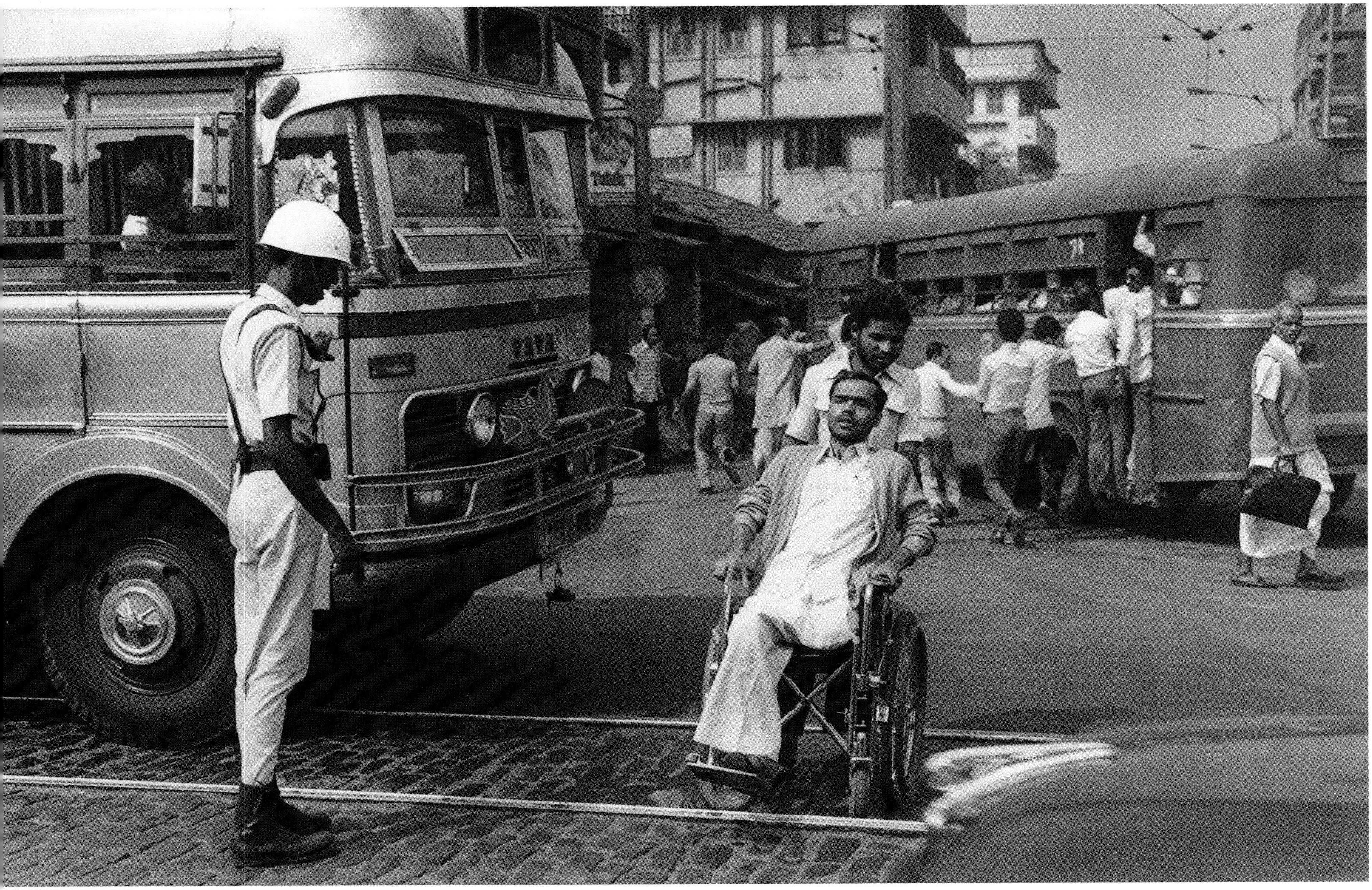

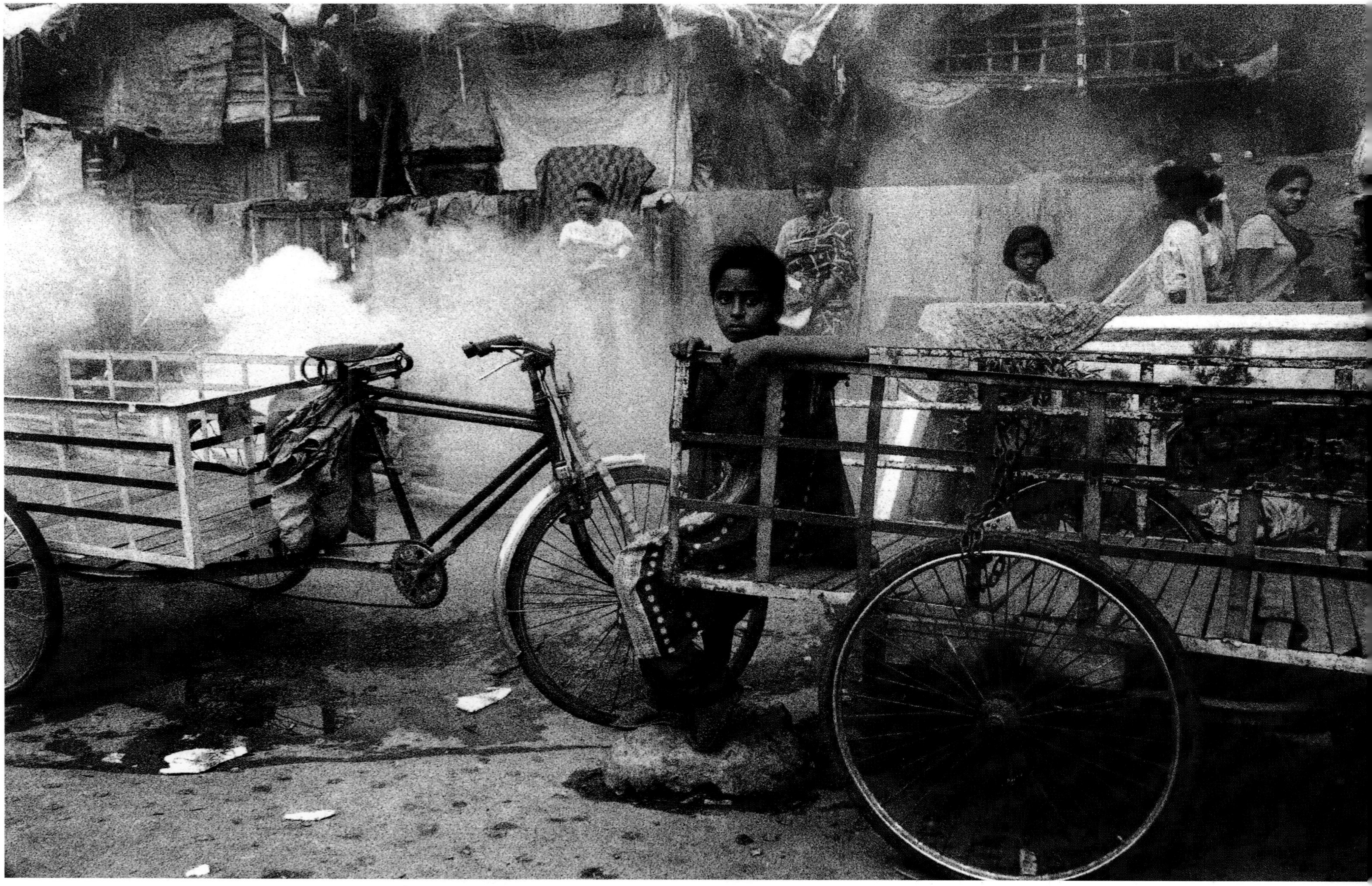

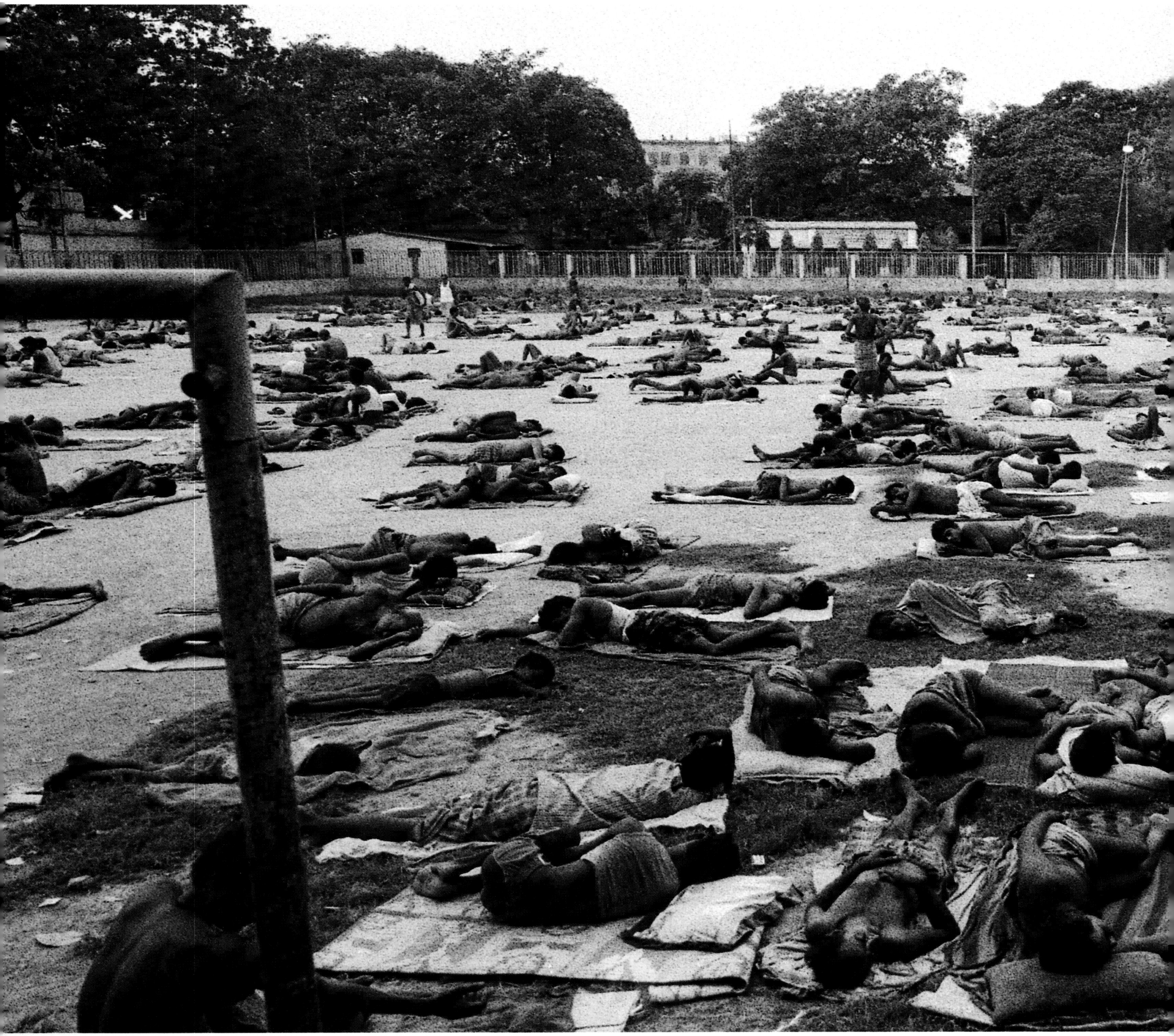

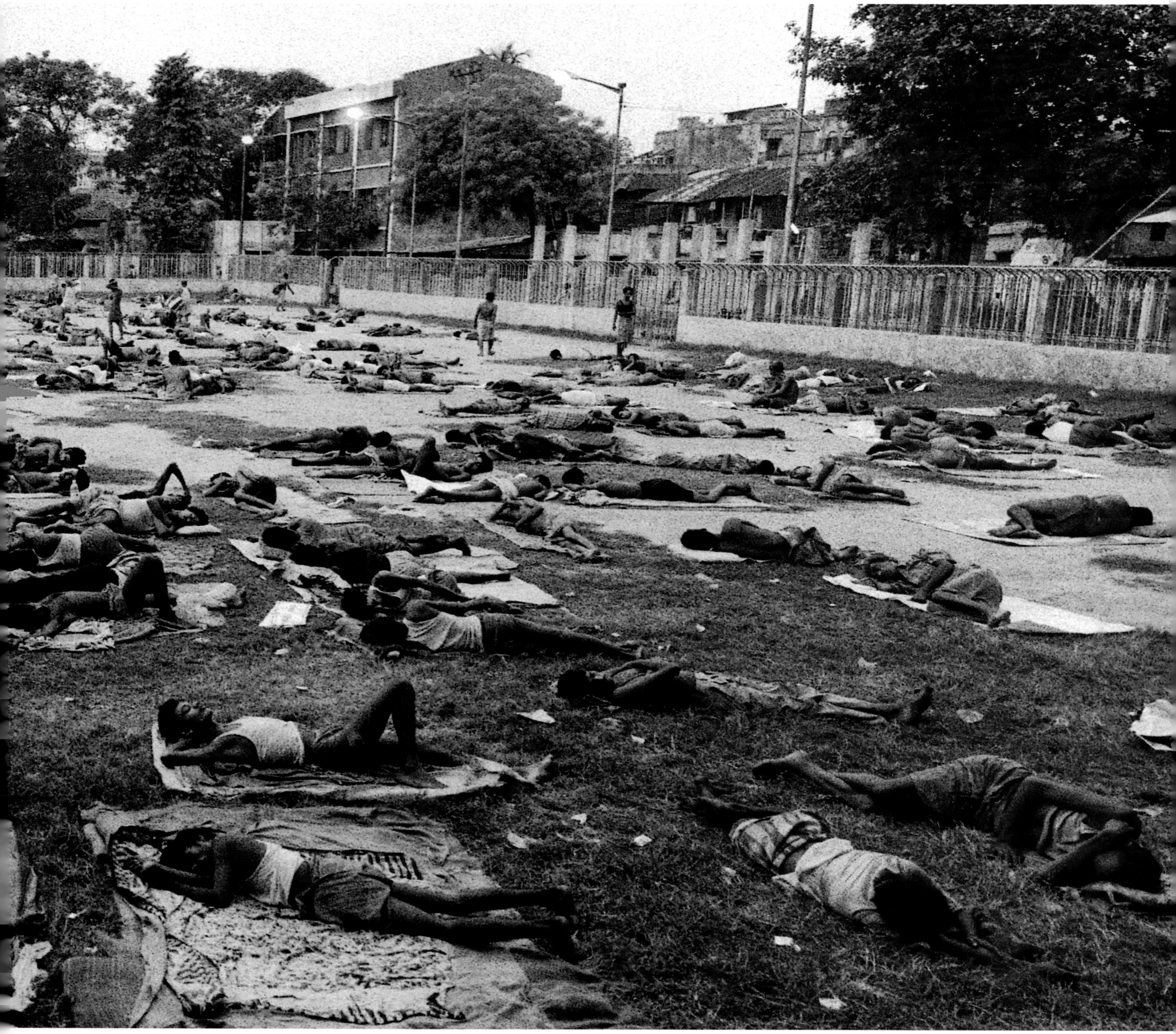

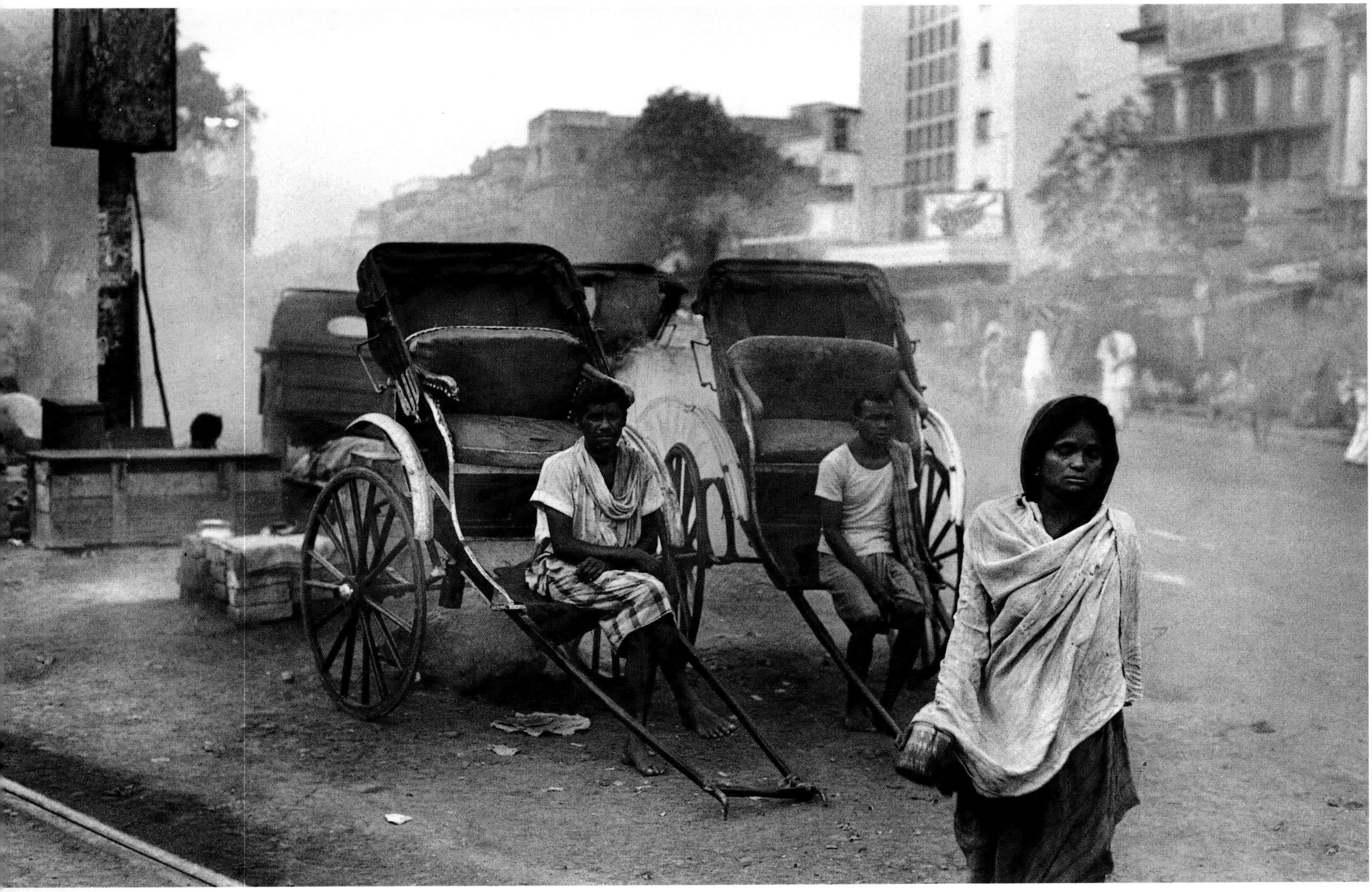

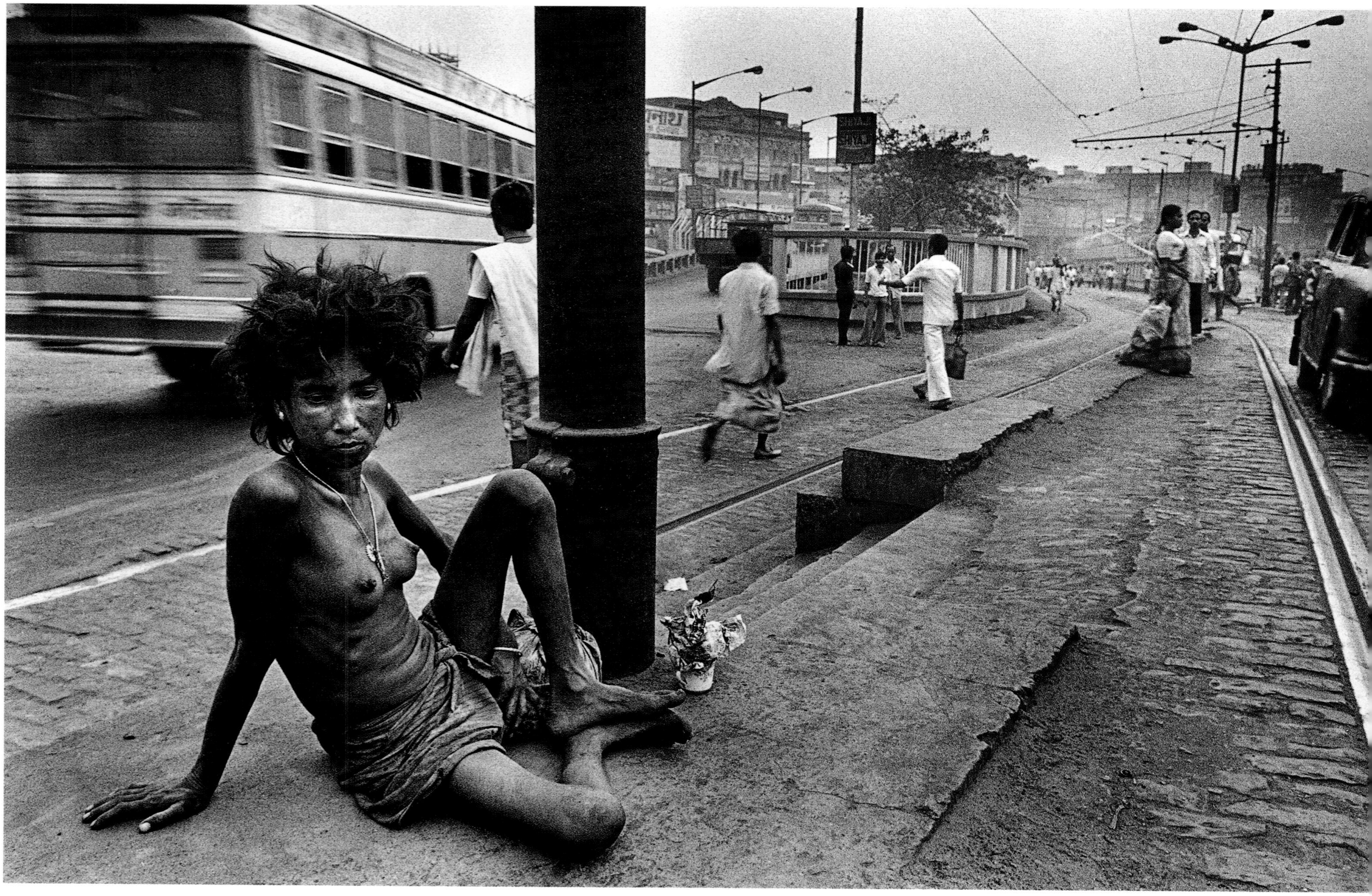

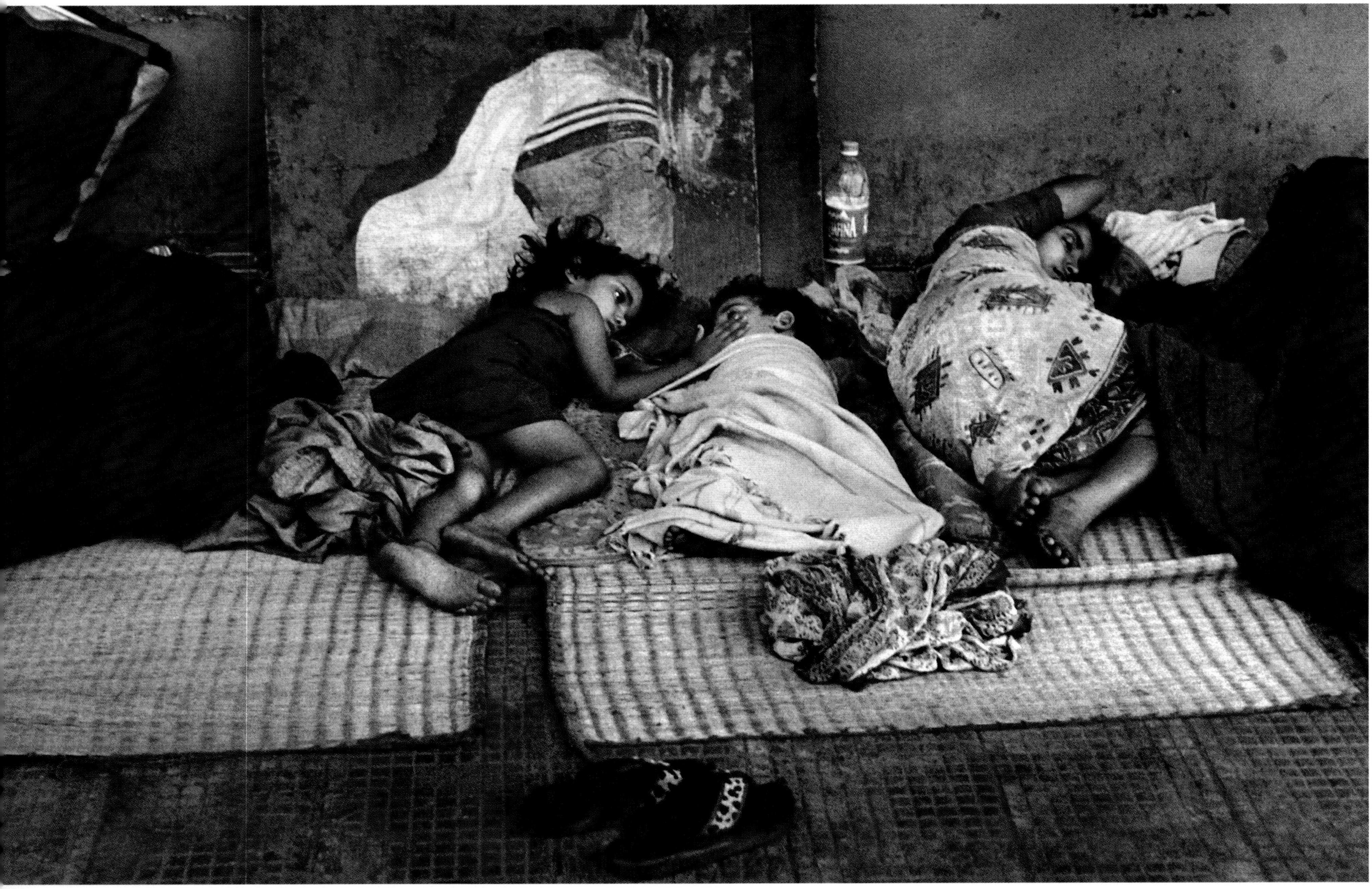

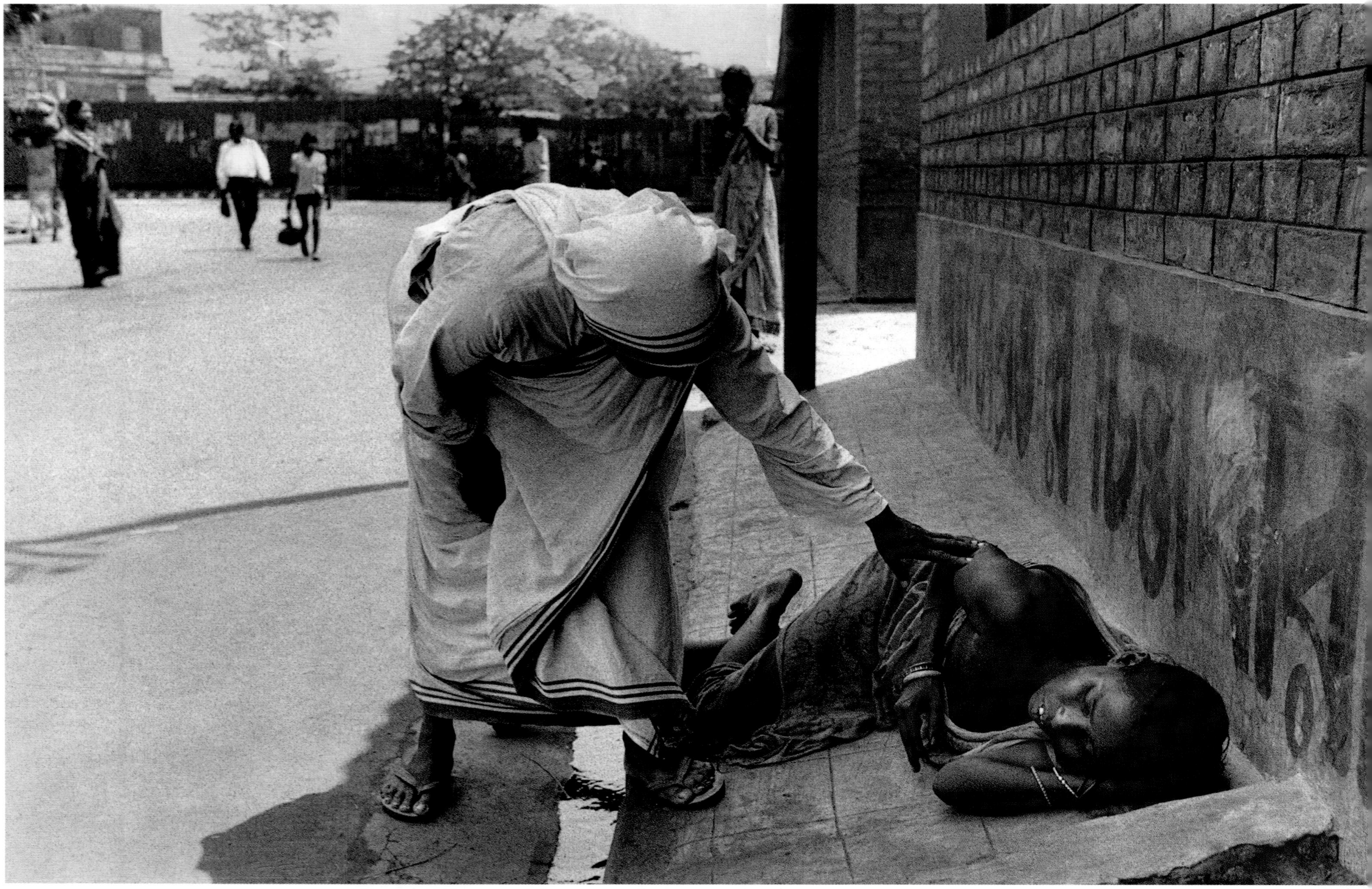

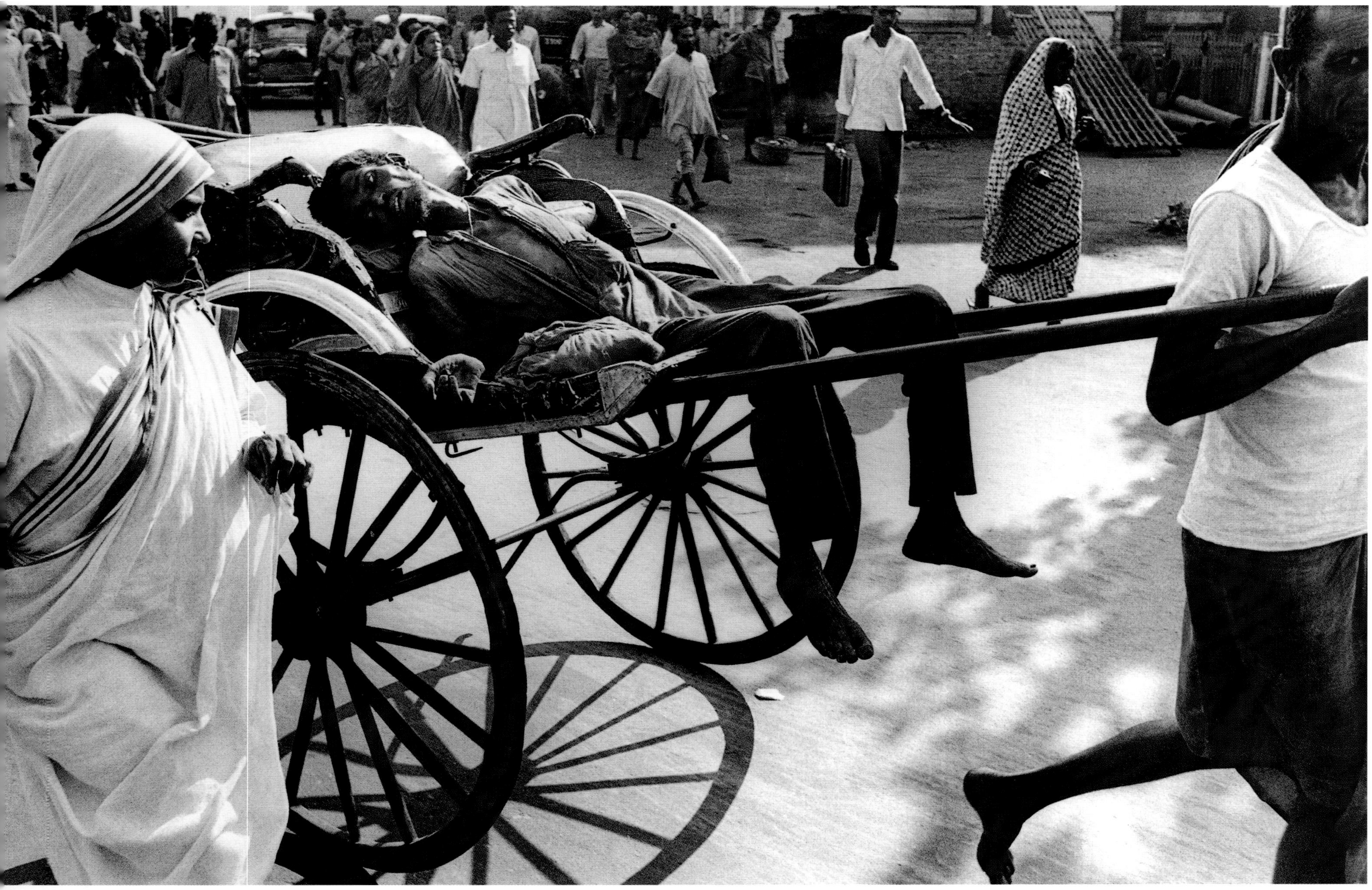

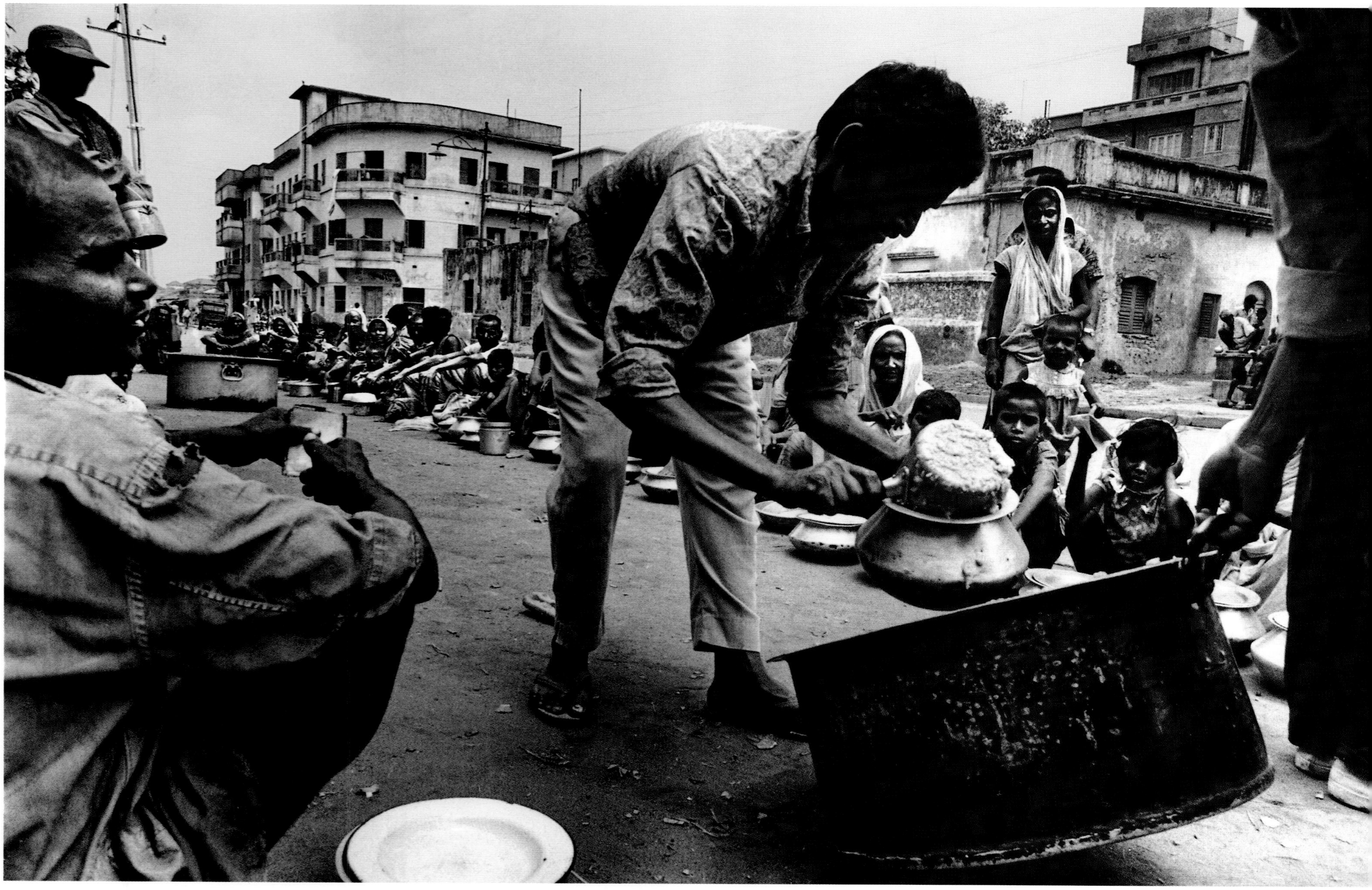

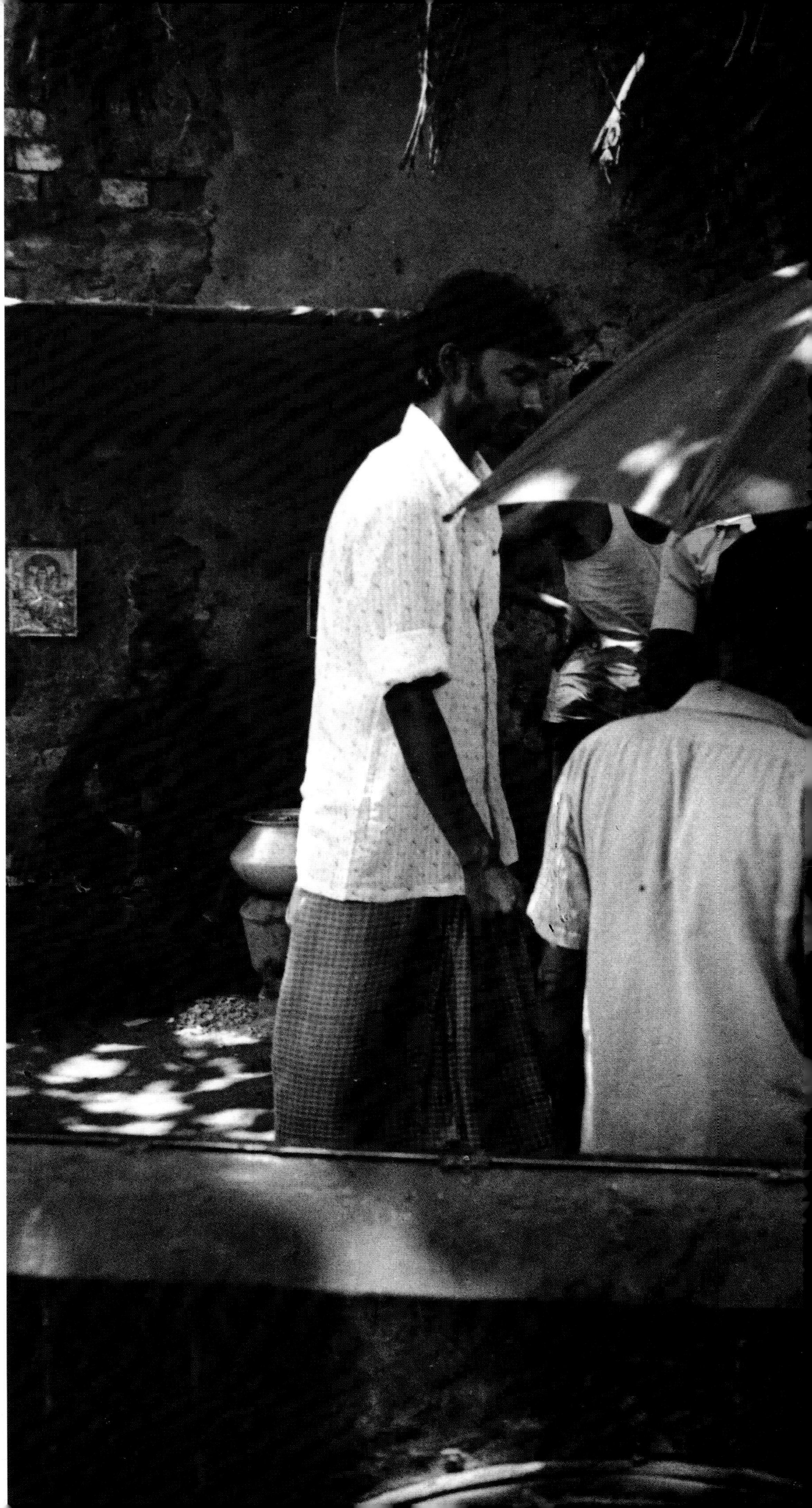

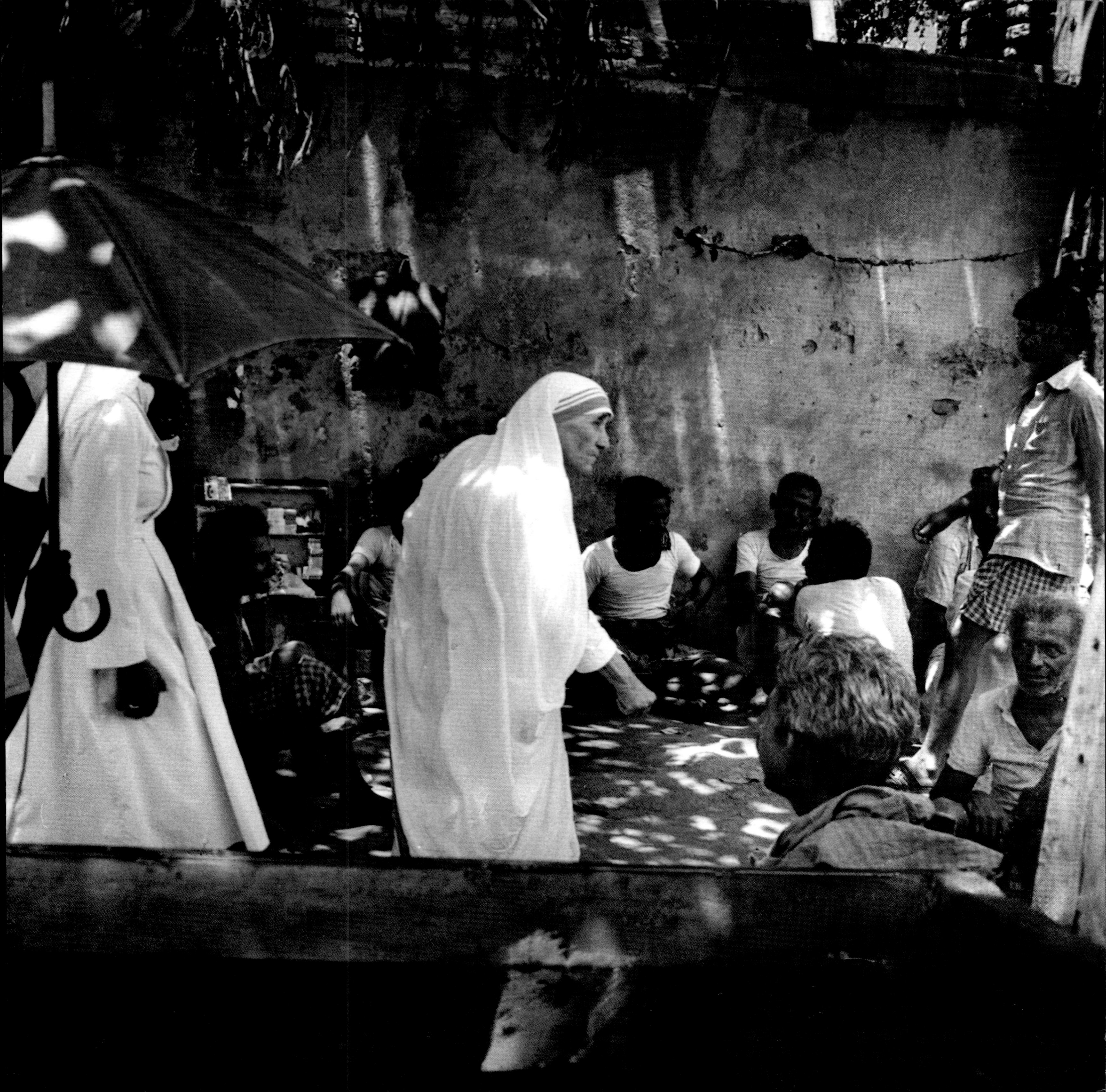

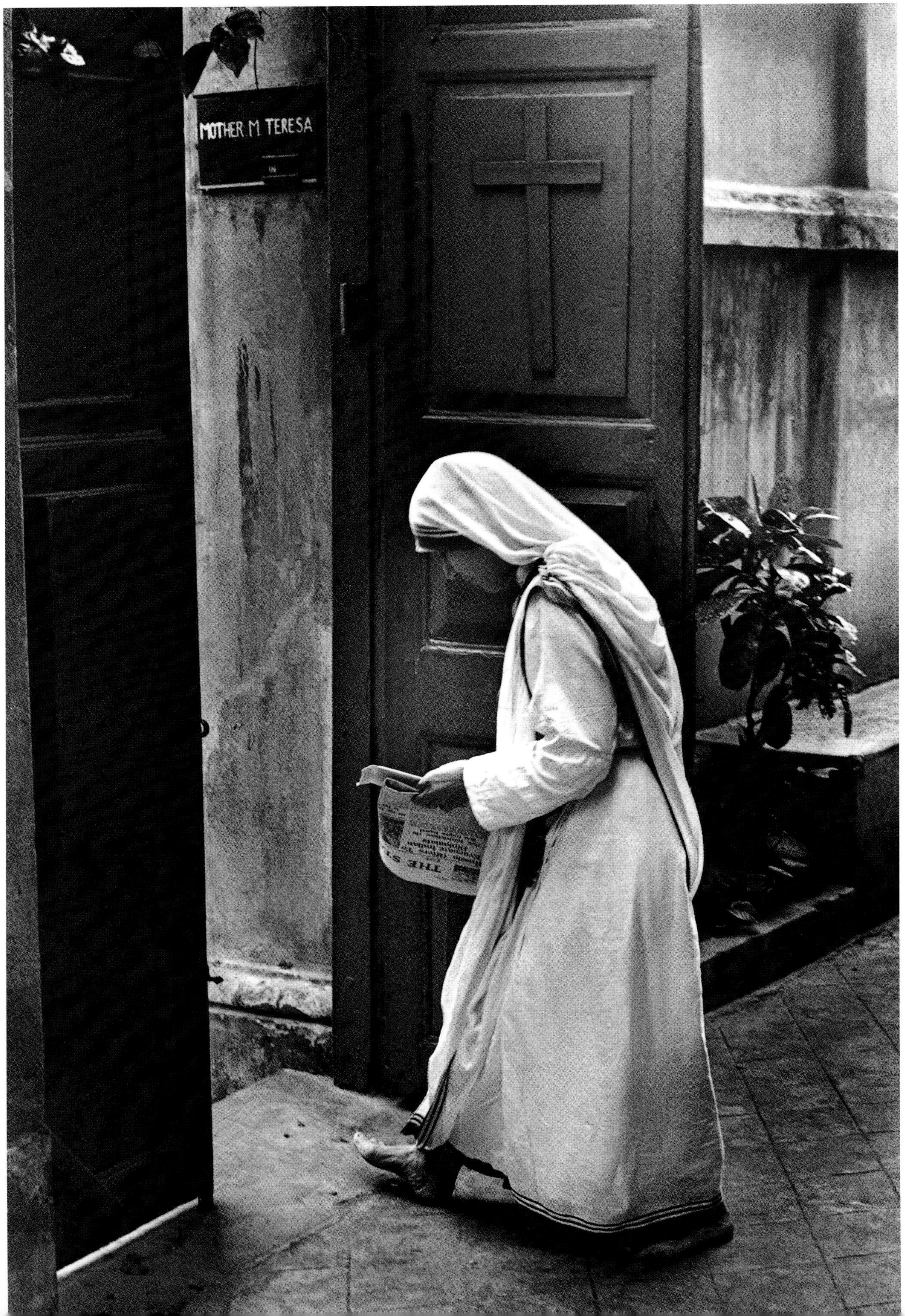
MOTHER M. TERESA

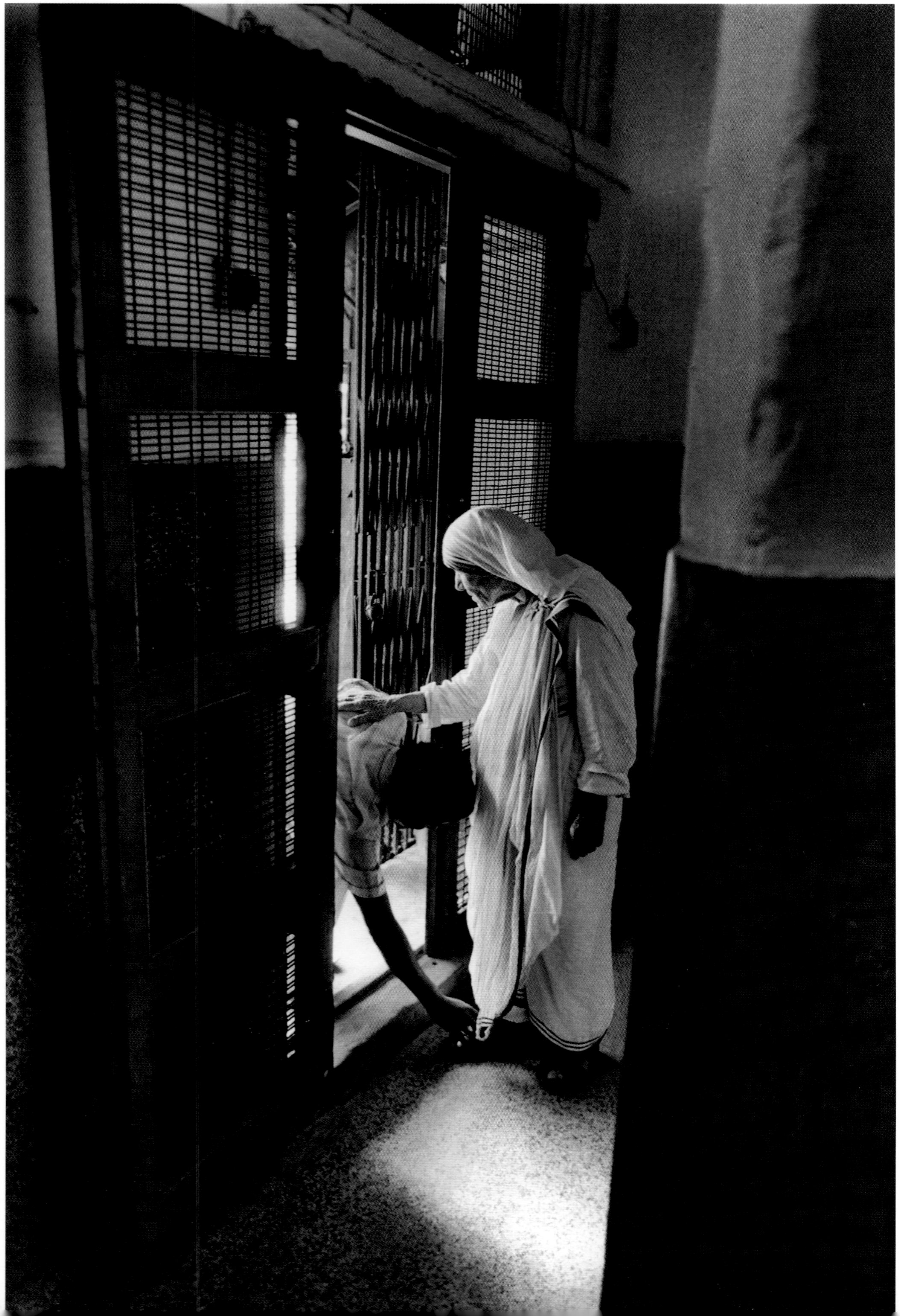

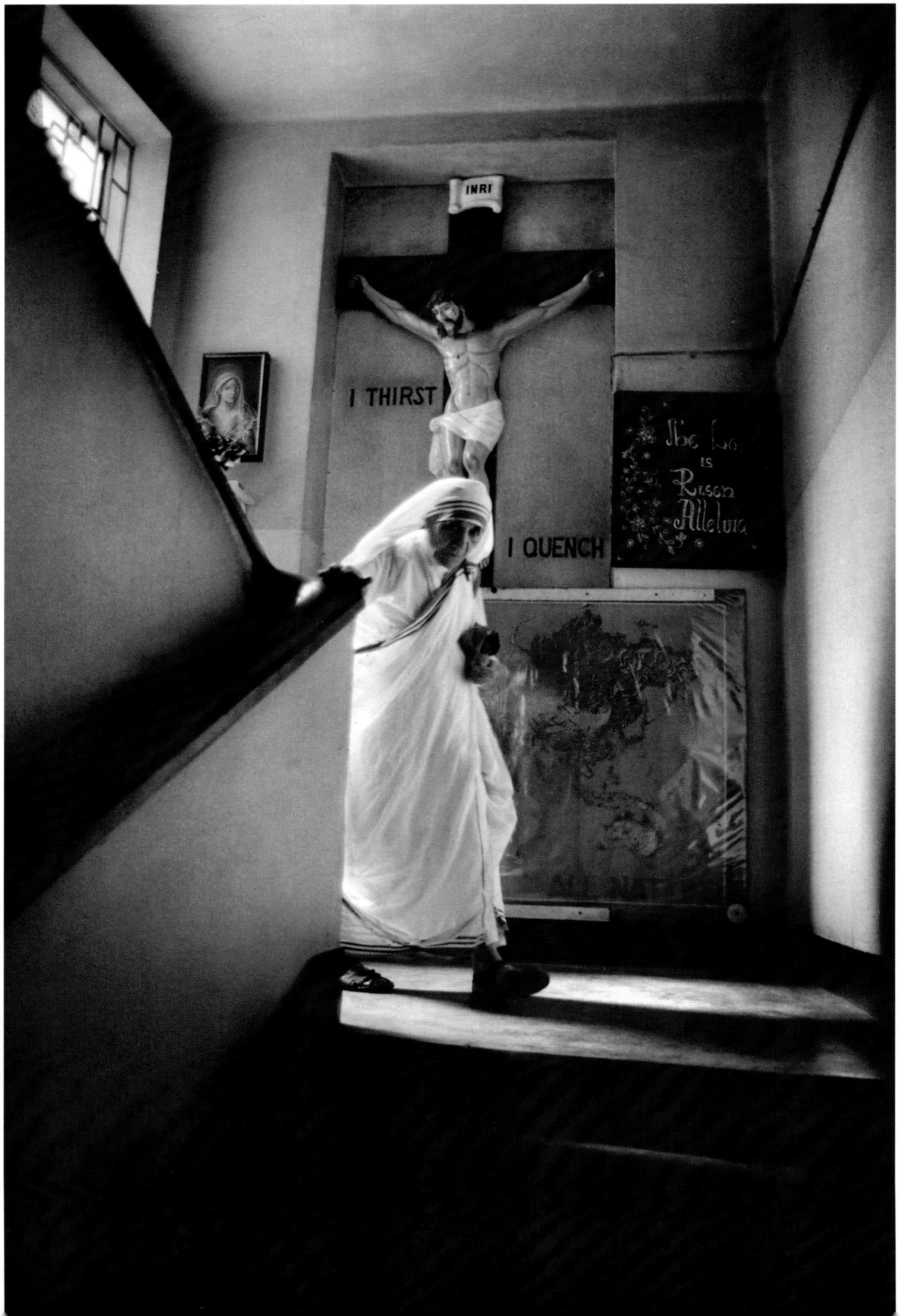
INRI
I THIRST
I QUENCH
is
Risen
Alleluia

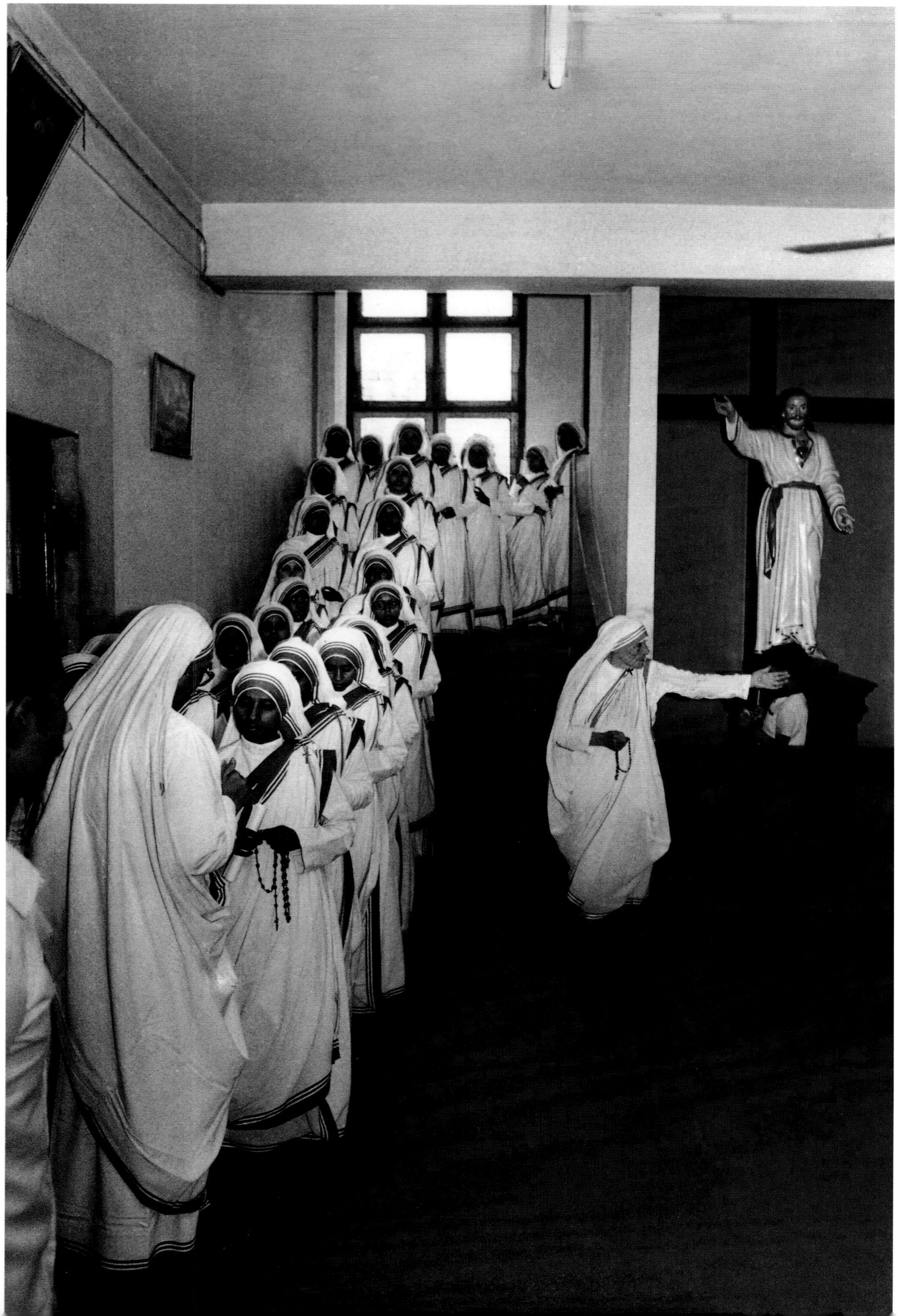

the first cause: melting with reason

THIS STORY GOES BACK TO THE EARLY SEVENTIES.

Remember Desmond Doig, Mother? It was with him that I first met you at your Home in Kolkata. Doig was a man of many talents and, at the time, editor of the now defunct *Junior Statesman*, the first magazine aimed at Indian youth. He was based in Kolkata and would often call me there to cover important assignments. When he began working on a story about your Missionaries of Charity, he asked me to come over. I was young, in my late twenties, and always eager to do something different.

Even at that time, the Missionaries of Charity were quite strict about giving access to photographers and journalists, whether it was in the Children's Home or the Home for the Aged. Permission was essential for taking pictures. Doig took me to the room that functioned as your office. He was talking to you about the story he proposed to write on your work. He told you (pointing toward me) that I was the photographer for the story.

In the course of this conversation, I caught a glimpse of three sisters who were standing on the first floor with prayer books in their hands. They were visible only with the flickering movement of the half curtain behind you. This was a compelling moment. Instinctively, I started taking pictures.

"What the hell on earth are you doing there?" you thundered. I was taken aback. "Mother, there are these sisters praying and they look like angels," I said, all excited. How you melted, Mother, and accepted that moment.

You reveal yourself in strange ways, Mother. That day, you made me realize how tough you could be, and also, oh, how soft when you saw reason.

Hereafter, I would watch my step and move to different areas to take pictures.

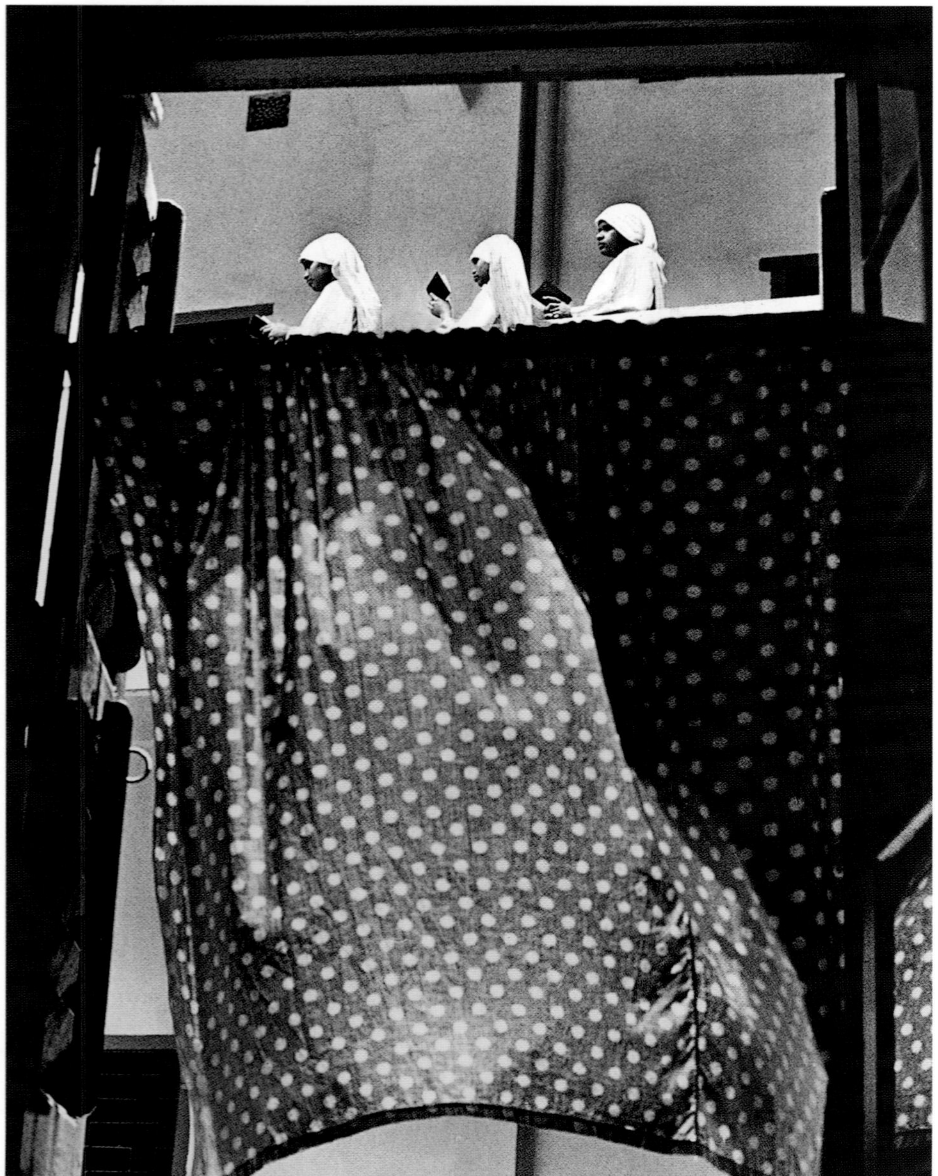

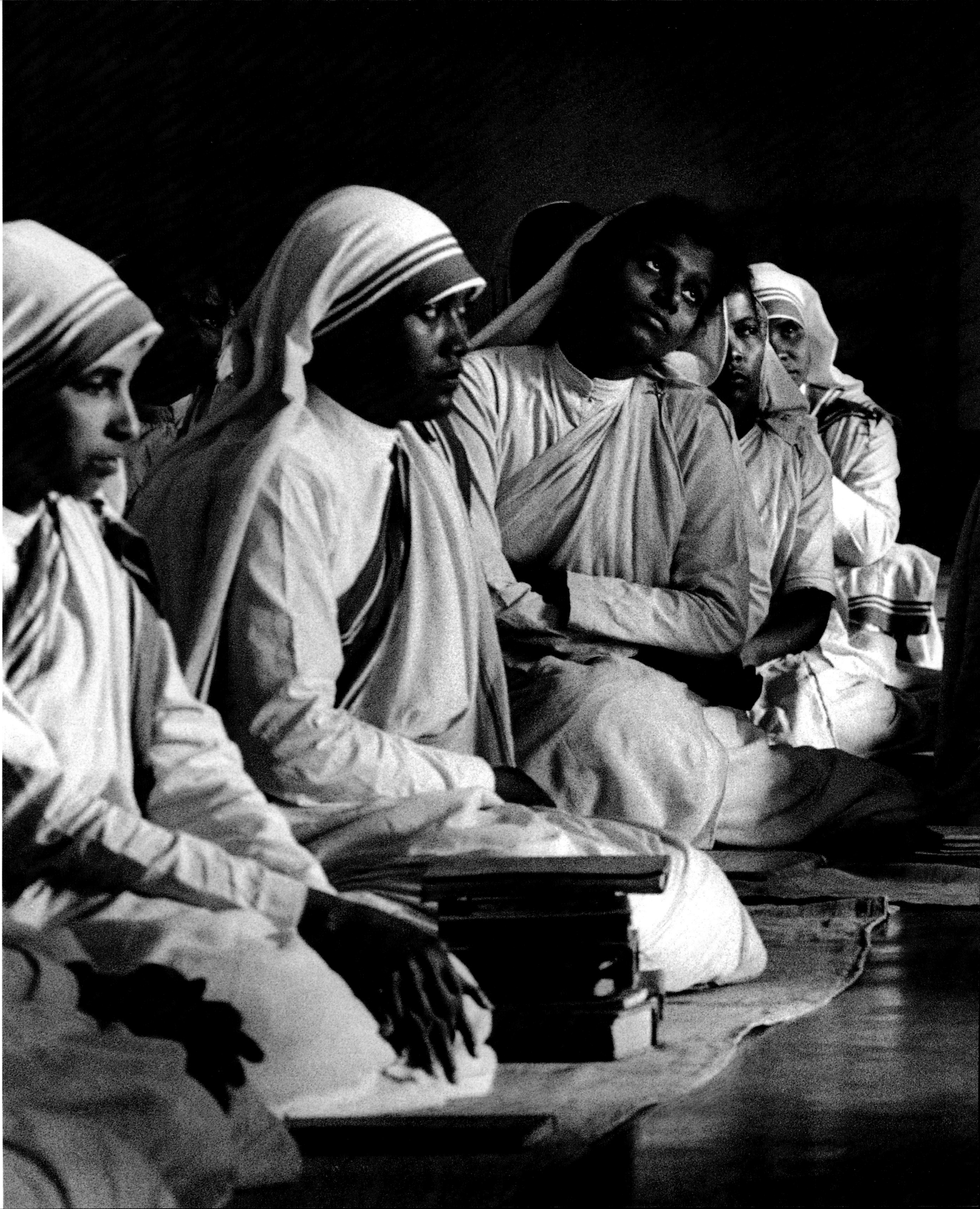

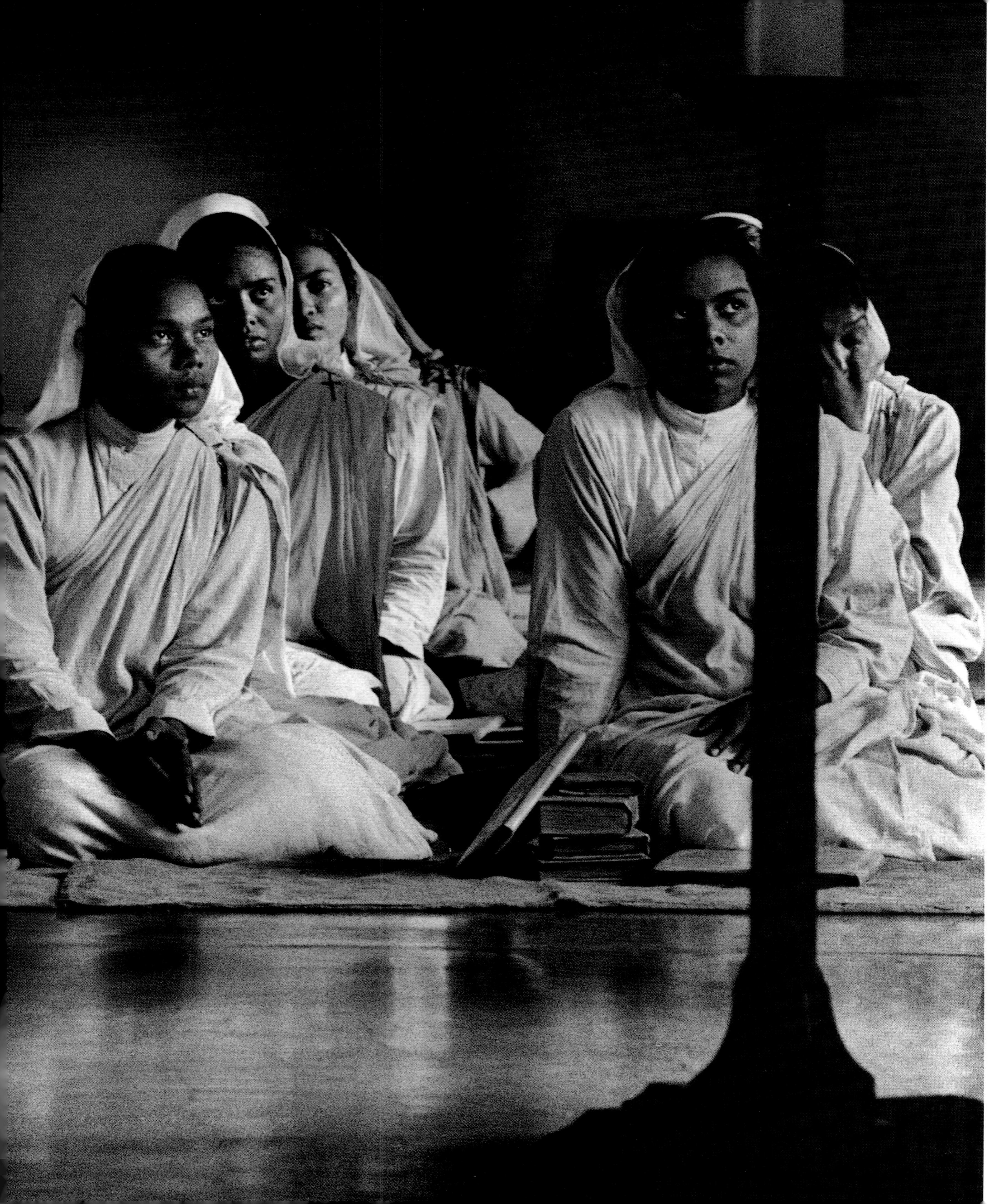

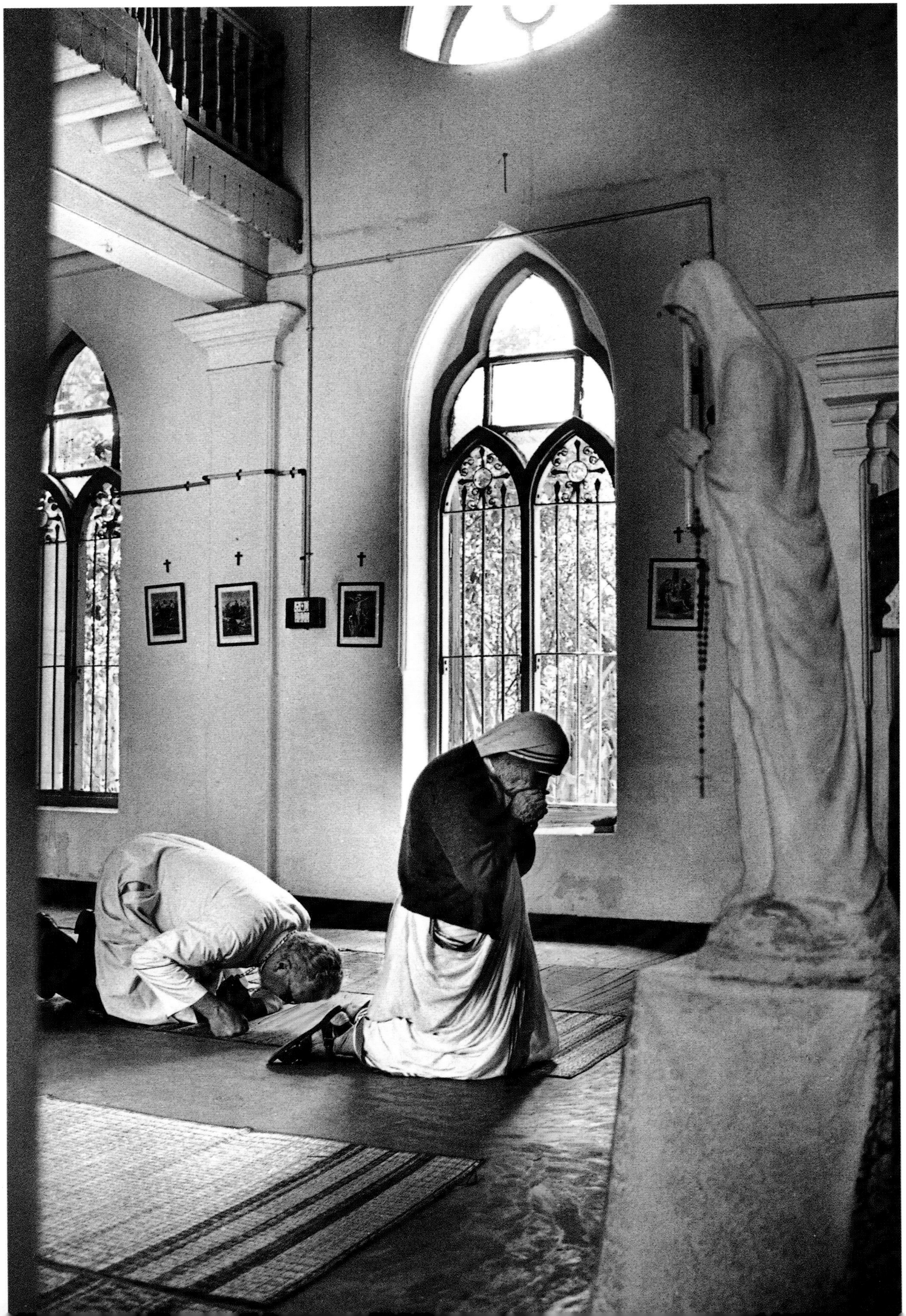

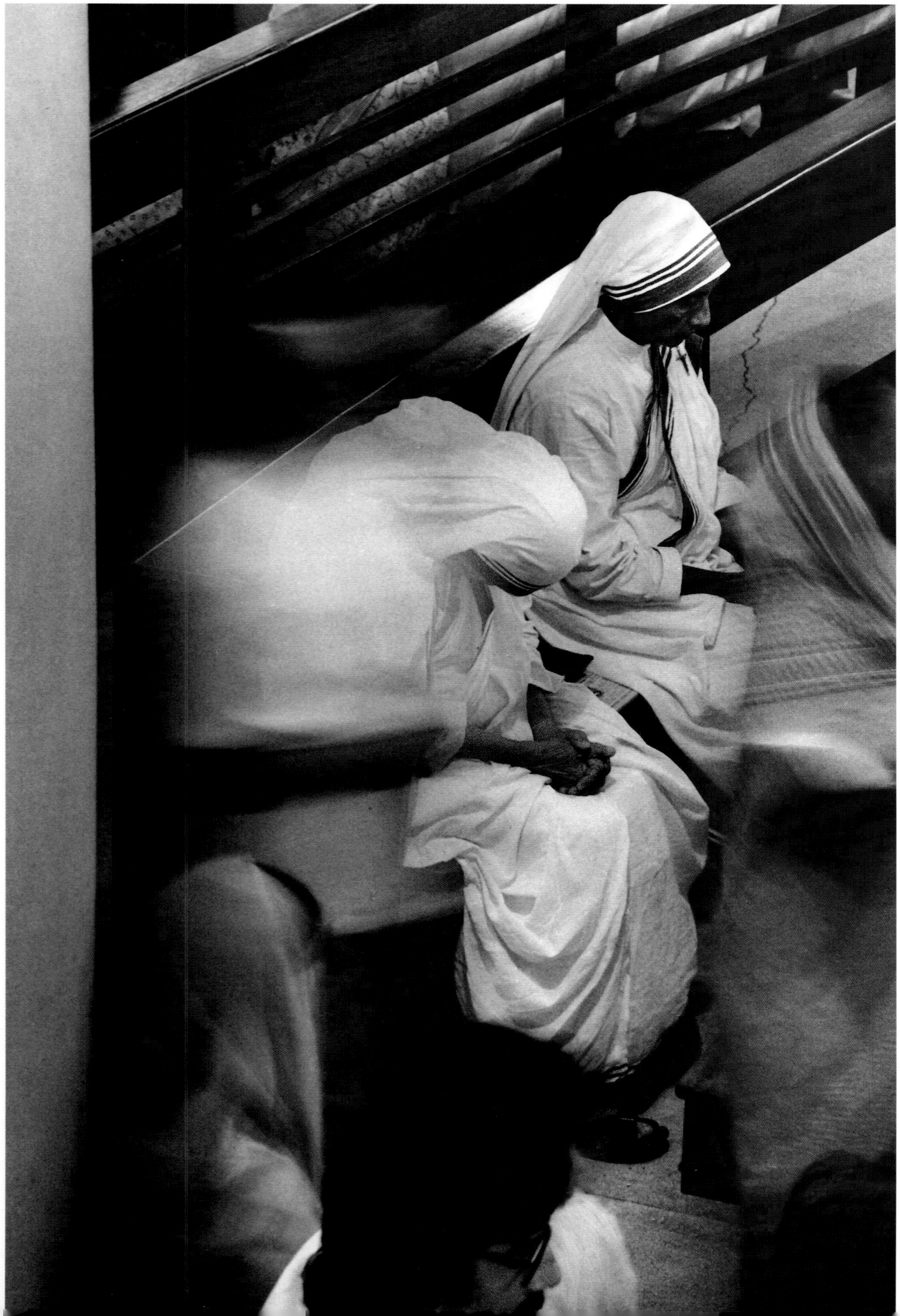

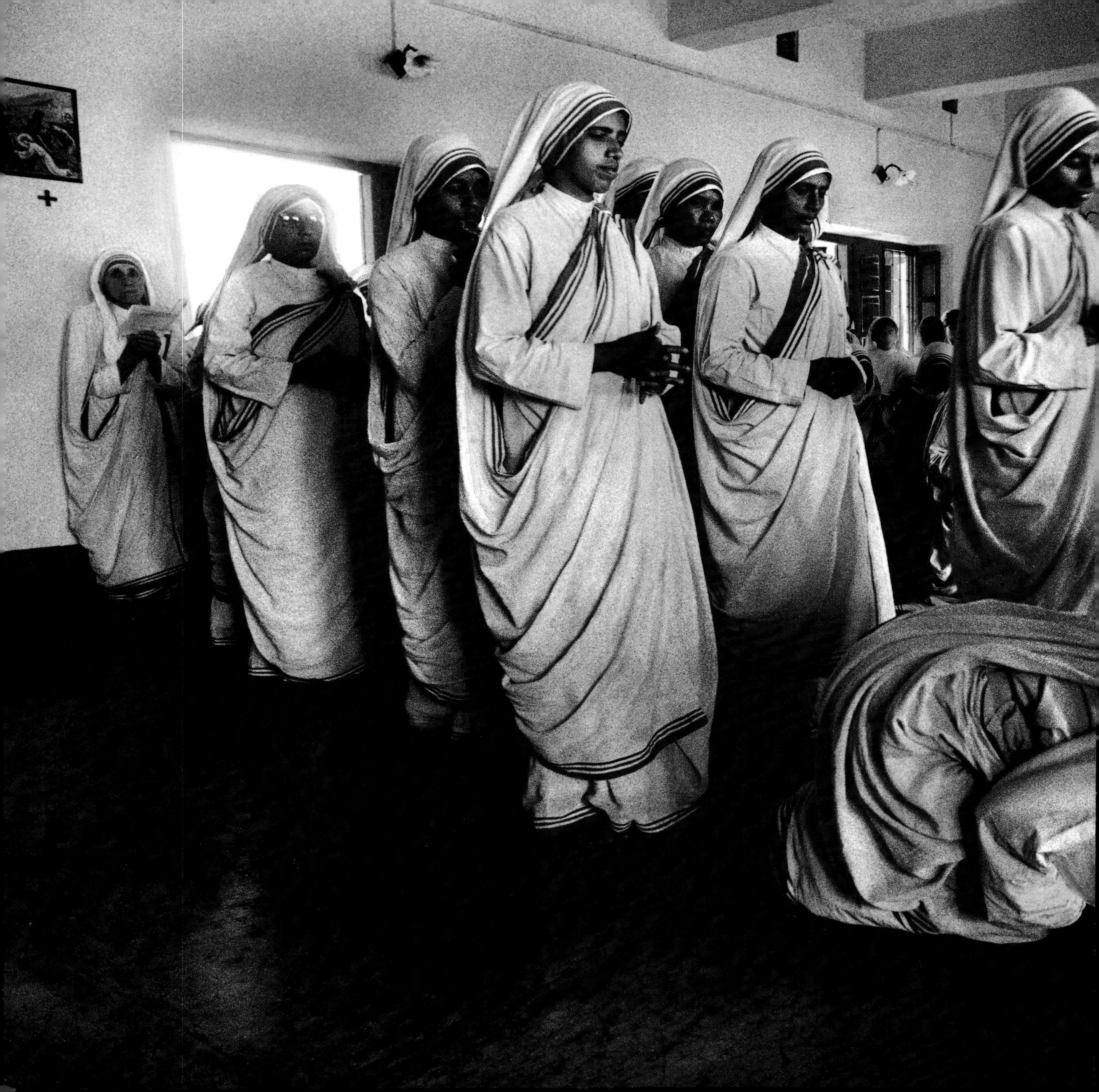

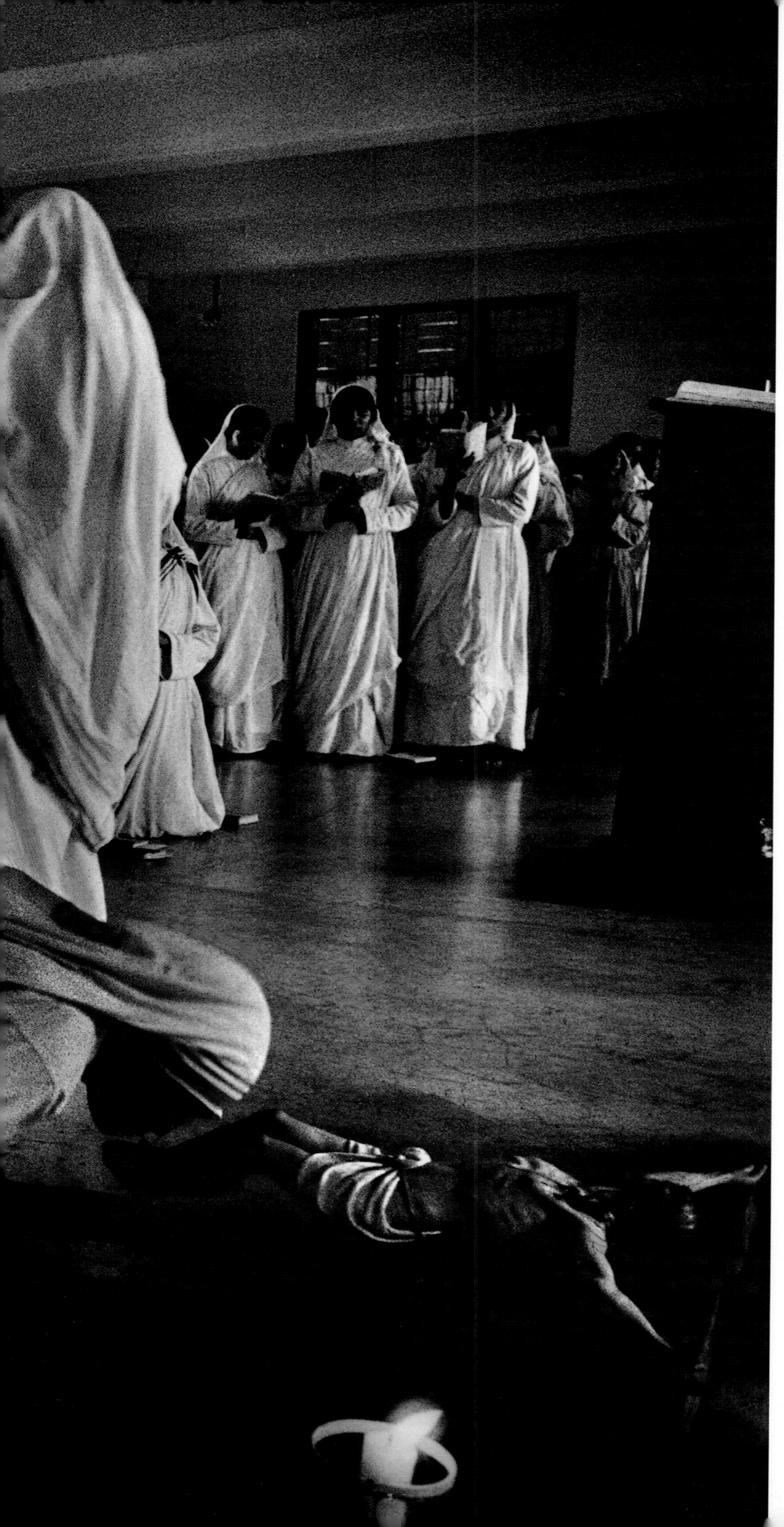

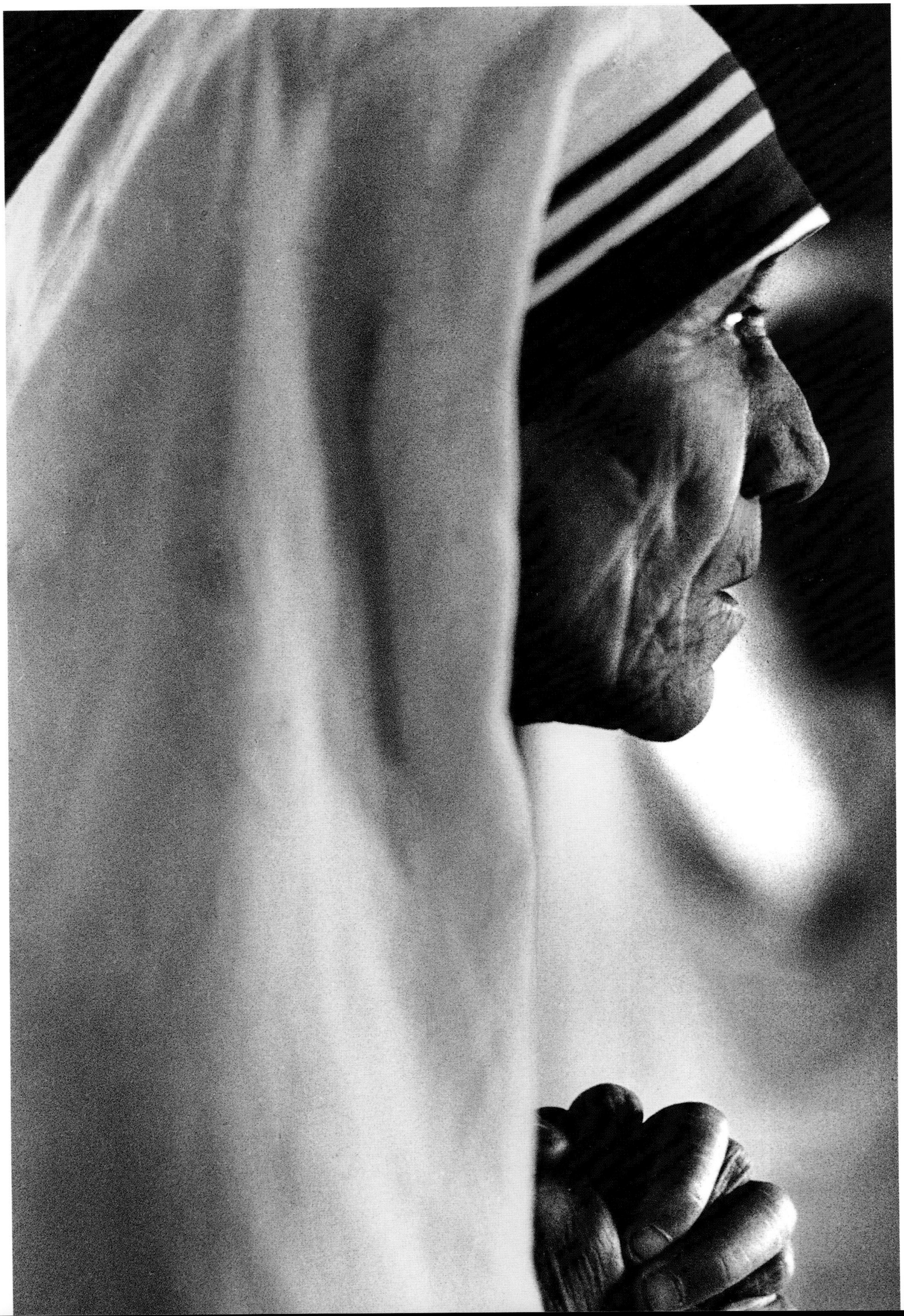

the divine error: inside the bosom of forgiveness

THE DAY BEFORE EASTER.

A day of deep prayer, of introspection, of solitude. You tell me there will be no shooting that day. "When we do our prayers we do not want anyone to be walking around and taking pictures. It disturbs the sisters and takes away the seriousness of the moment," you said.

Dear Mother. Of course you made sense.
But I was shattered. I was unprepared for this rejection. If I could not shoot while you were in prayer, then how was it possible for me to record the Divine Connection? Dear God! Had my story come to an end even before it could begin? Was this just another assignment after all? I was at a loss. But had I really lost? Mother, you had logic on your side this time, but on my side I had suffering. Through my despair, came an awakening that had been so far asleep.

It emboldened me to say to you, "Mother, you often say that you nurse the poorest of the poor because you were not there when Jesus was suffering, and thus, while nursing the poor, you actually nurse Jesus. This is one of the two routes through which one can establish direct connection with Him. The other route is prayer. I have never met Him, never seen Him, but I see Him only when you do your prayers; Jesus comes to dwell in your eyes. If I can't photograph this, then how can I establish this connection and share it with others? My story will remain incomplete."

the divine error: inside the bosom of forgiveness

YOU AGREED ON THIS CONDITION: "YOU WILL SIT IN ONE PLACE TO TAKE PICTURES."

In your magnanimous way, you asked me to come the next morning a little before six o'clock.

I could feel your love that joyous morning as you led me to the prayer room and showed me the place from where I could take pictures. From here, I was directly across from you as you started praying. I began to shoot. Soon, I realized that without eye contact, my own prayers would never be answered! Mother, I need to capture that meditative intensity in your eyes.

I was hesitant to move. I struggled within myself. Your words still rang in my ears. The spell of the moment compelled me to move; when you were in a trance, the Lord was everywhere. I took pictures, and then came back. At the end of the prayer, as the sisters moved in a line to kiss the feet of the Lord once again, I moved, and from quite a distance, got those pictures too.

I moved toward you, with the burden of my guilt and implored your forgiveness with my eyes for having failed to keep my word. "Mother, I am sorry, I could not remain in one place as you had asked me. Please forgive me," I said.

You took my hands into yours, looked deep into me and said, "God has given you this assignment. You must do it well." Mother, how I thanked you for forgiving me. How I thanked you for showing me a Divine Connection to my work. Only you could draw such enrichment from error. I was blessed.

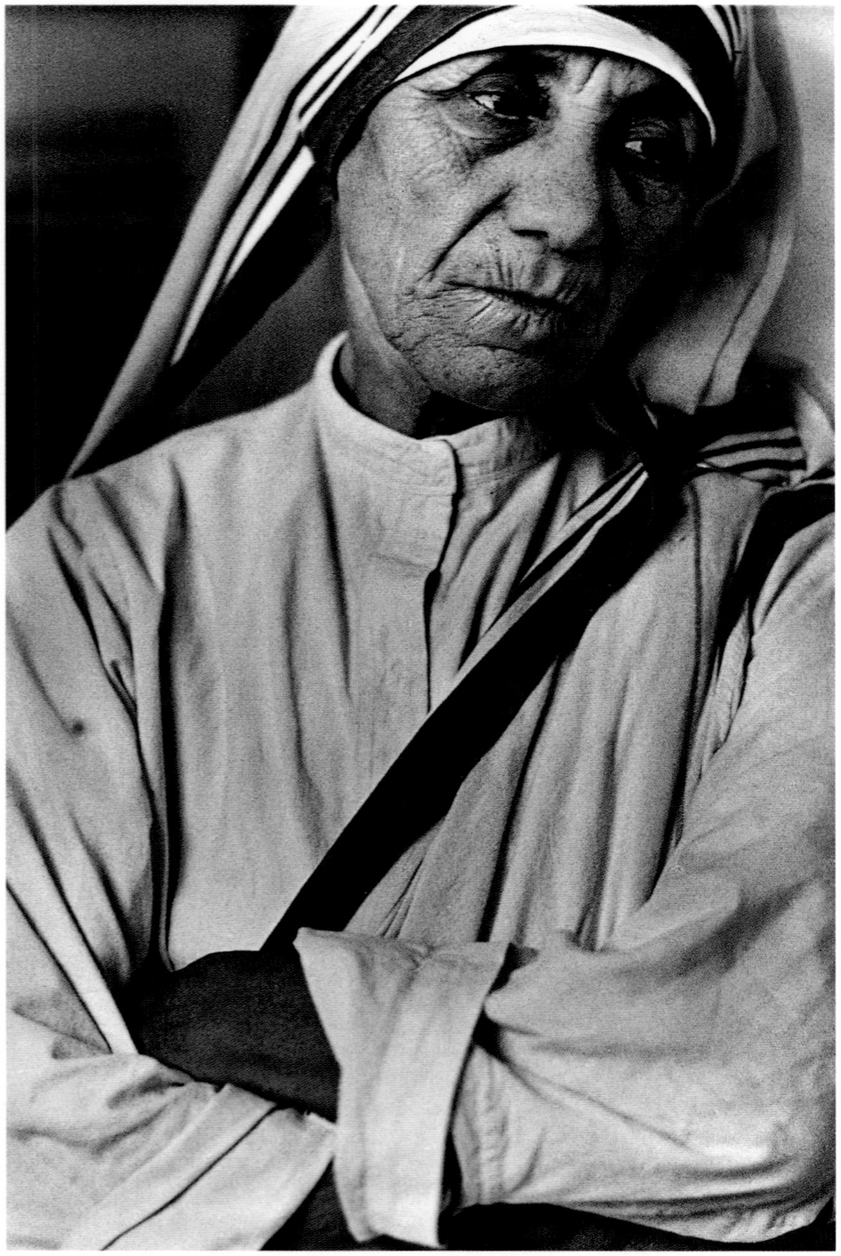

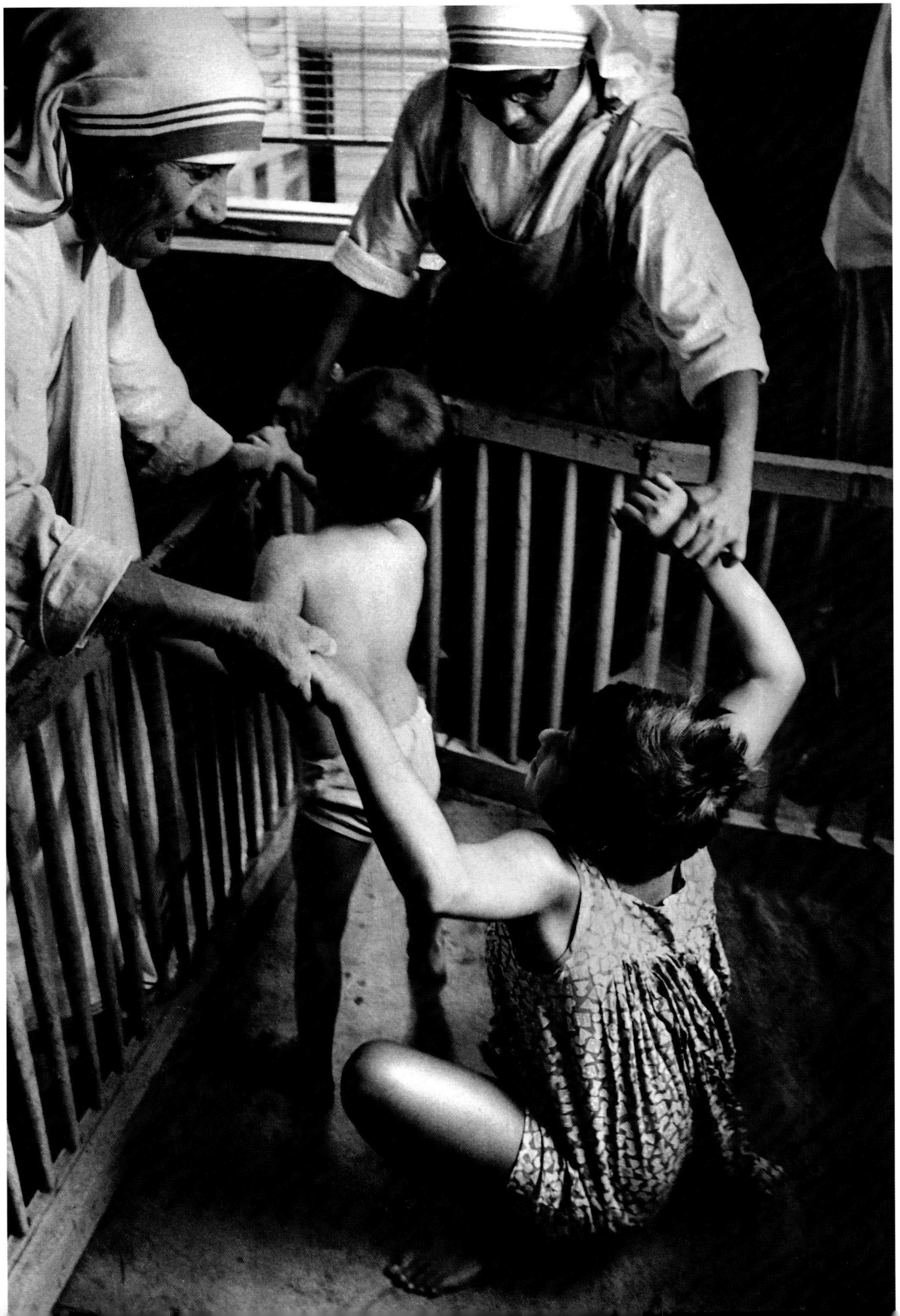

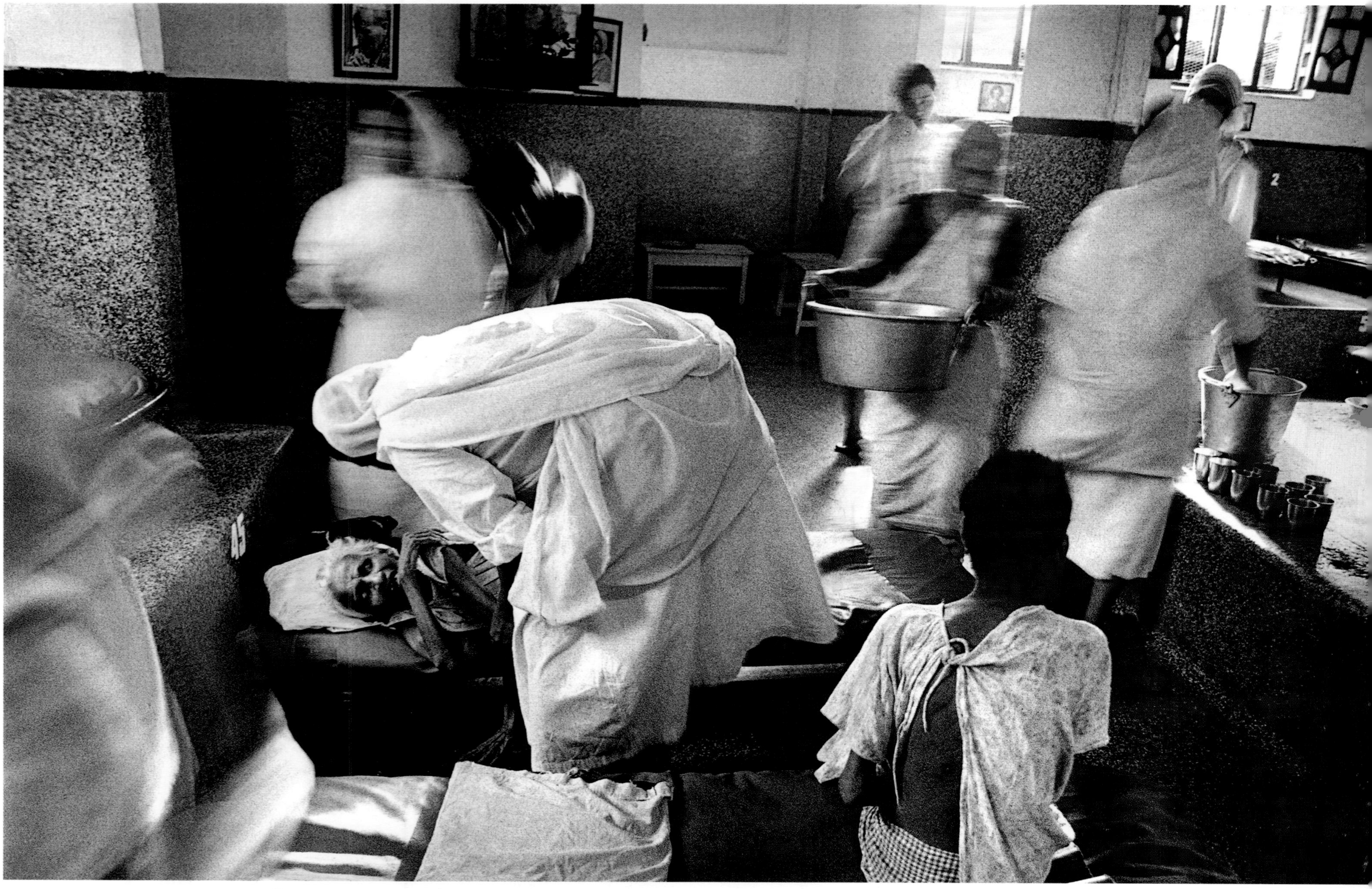
45
2

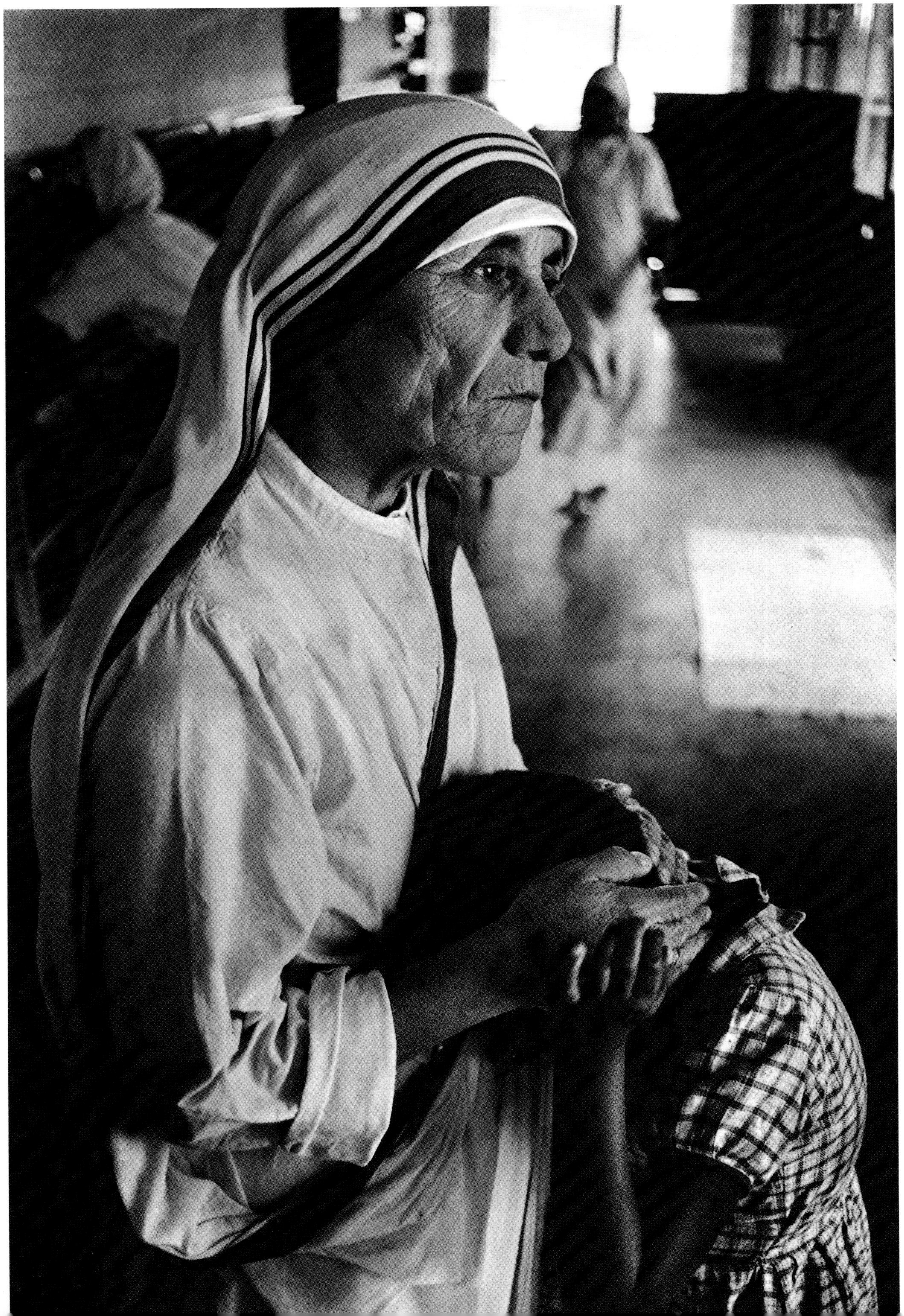

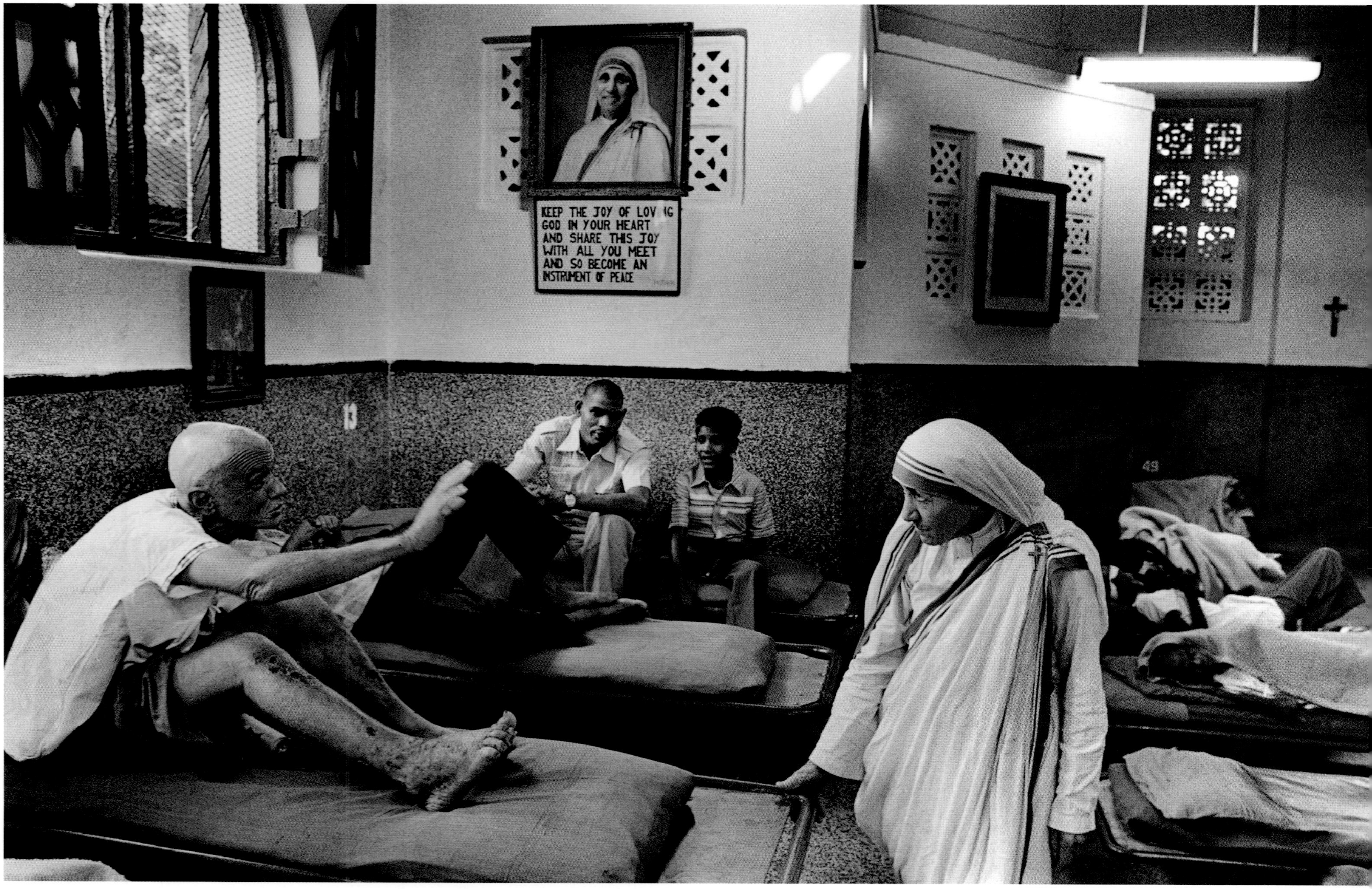
KEEP THE JOY OF LOV IG
GOD IN YOUR HEART
AND SHARE THIS JOY
WITH ALL YOU MEET
AND SO BECOME AN
INSTRUMENT OF PEACE
13
49

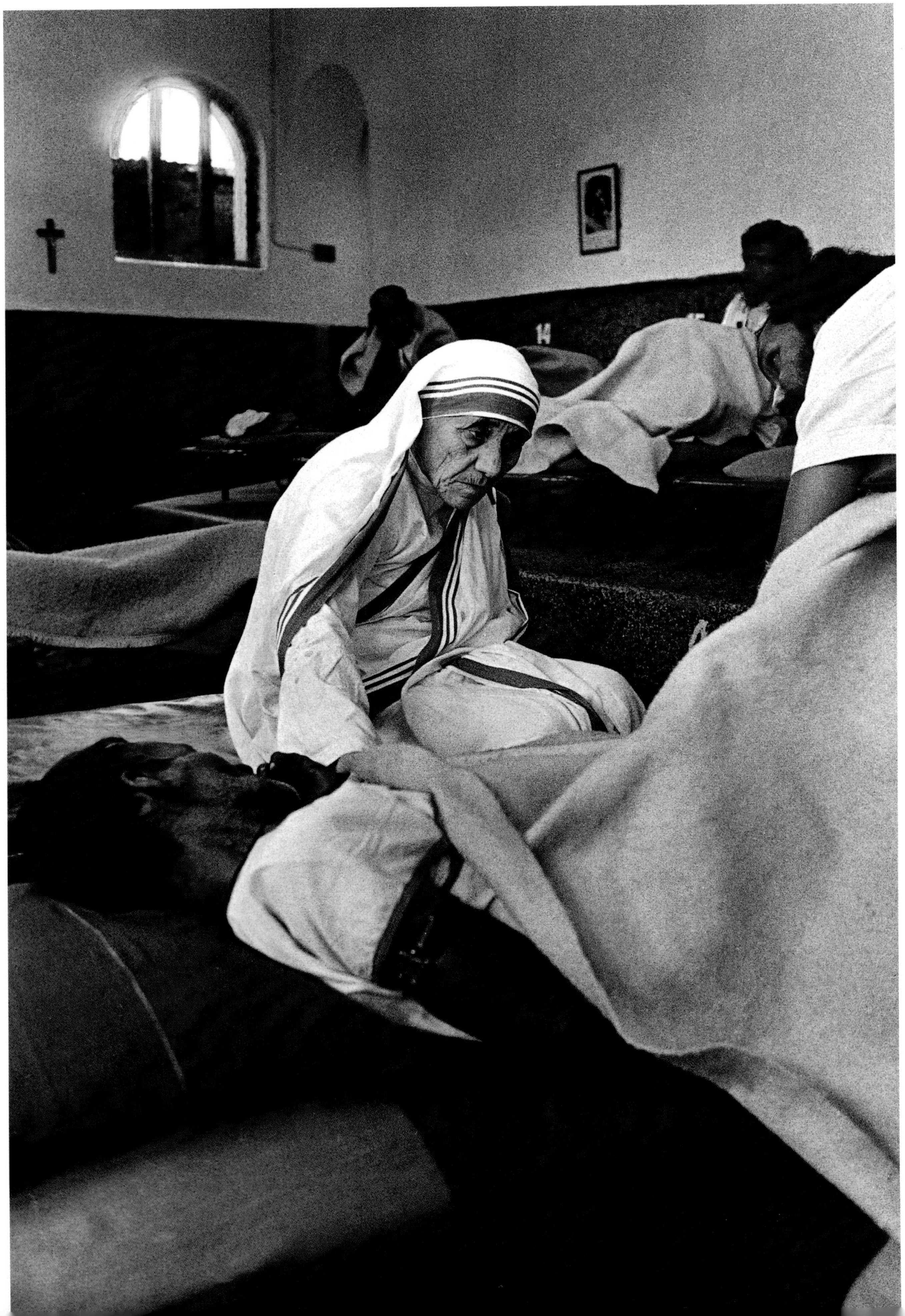

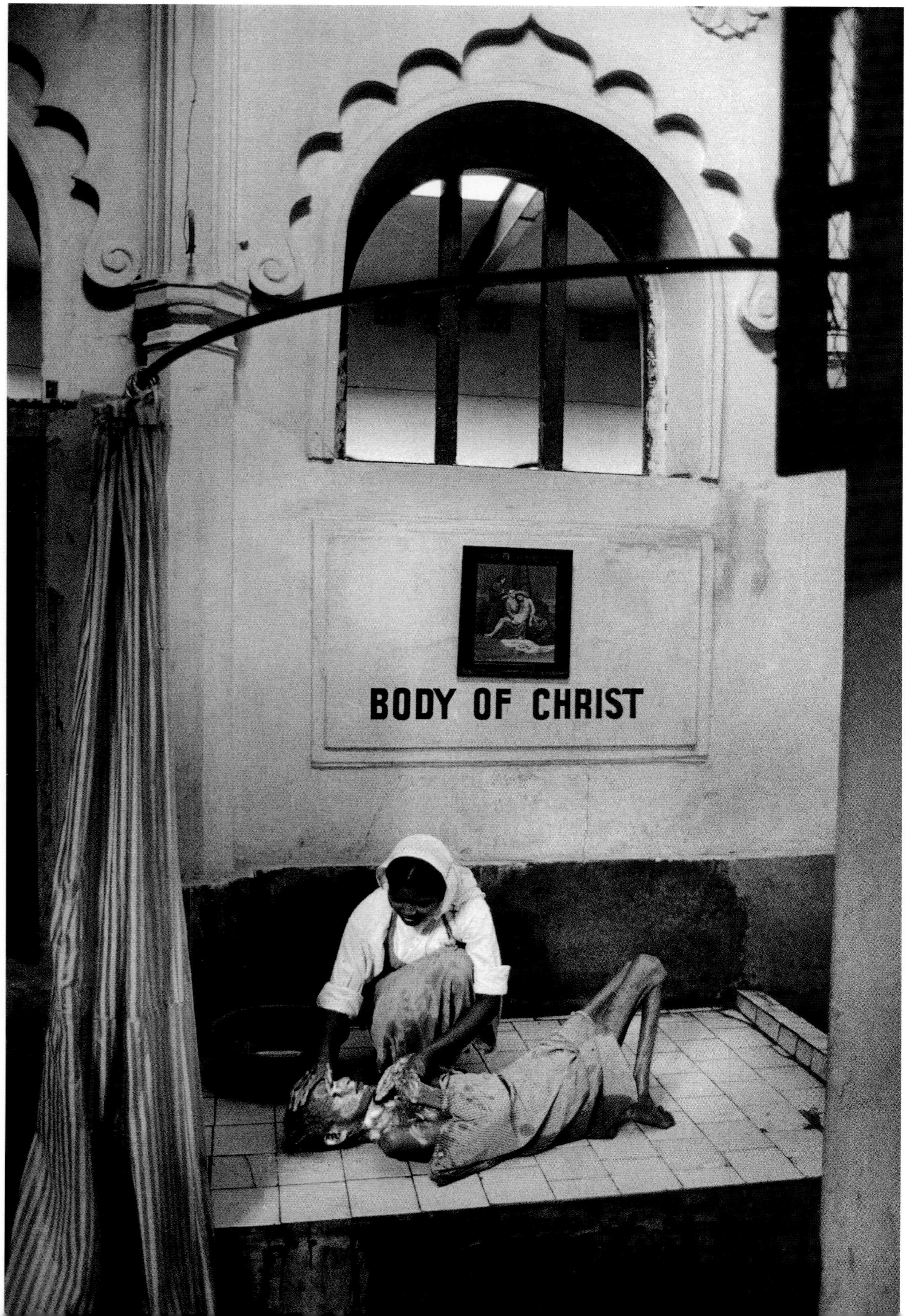
BODY OF CHRIST

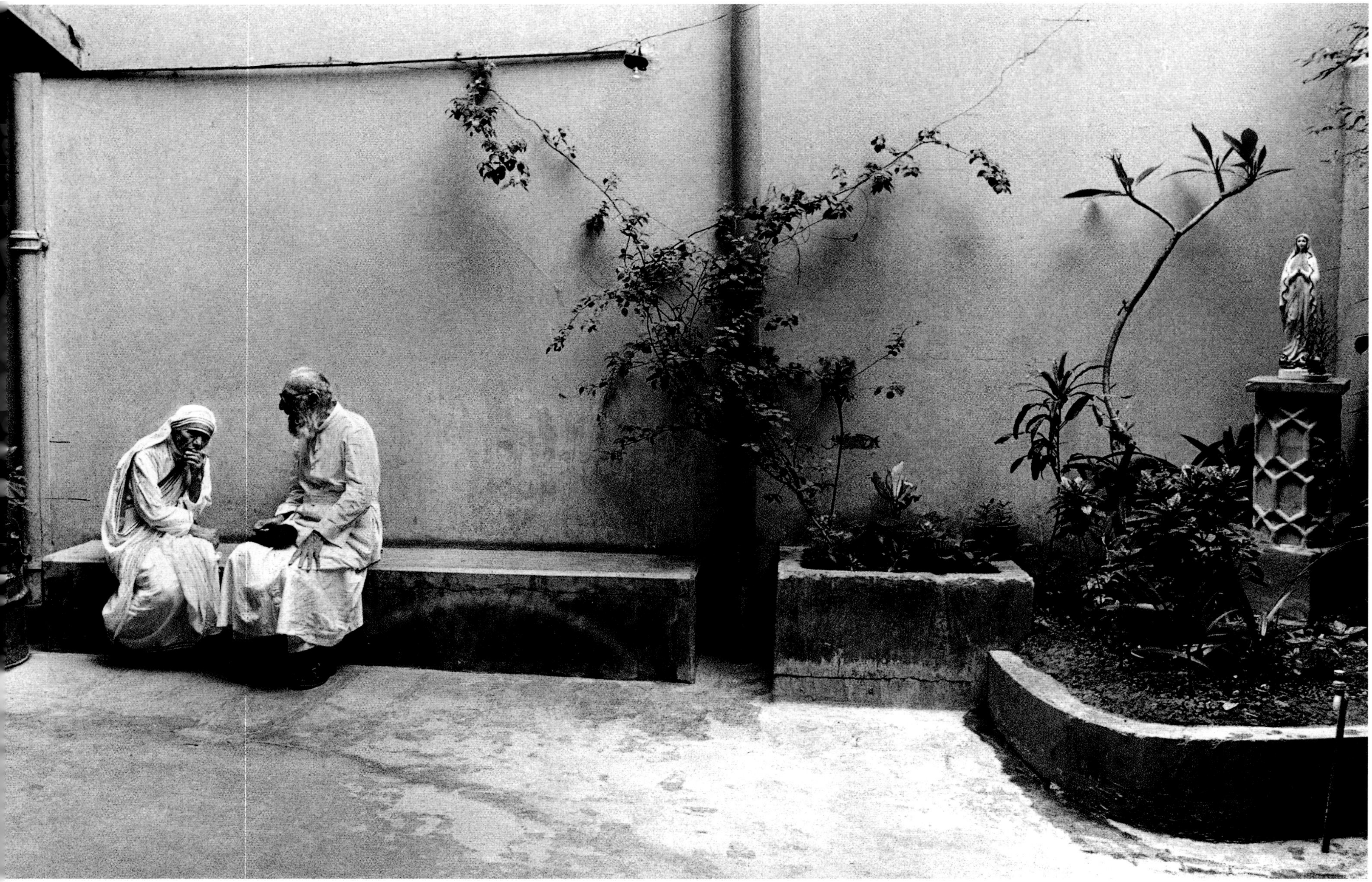

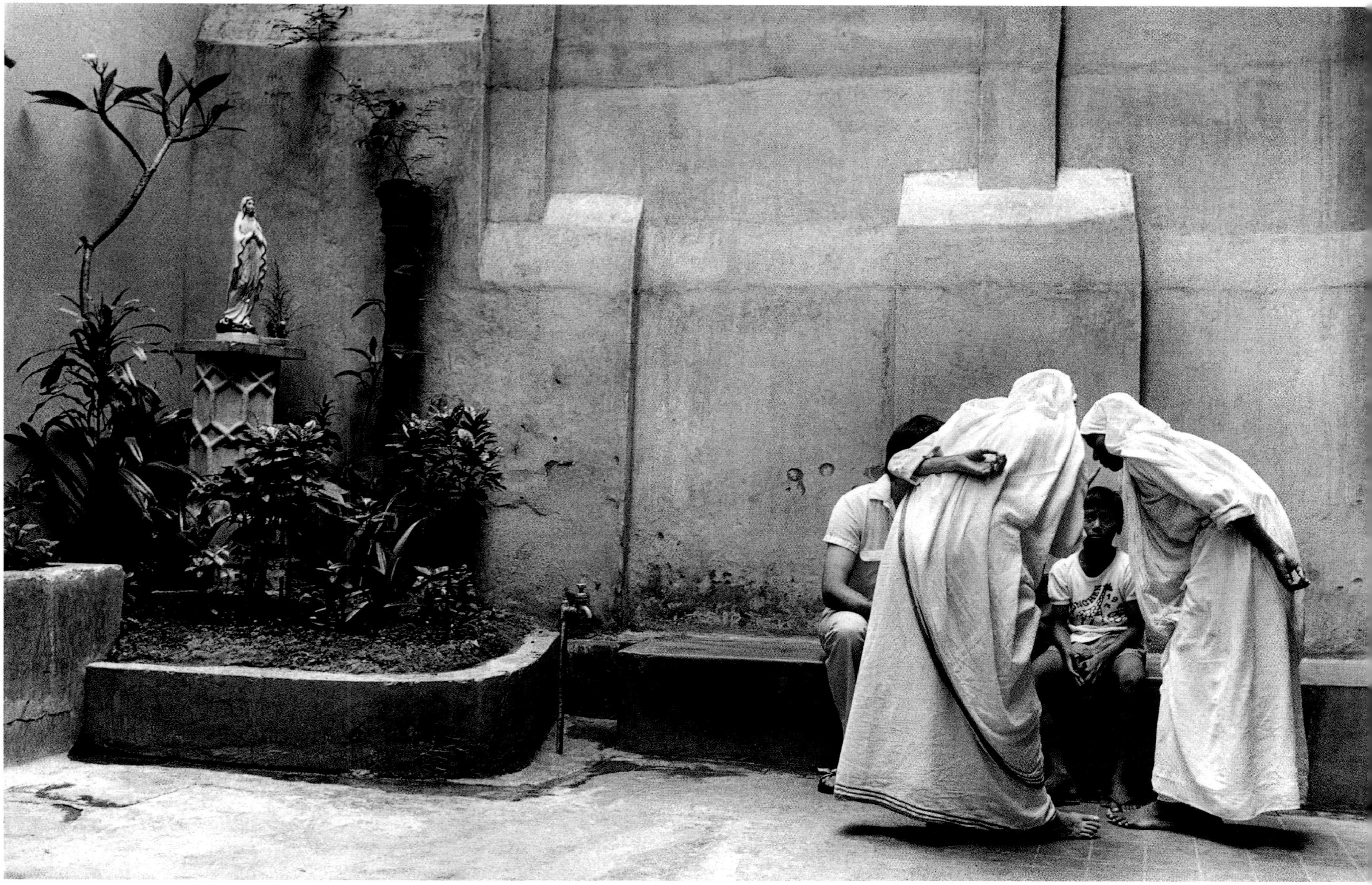

the winning handclasp: the mother of all graces

THE POPE WAS TO VISIT YOUR HOME FOR THE AGED AT KALIGHAT.

Quite naturally, security and other procedures were very strict. Permission was needed to take pictures.

You directed me to a bishop who was in charge of these administrative matters.

I approached him with my request and told him that I knew Mother and she had asked me to get in touch with him. He told me to wait outside his office.

You happened to arrive there as I was waiting. The Bishop spotted me and said to you, "This man says that he knows you and . . ." Before he could complete his sentence, you took my hands in yours and said in your winning way, "Even I know him!"

That settled everything for me.

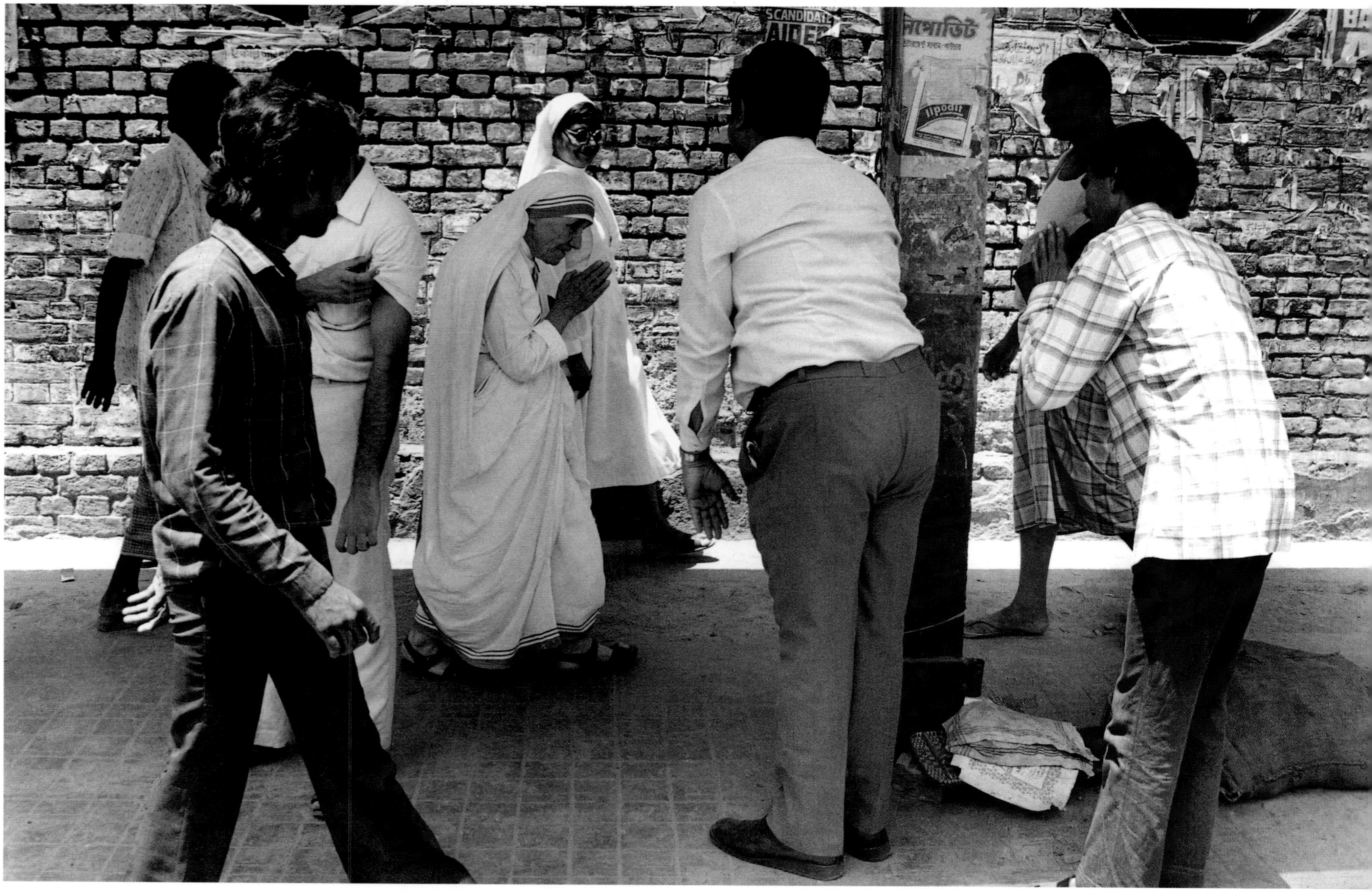

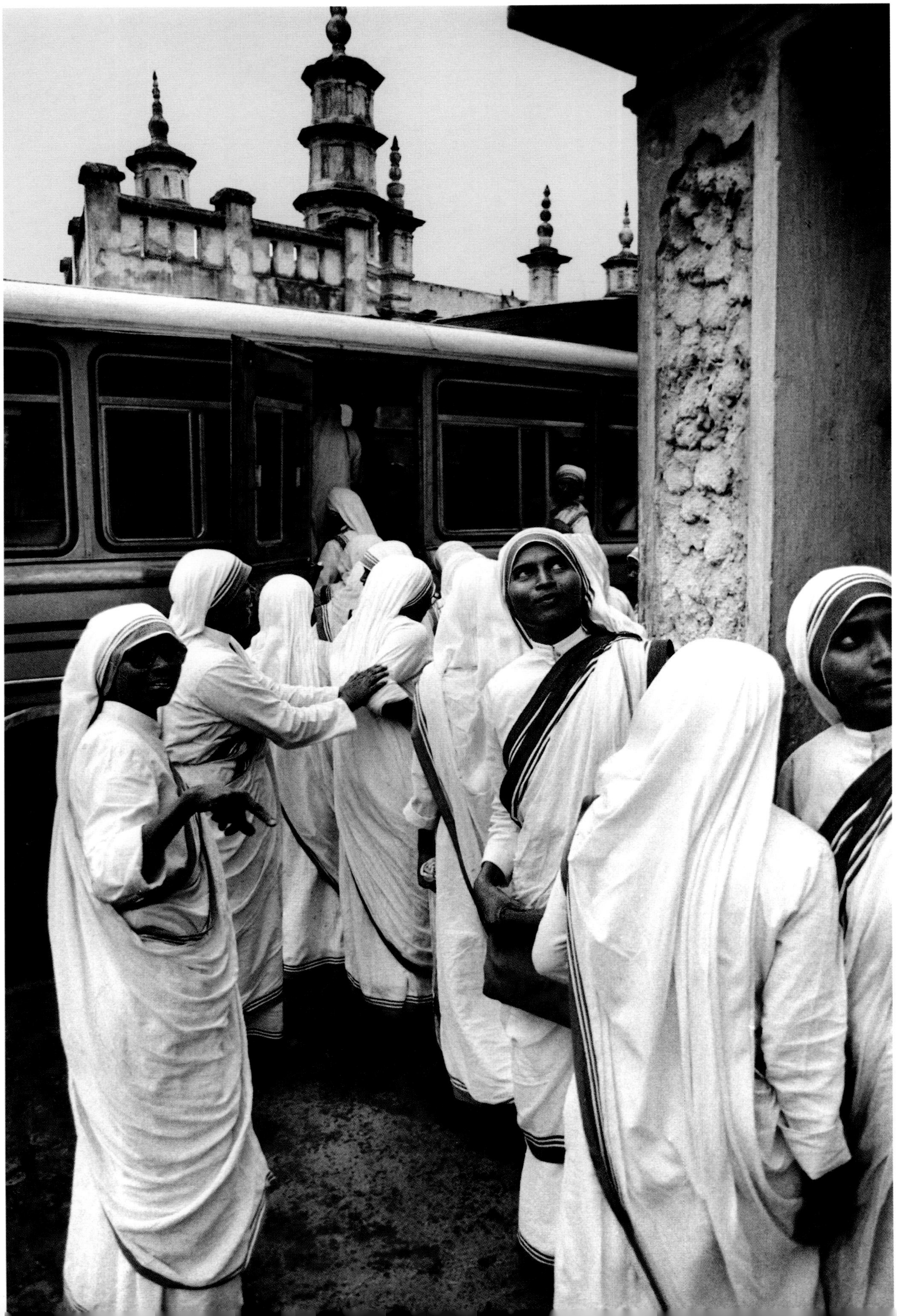

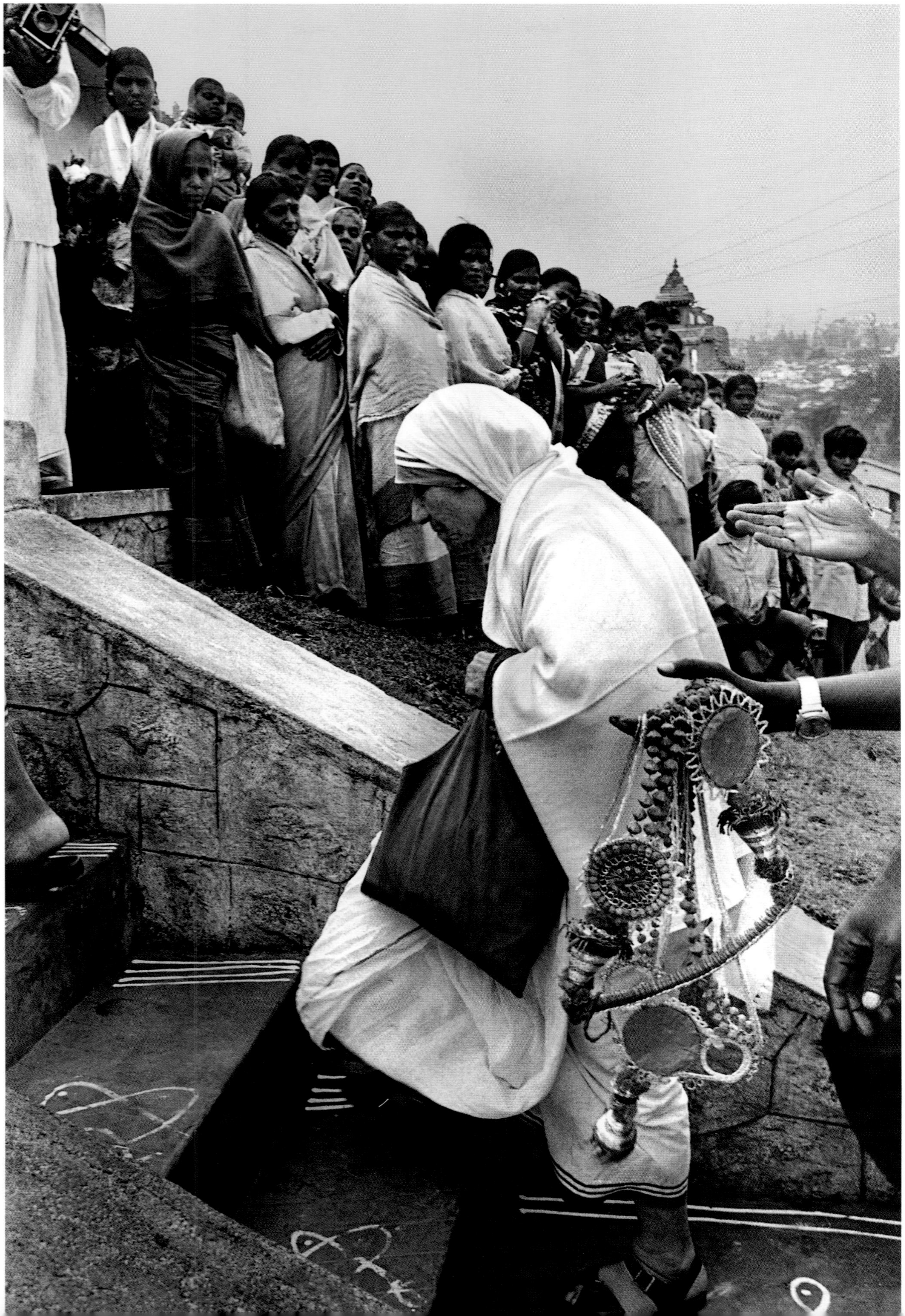

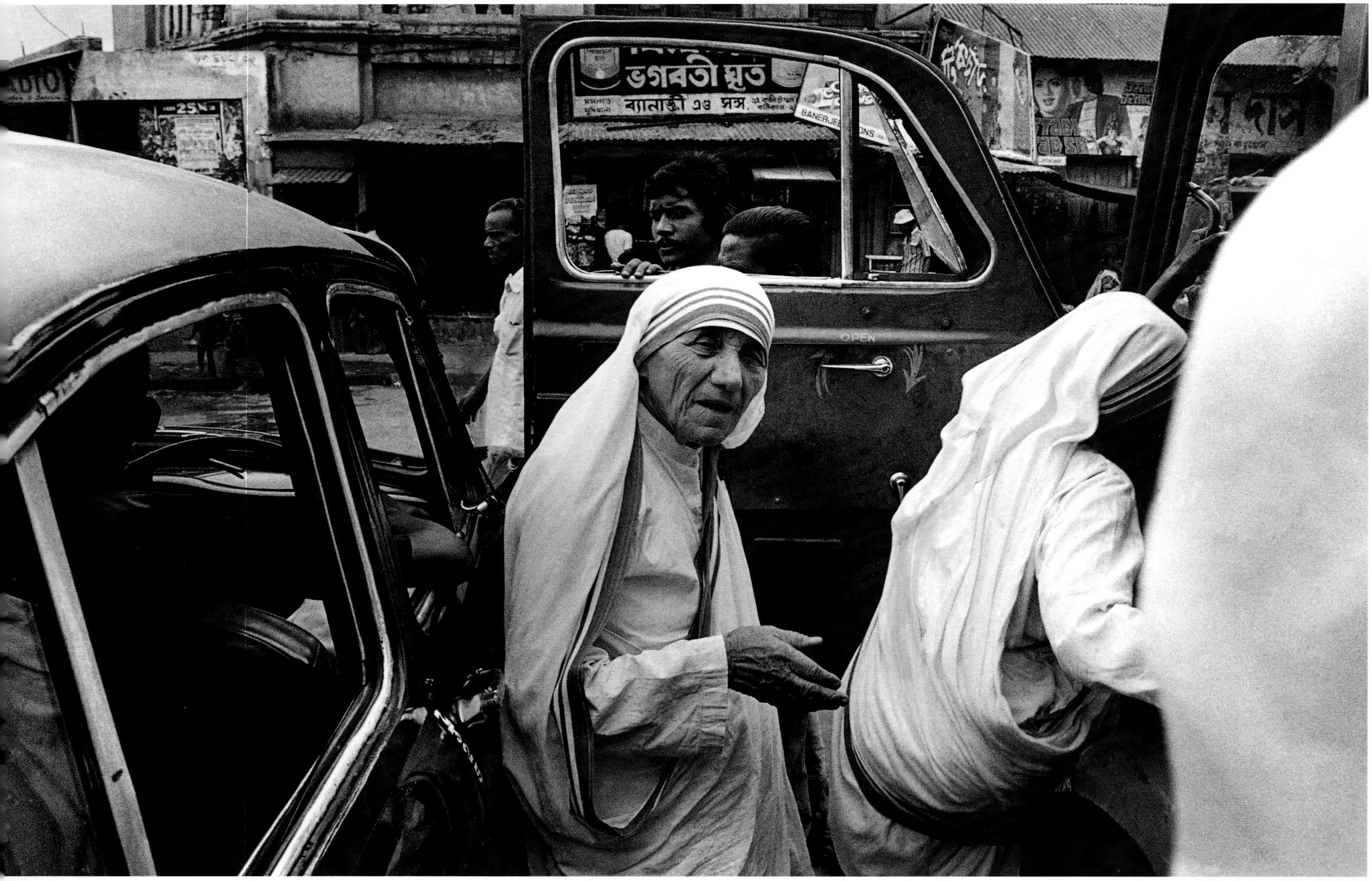
ভগবতী ঘৃত
OPEN

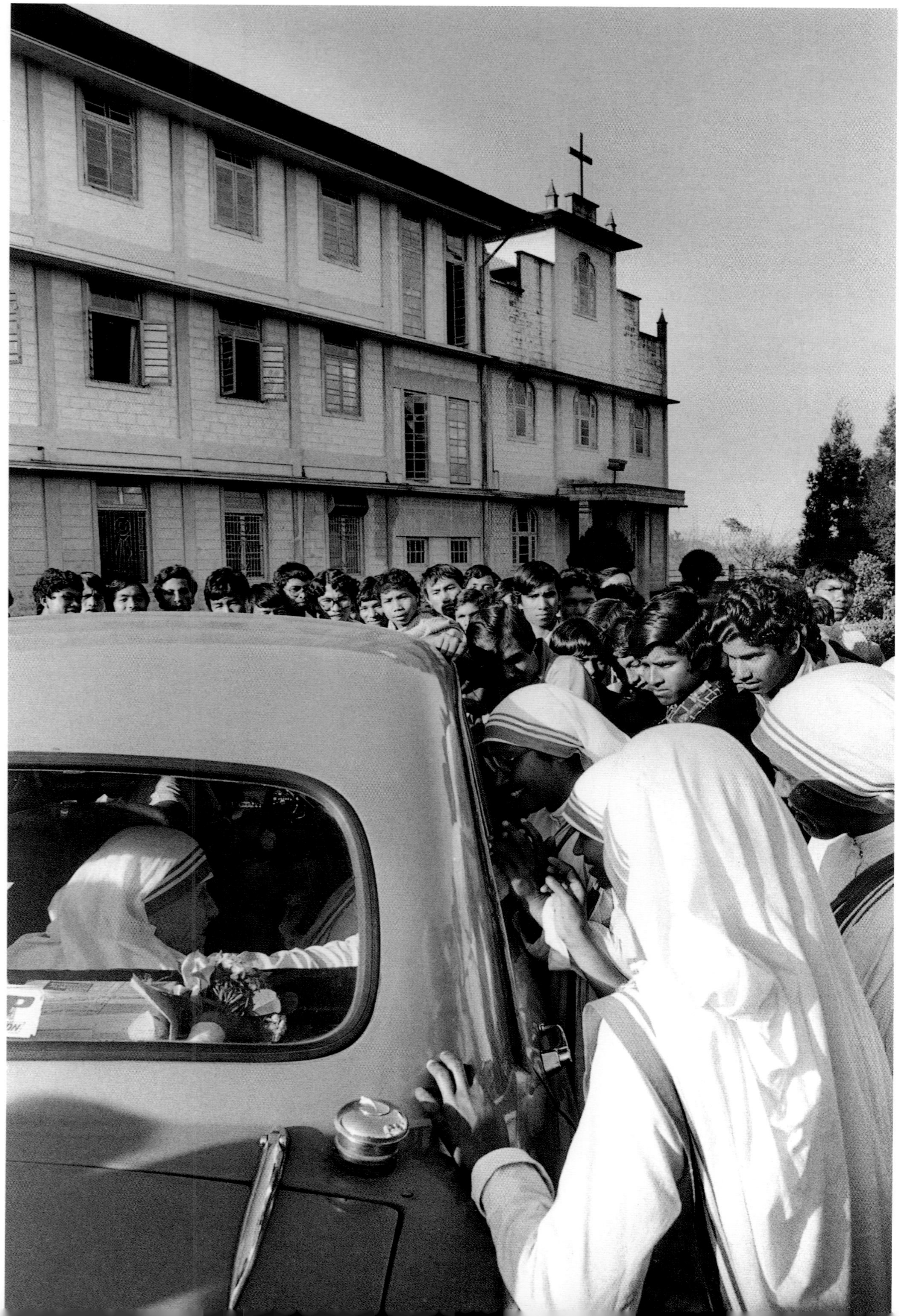

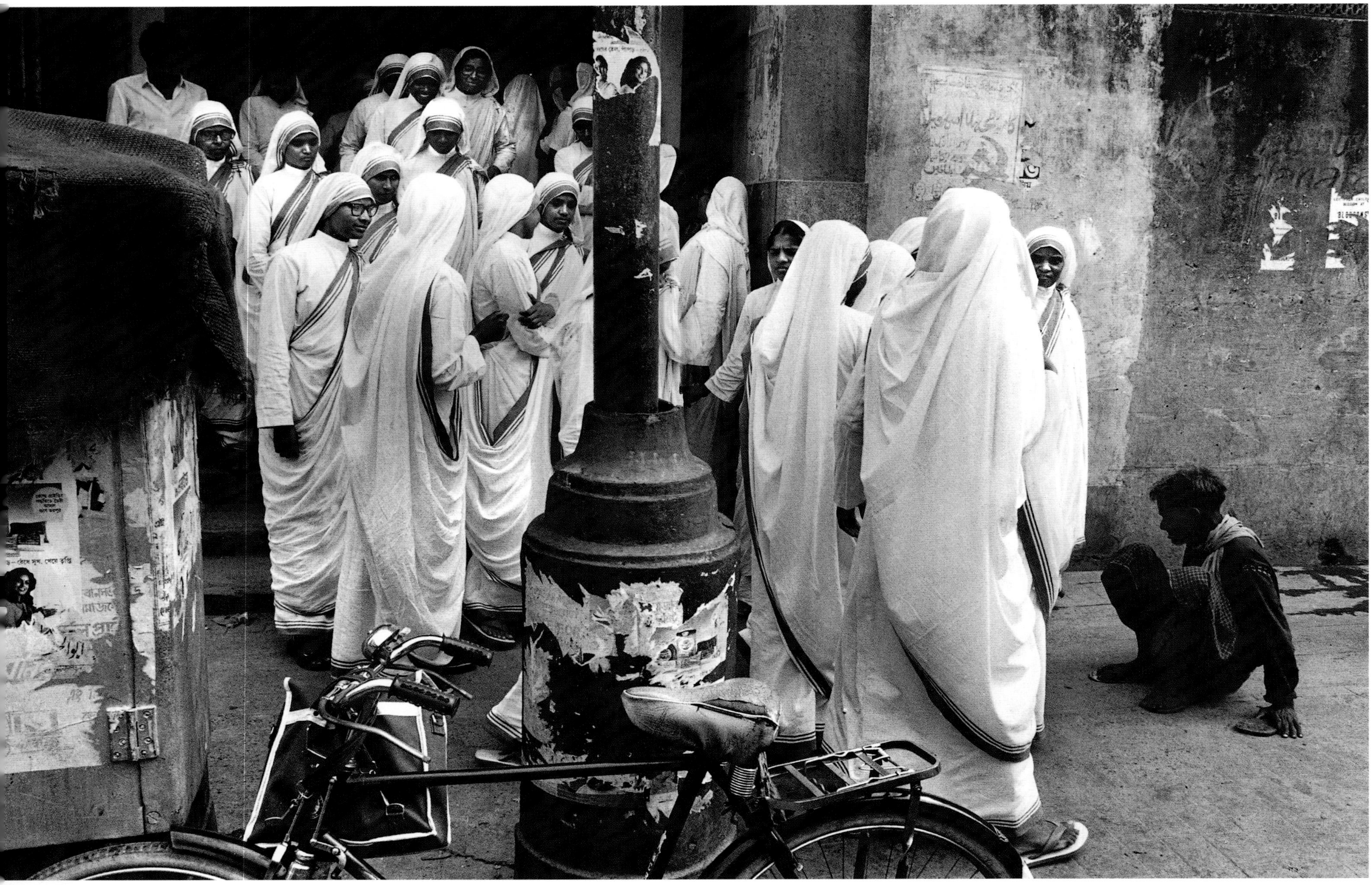

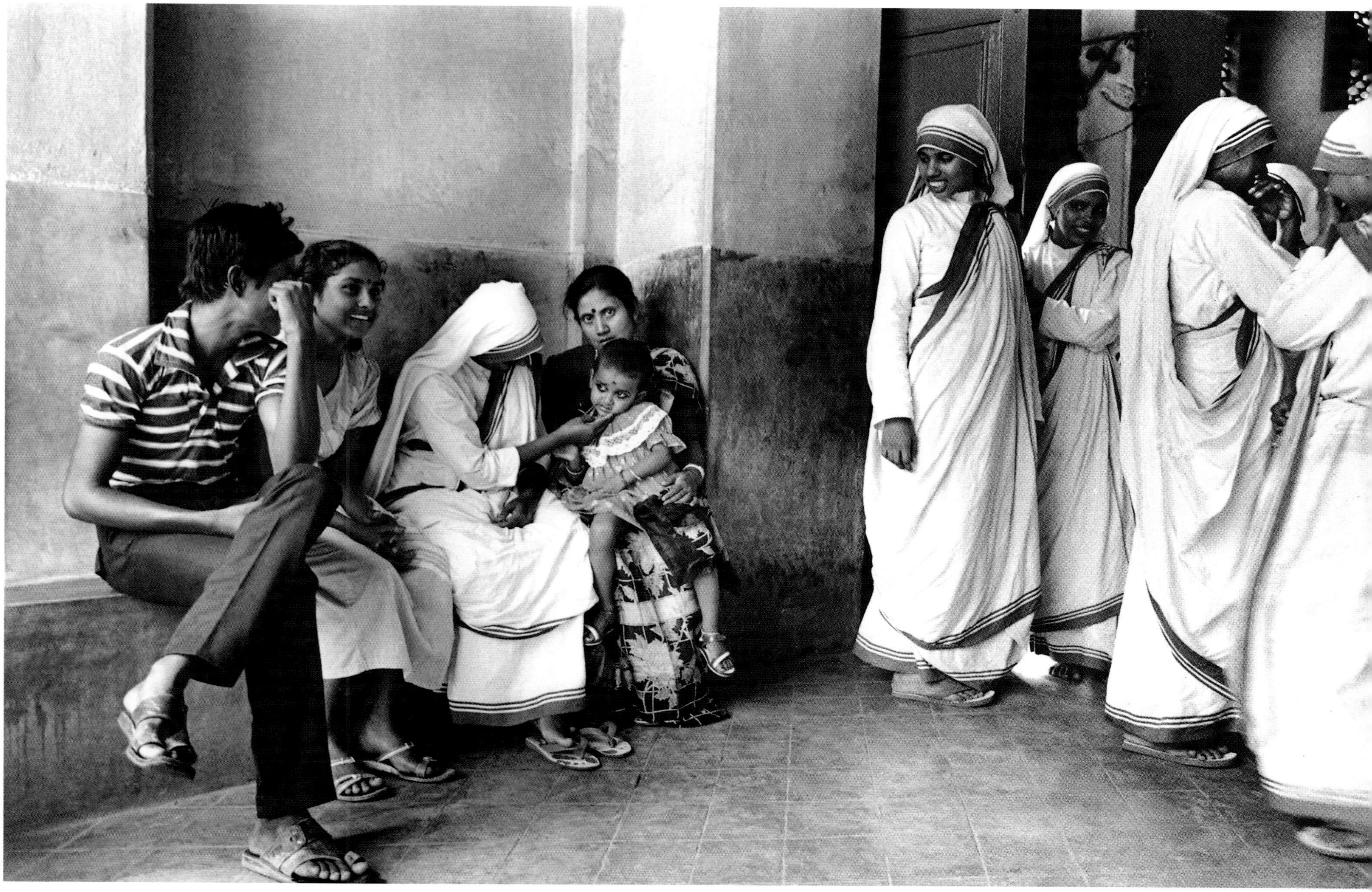

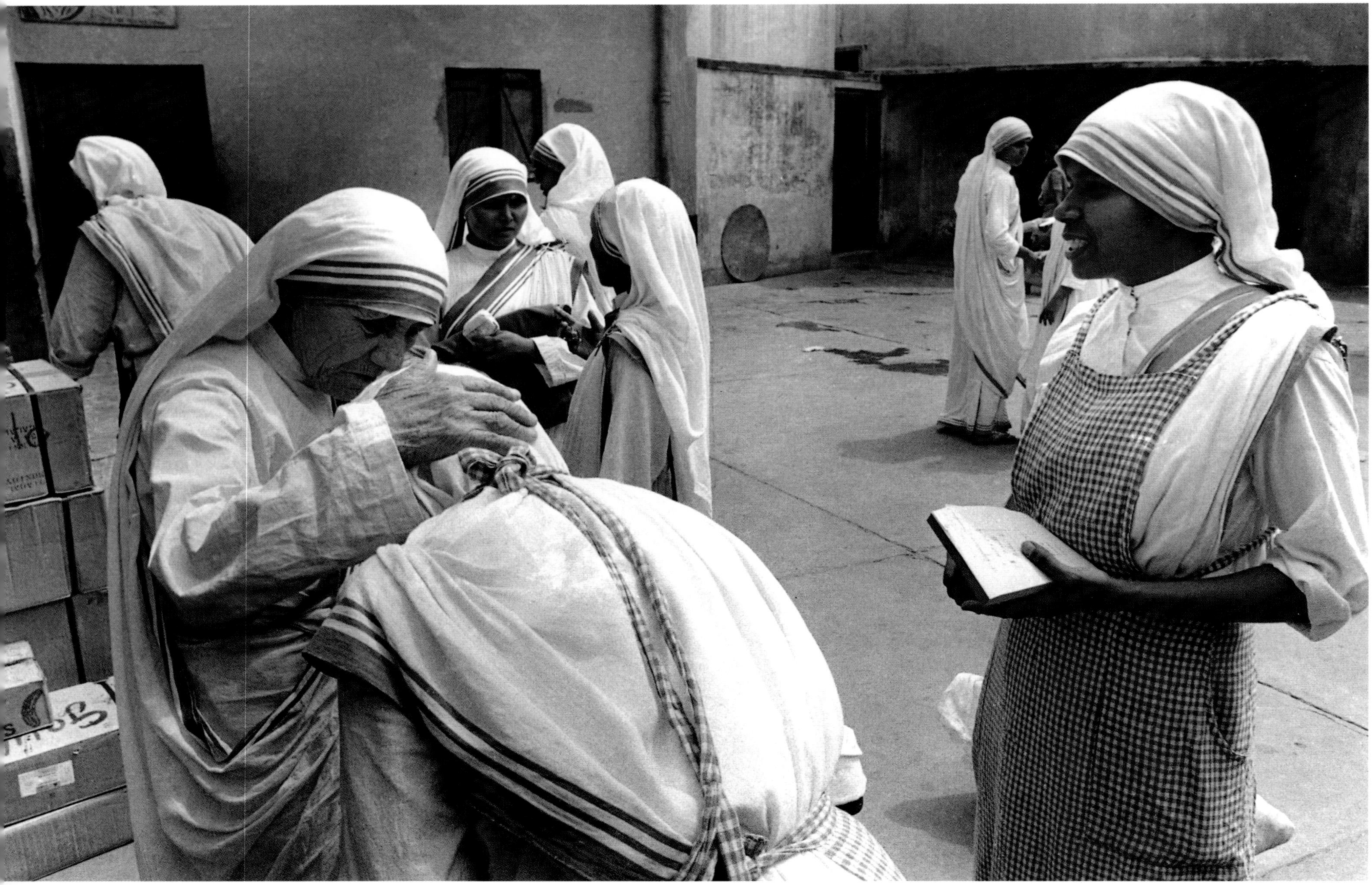

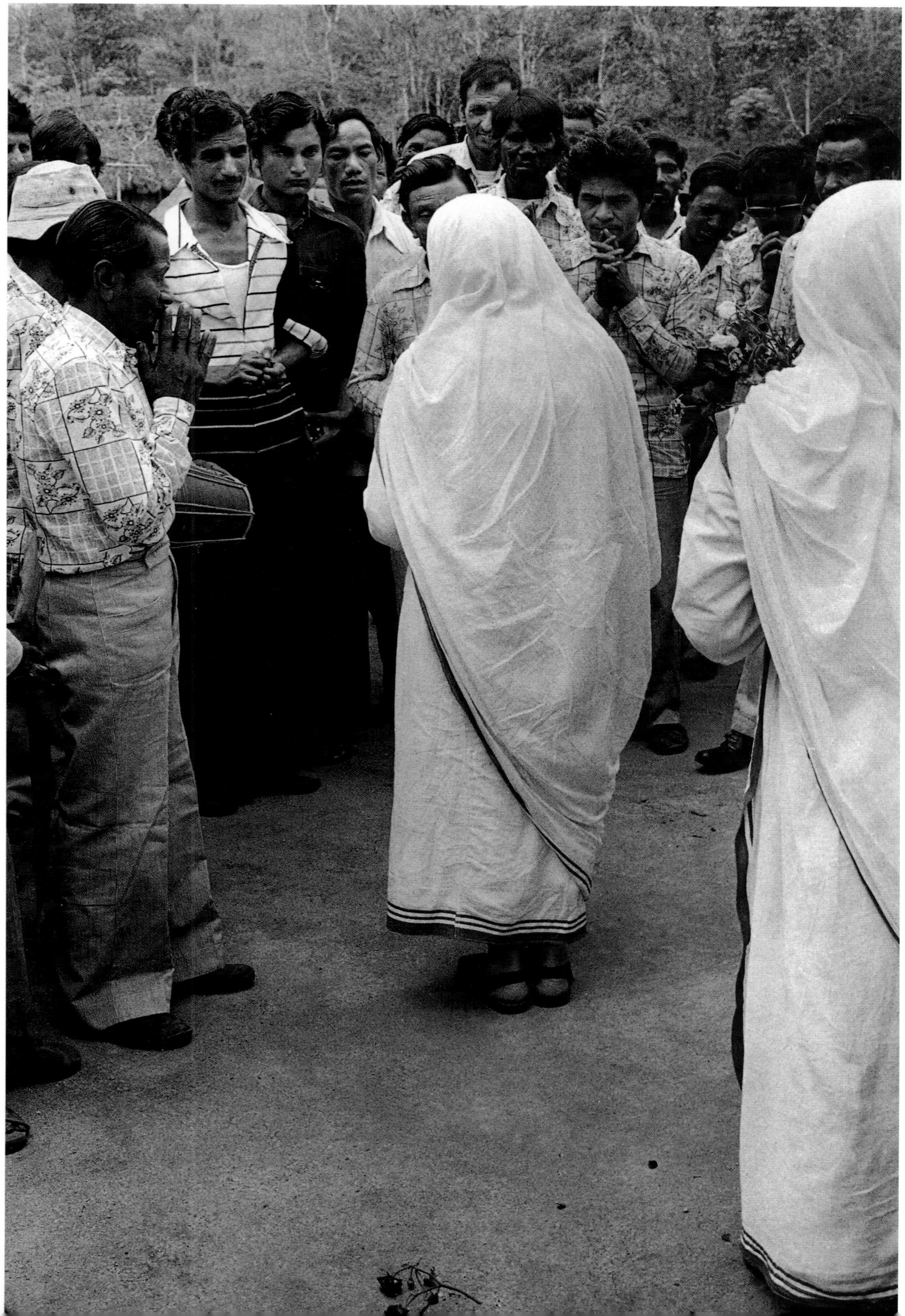

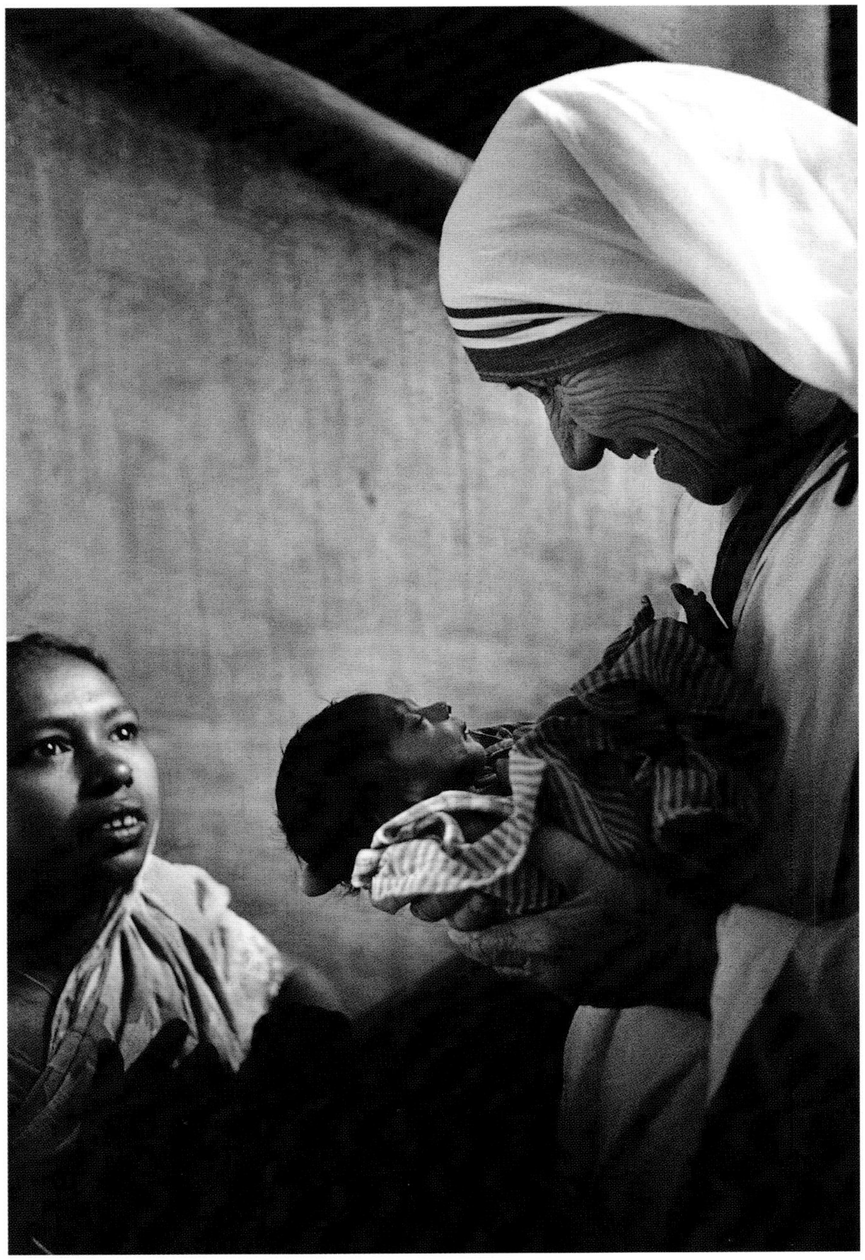

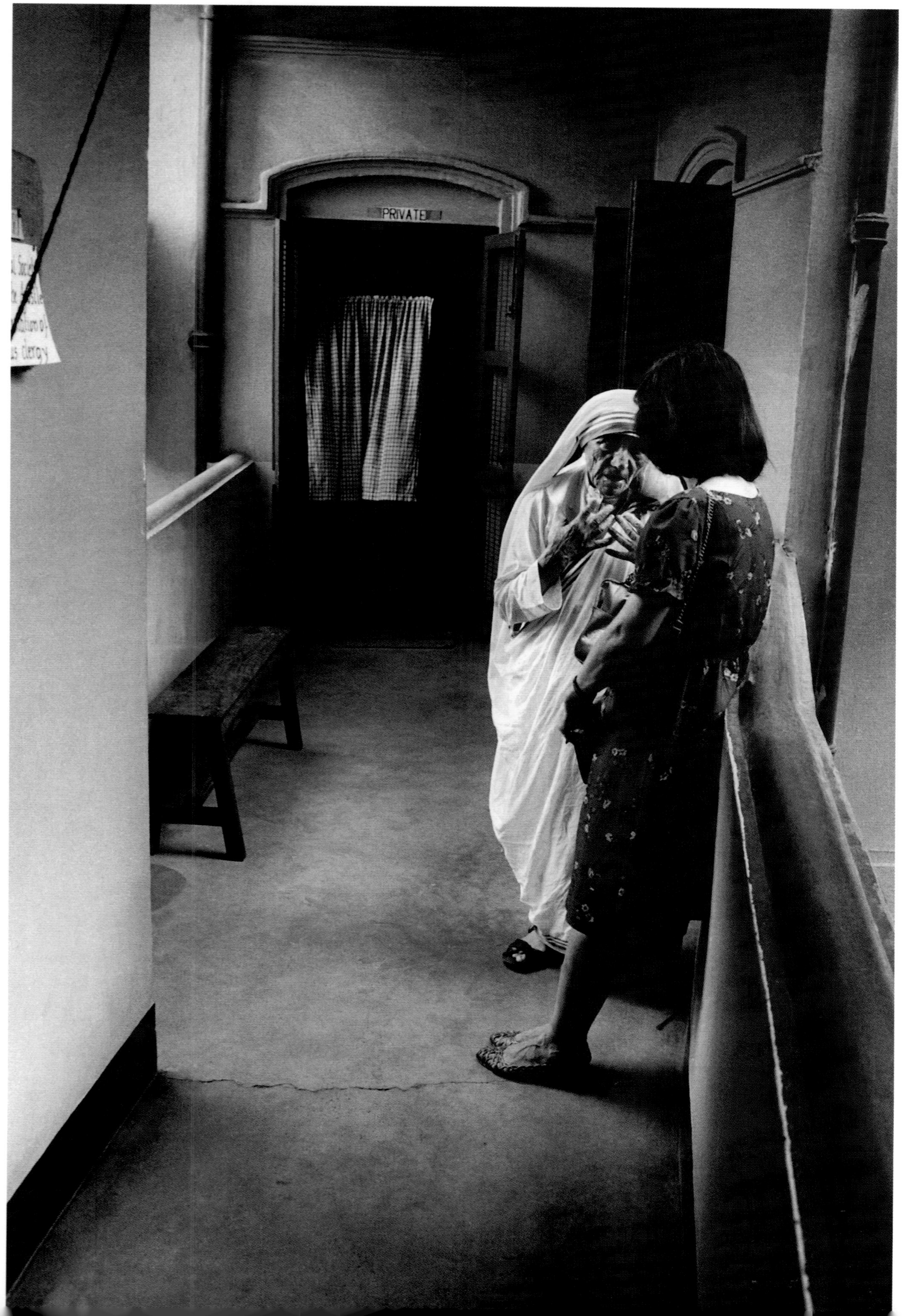
PRIVATE

a good brahmin: the soul of service

MOTHER, IN YOUR LOVE FOR THE POOR, I SAW YOU SERVING CHRIST IN THE TRUEST AND MOST MAGNANIMOUS SPIRIT OF THE LORD.

Each time you met anyone at home or on the streets, for shelter or for love, you transformed their existence into loving care.

Once, an old Brahmin woman was dying on the streets of Kolkata; the sisters of the Missionaries of Charity wanted to pick her up and bring her to their Home for the Aged. The woman, however, insisted she couldn't be touched by anyone except a Brahmin. This story was narrated to you, and you decided to bring the dying woman under your own personal care.

As you were about to touch her, the dying woman asked if you were a Brahmin. In recounting this episode, you asked yourself, "Who is a Brahmin? I felt anyone who serves his people is a good Brahmin so I said, 'Yes, I'm Brahmin'." And you brought her home.

a true indian: pride of the poor

OH MOTHER! NO OTHER INDIAN HAS MADE ME SO PROUD AS YOU DID THAT DAY.

The day I was photographing you at Kalighat, in the Nirmal Hriday Home for the Aged, you were busy attending a sick person.

A sister came to tell you that a Swiss banker wanted to see you. You acknowledged the message, but continued to nurse the ailing old woman.

After you finished nursing, you met the Swiss gentleman who made an offer of a hefty donation to you. But there was a touch of arrogance in his attitude.

You heard him patiently and then told him, "I am sure there are old people in your own country who also need a home and care. Why don't you do something there? My people give me enough money to look after the poor in my own country."

As I watched and listened, I felt pride in being an Indian as I'd never felt before.

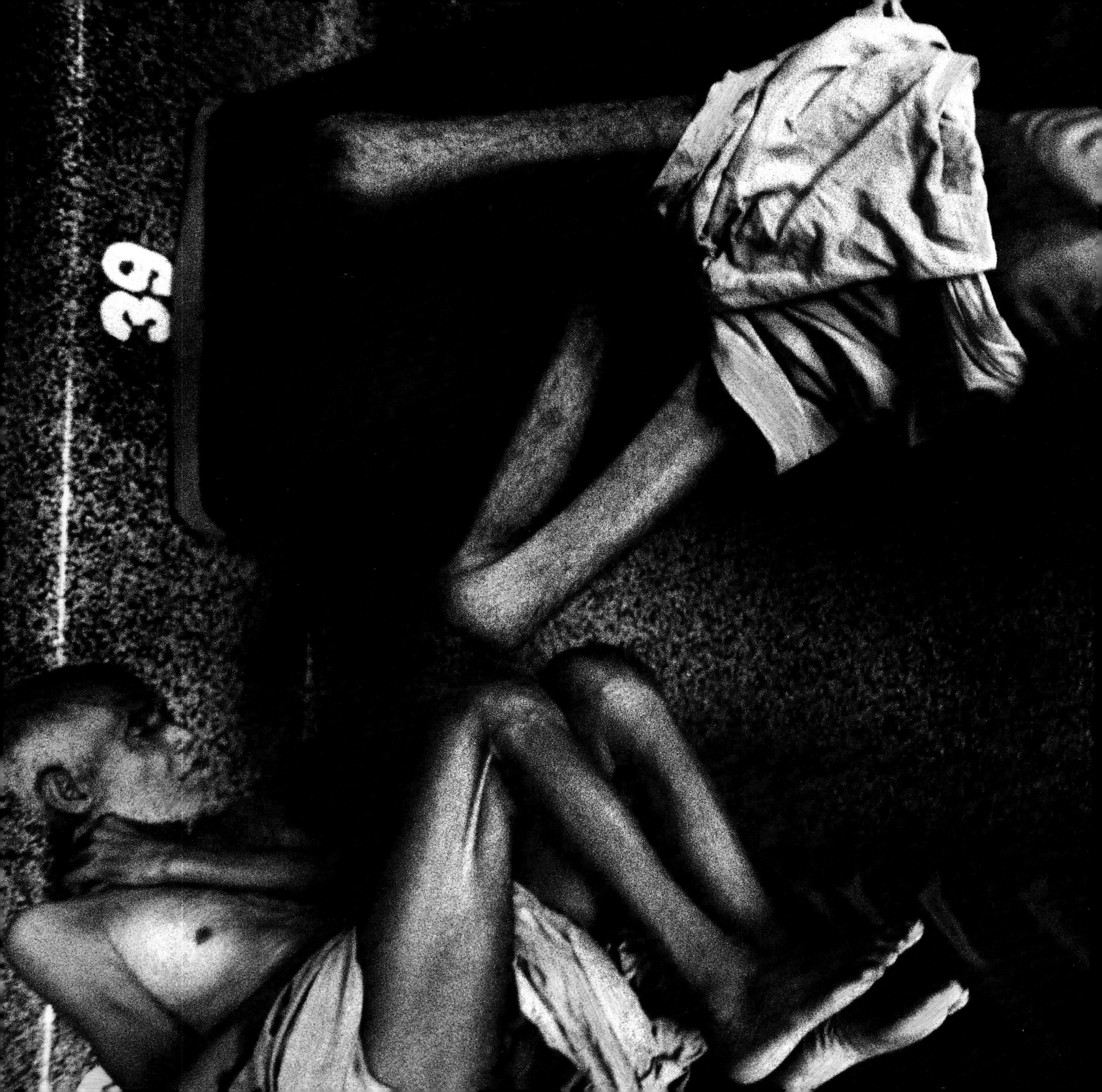
39

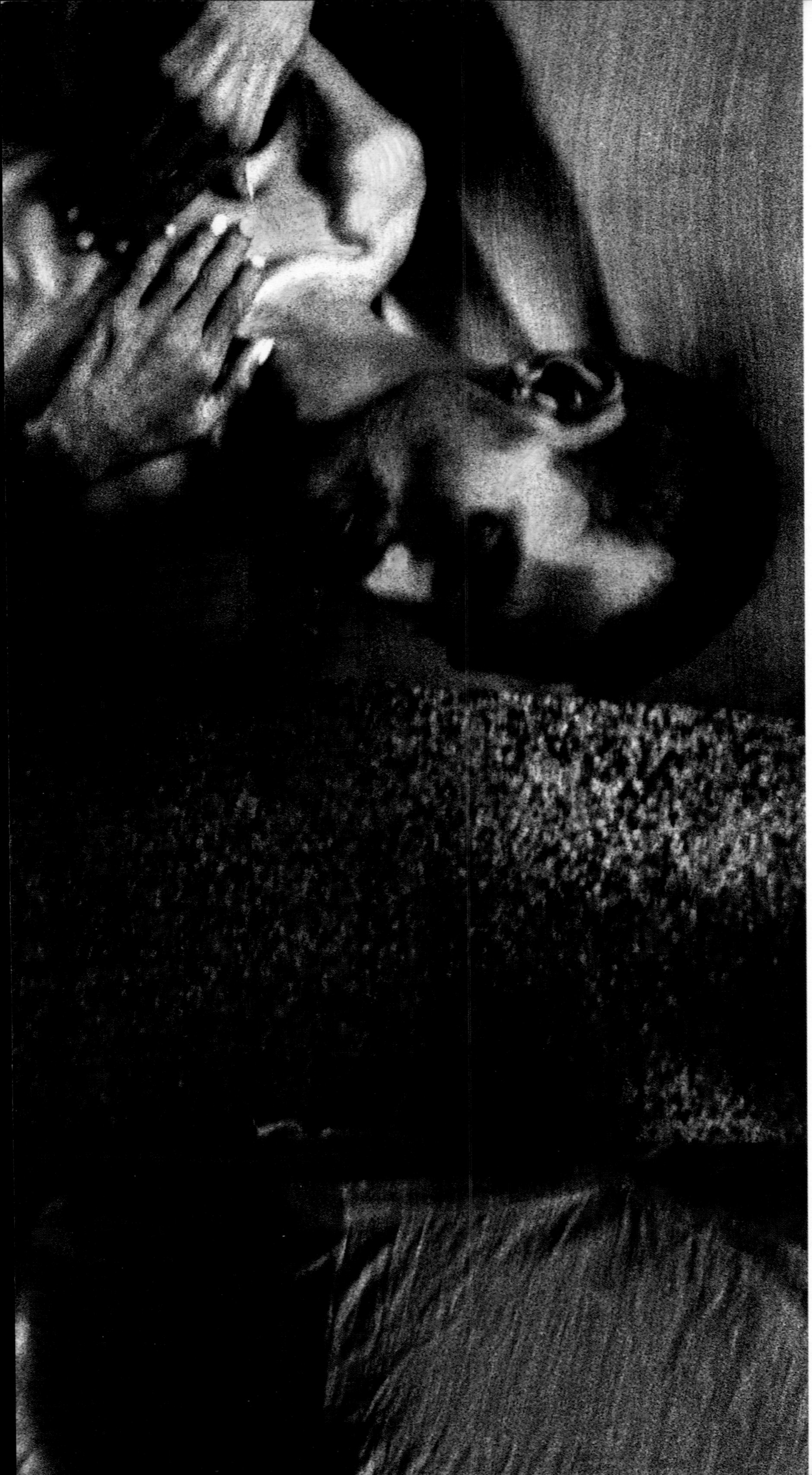

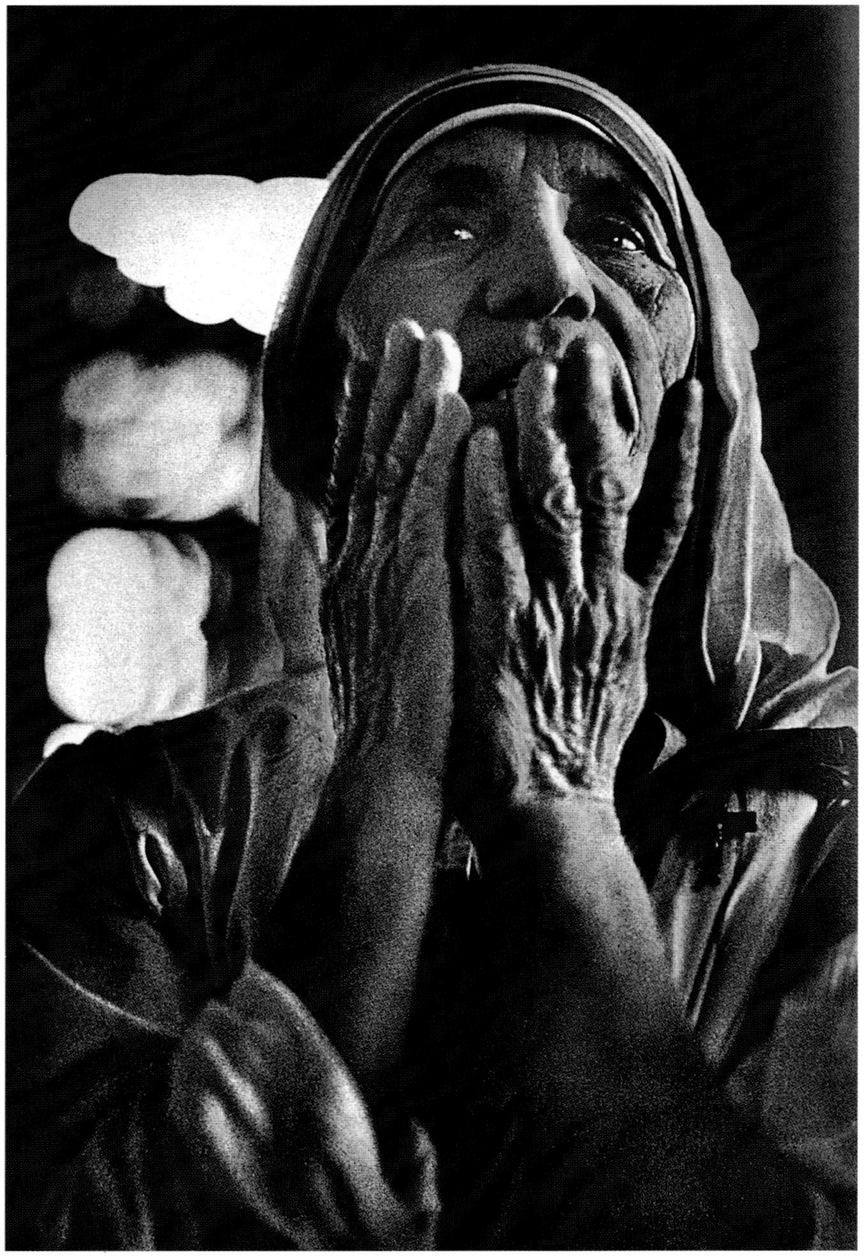

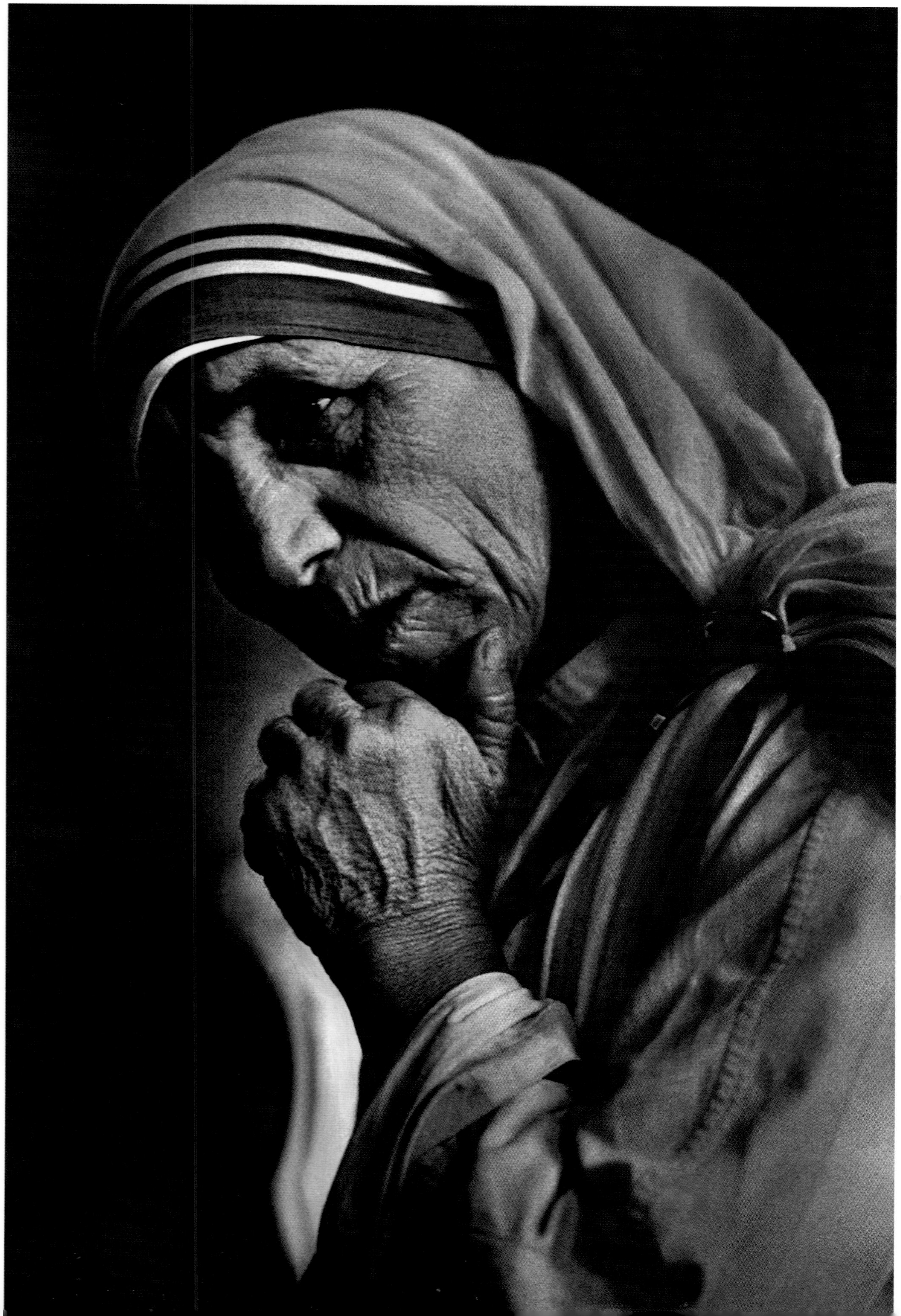

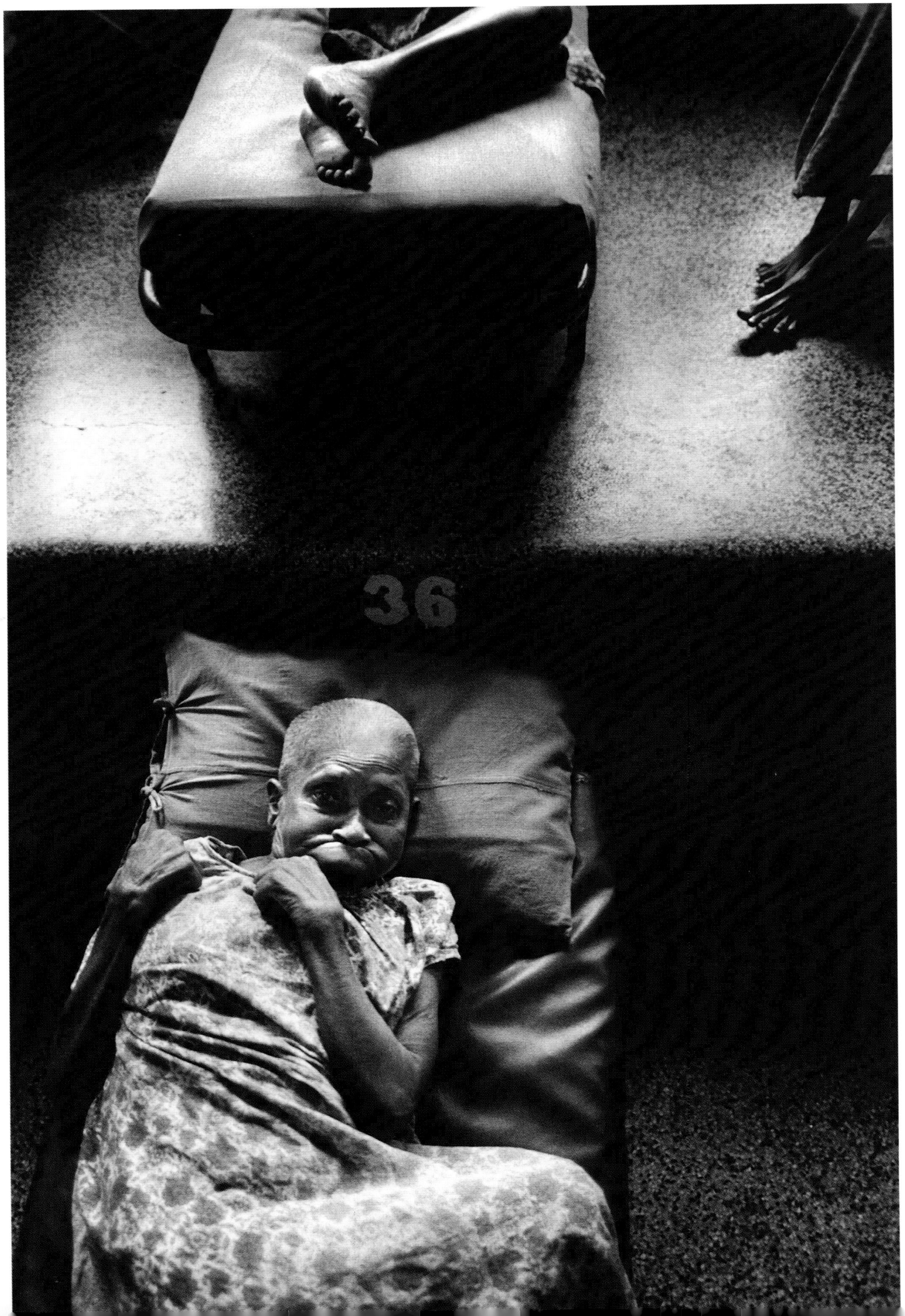

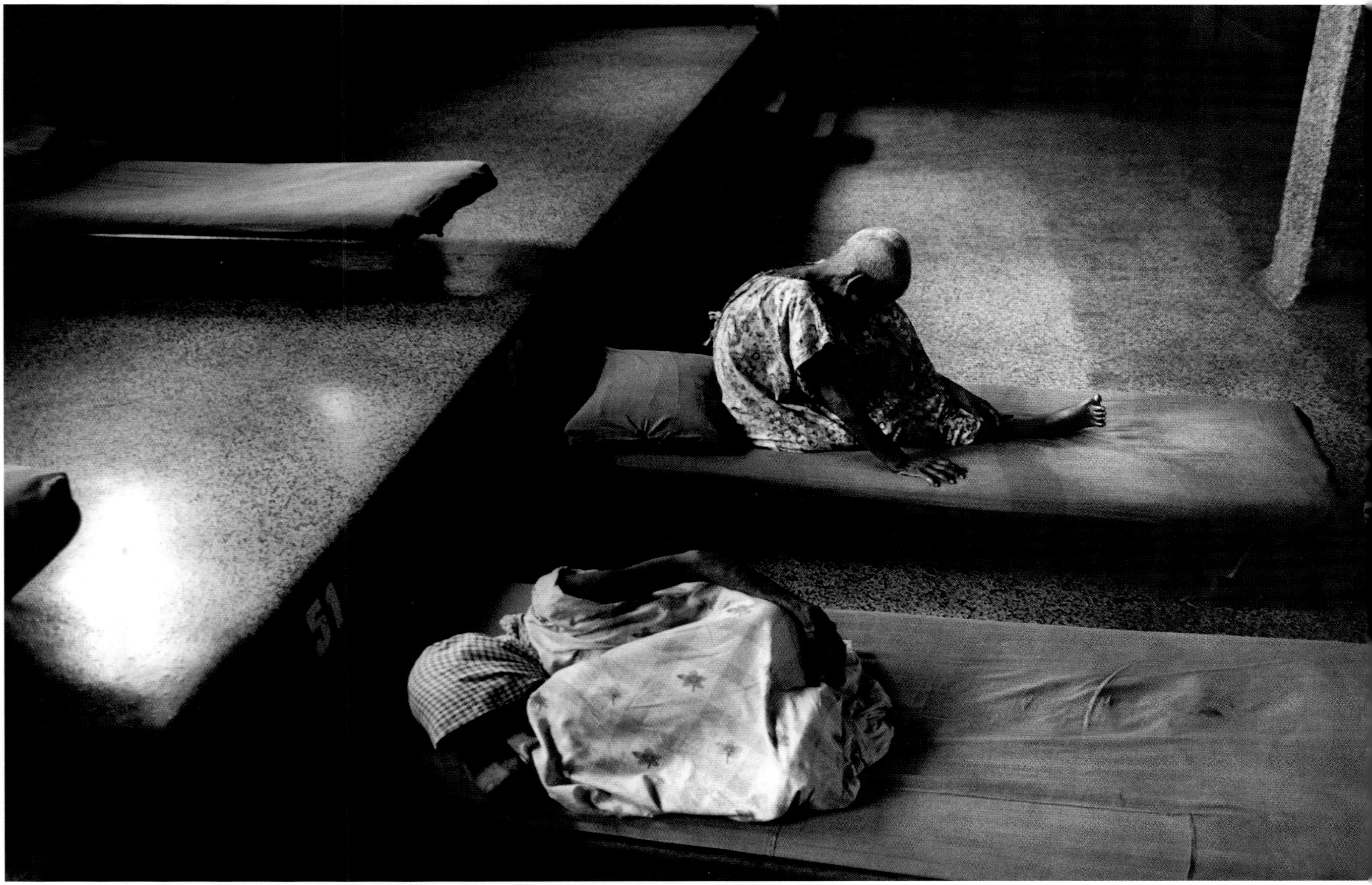
51

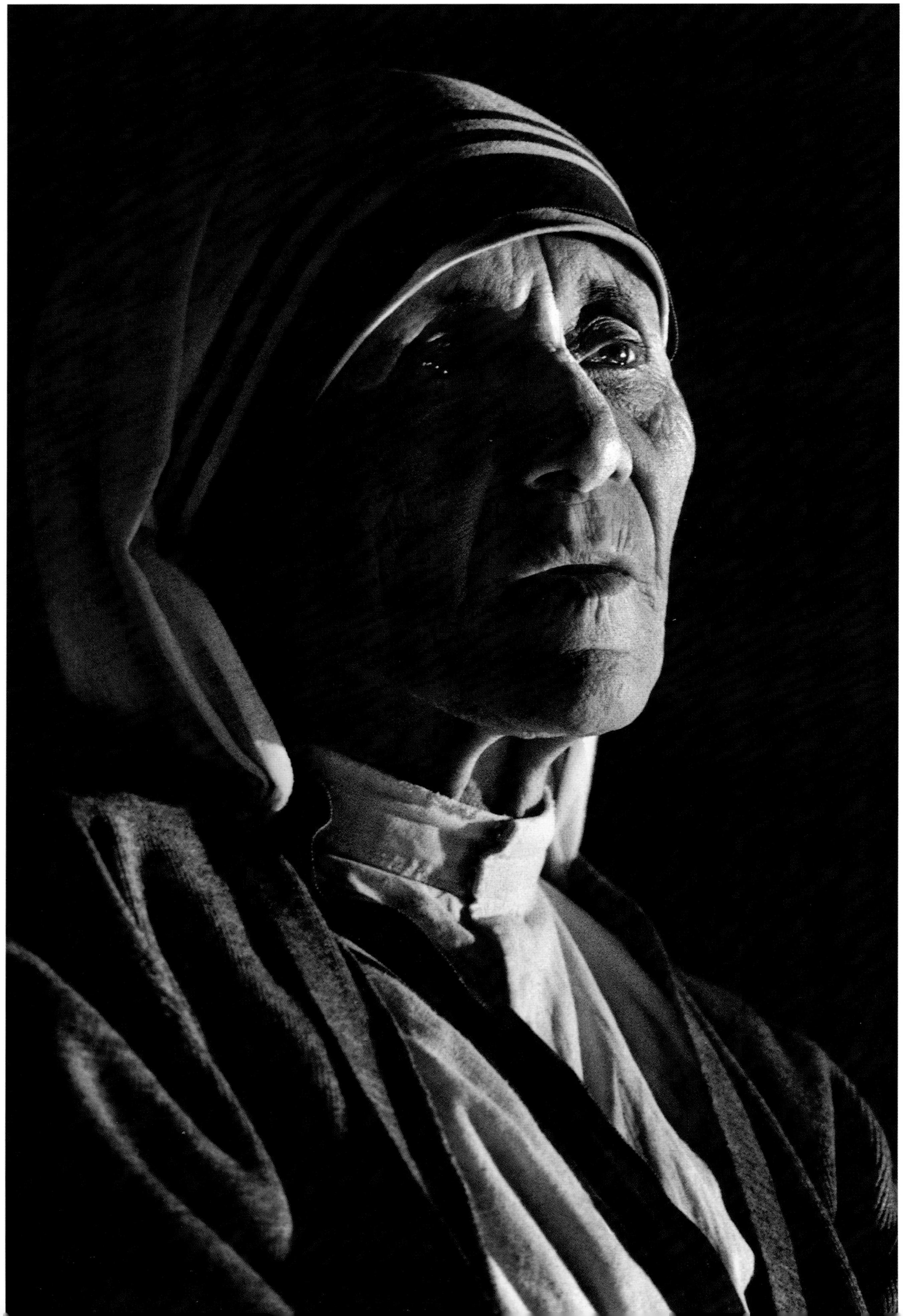

never forsaken: prayer's glorious path

THIS GOES BACK TO THE TRYING TIMES WHEN MILLIONS OF PEOPLE FROM BANGLADESH WERE BEING DRIVEN OUT FROM THEIR HOMES TO BECOME REFUGEES ACROSS THE BORDER.

There was distress all over. It was not possible for you, Mother, and your sisters, to stay away from this crisis of humanity.

There were innumerable hardships in the process. "My sisters will put up with everything; they will spend all their time, and do their duty, but they will have to come back every evening for their prayers to rejuvenate their spiritual energies," you told the authorities in charge of the relief work. Such is the spiritual power of everyday prayer.

Daily prayer could not be forsaken at any cost. It energizes that divine connection with the faith and sustains everything.

another mother: and a son's promise

MOTHER, I HAVE A STORY TO TELL YOU.

I could not but help get emotionally involved in the plight of the people who were under your care. Almost everyone had a painful past. There was an old and fragile lady who would always be yearning for her son. She would get cross with the sisters for not bringing him to her. Now I had no knowledge as to where her son was. I could not help her. So I decided to tell her a comforting lie, a harmless one.

I affectionately held her hand and told her that I was her son and I was sorry that it had taken me so long to come. She forgot about all her pain and tears, and showered her affection on me. She even chided me for having gone away without caring for her and then commanded, "Go and get me some cigarettes."

I took permission from the sister in charge and brought her cigarettes. I assured her that I would not leave her again. Thereafter, she would proudly tell other occupants that her long-lost son had come back. She was a changed human being. A few days later, she died old and fragile.

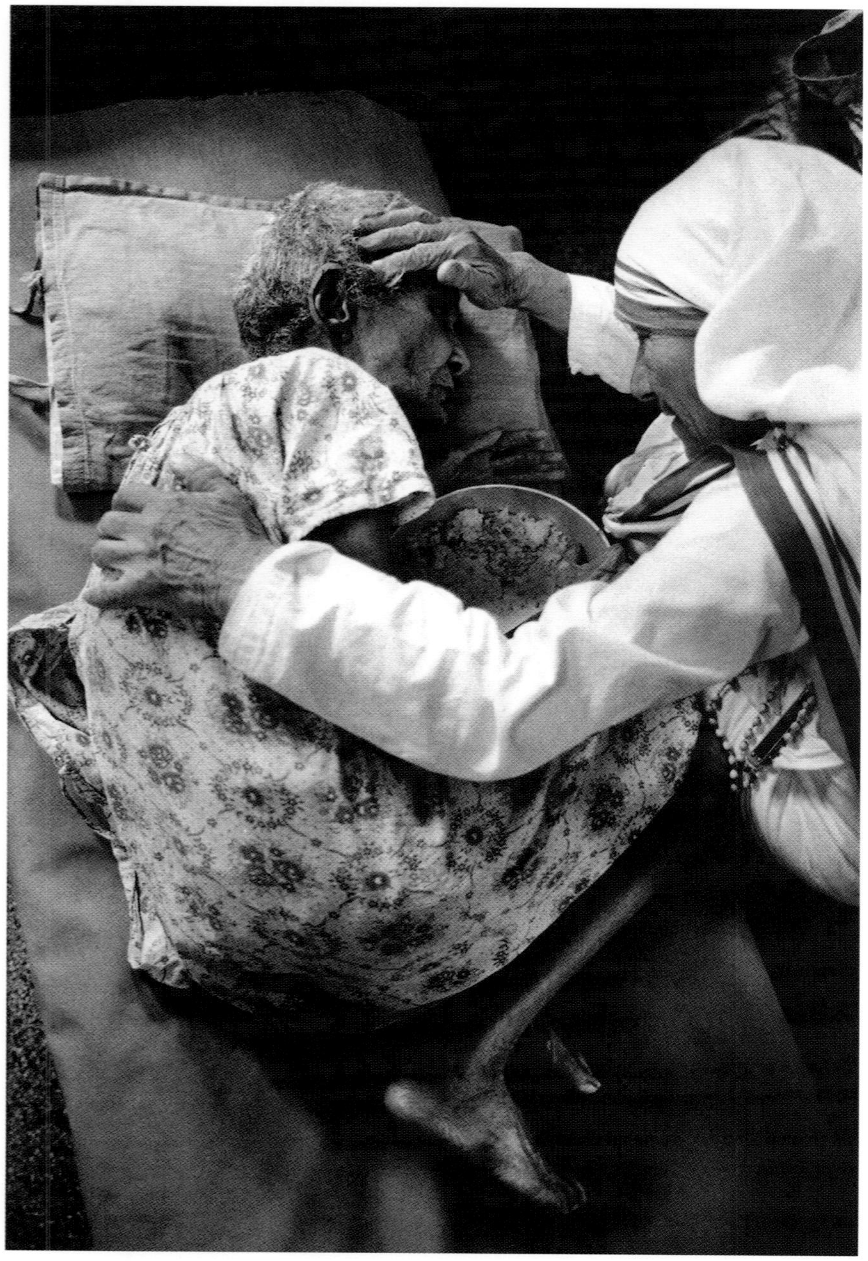

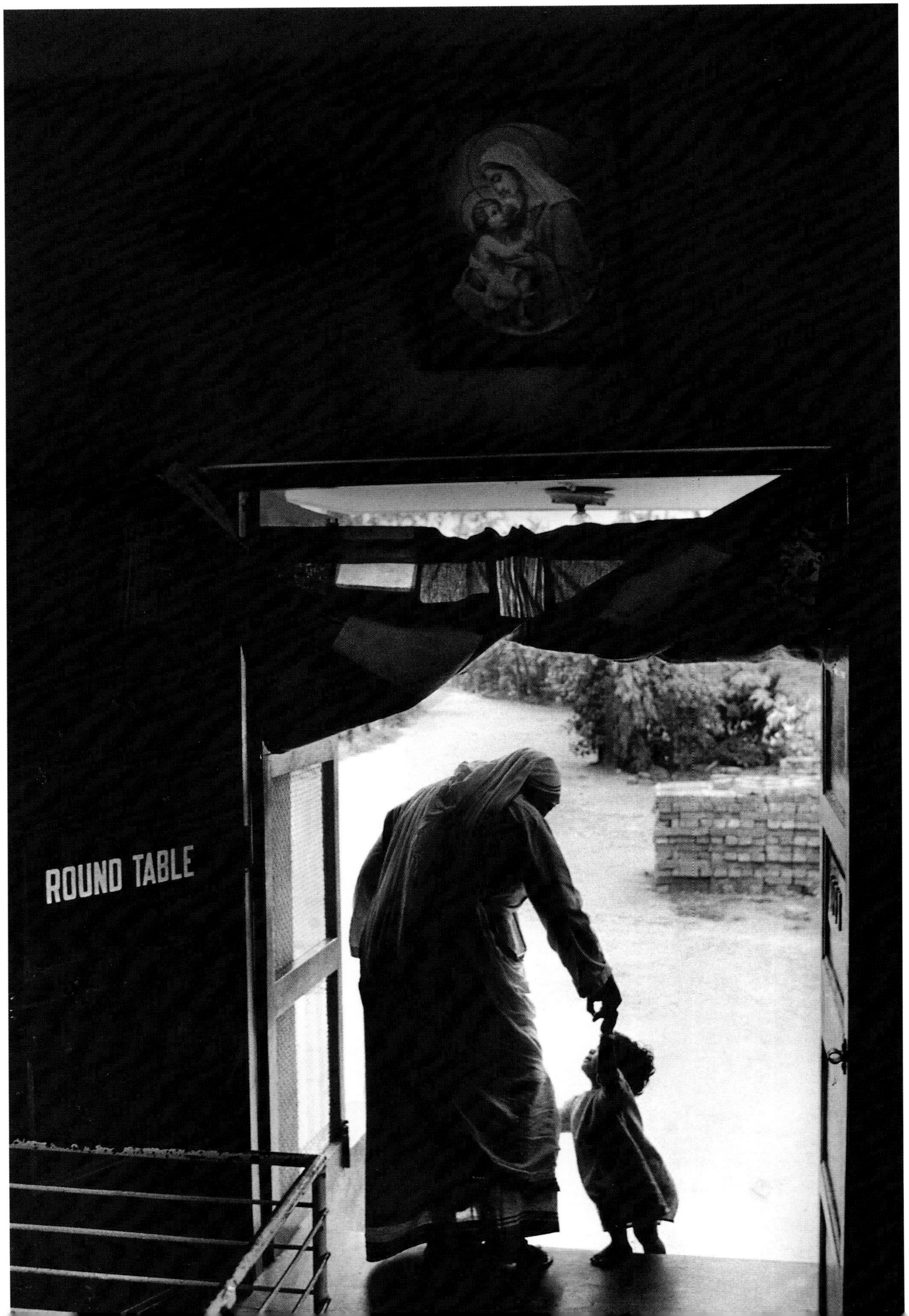
ROUND TABLE

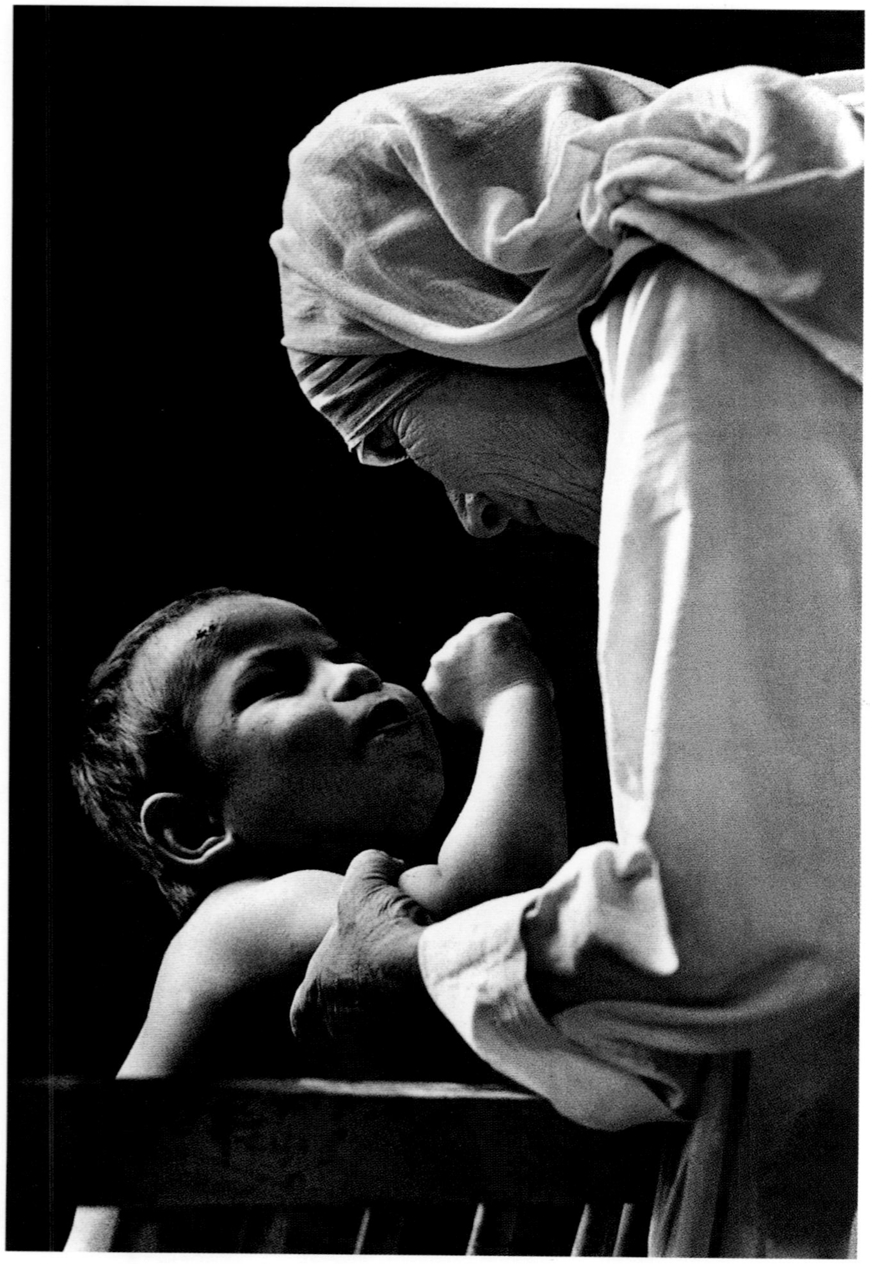

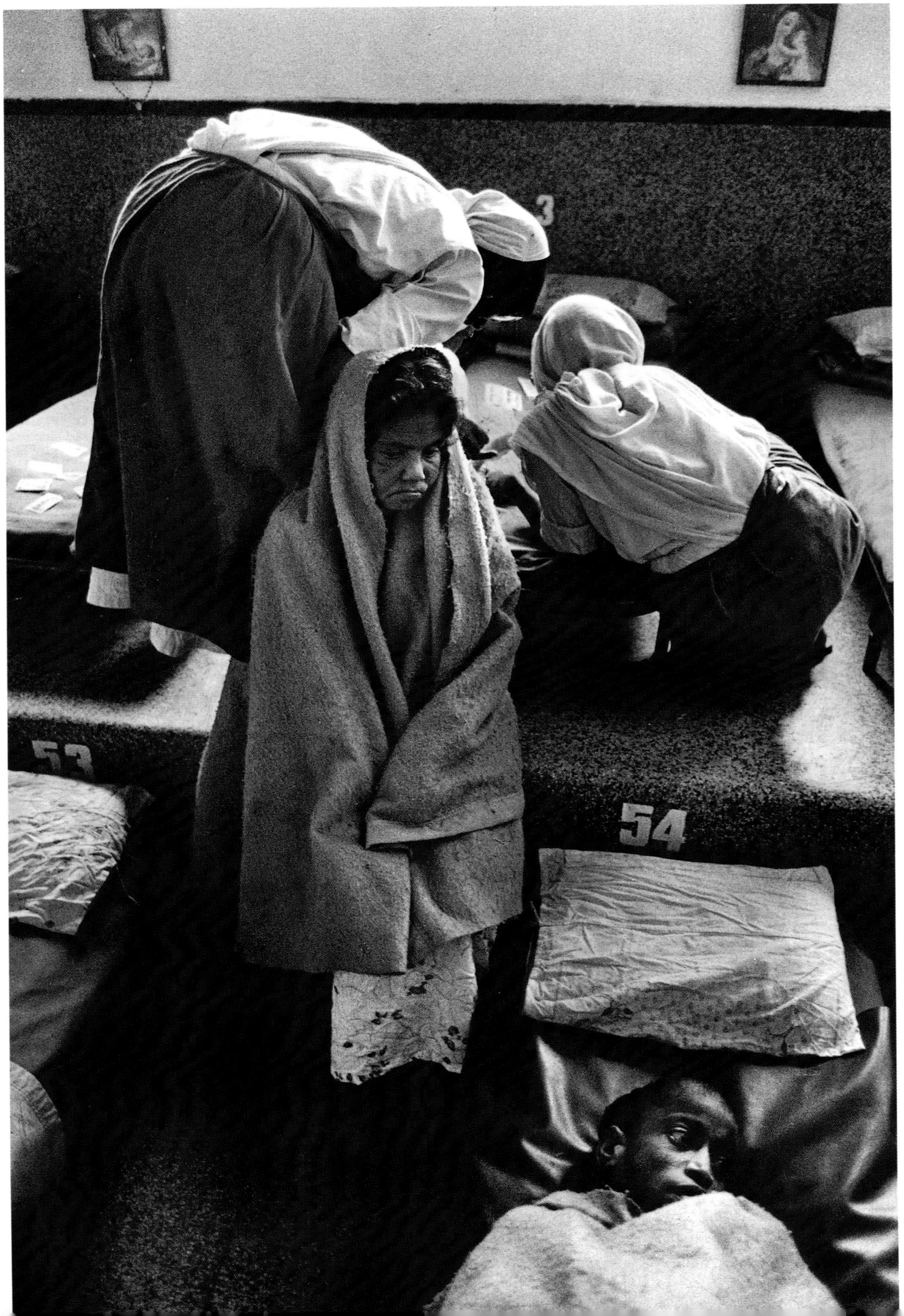

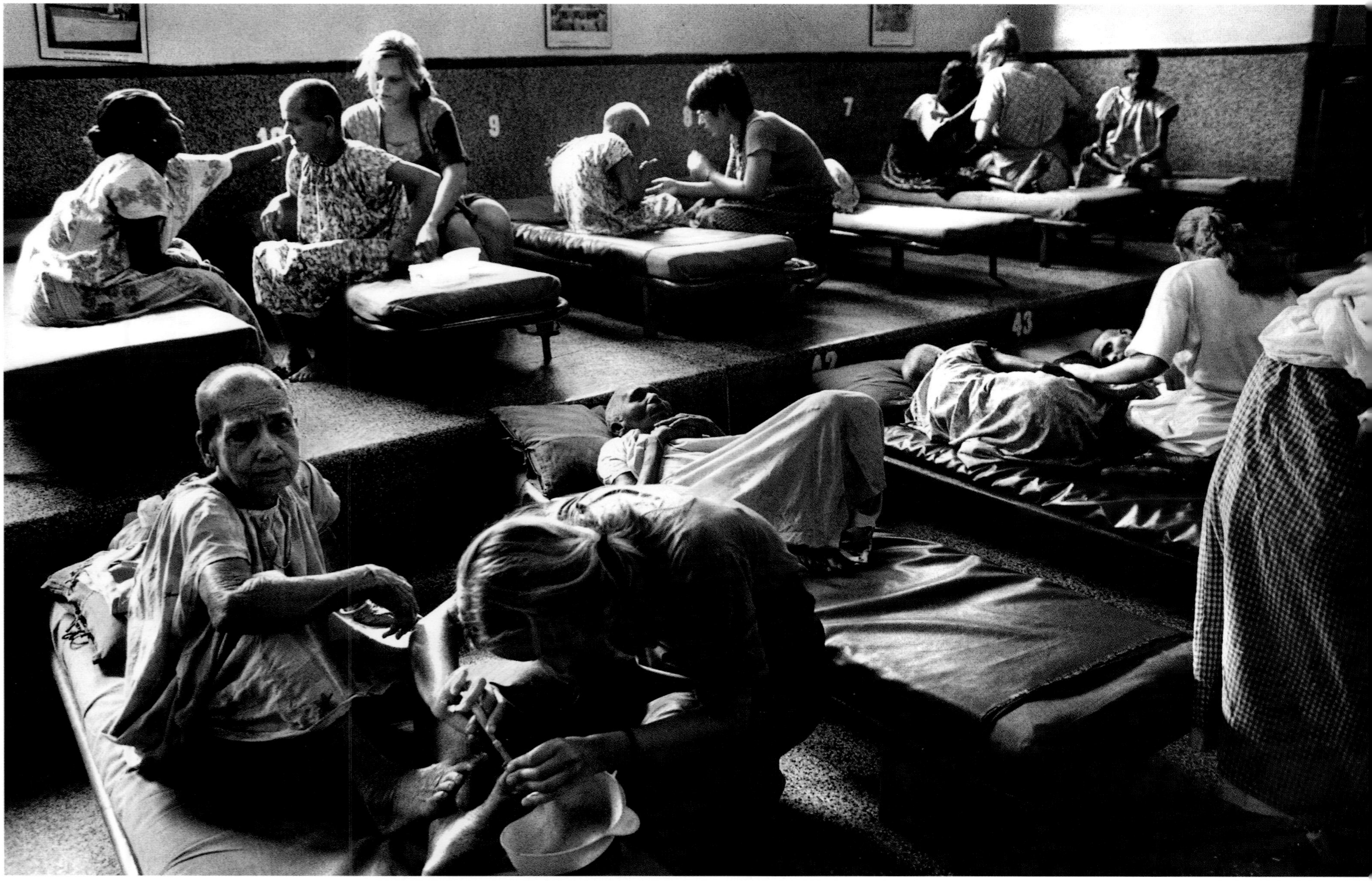

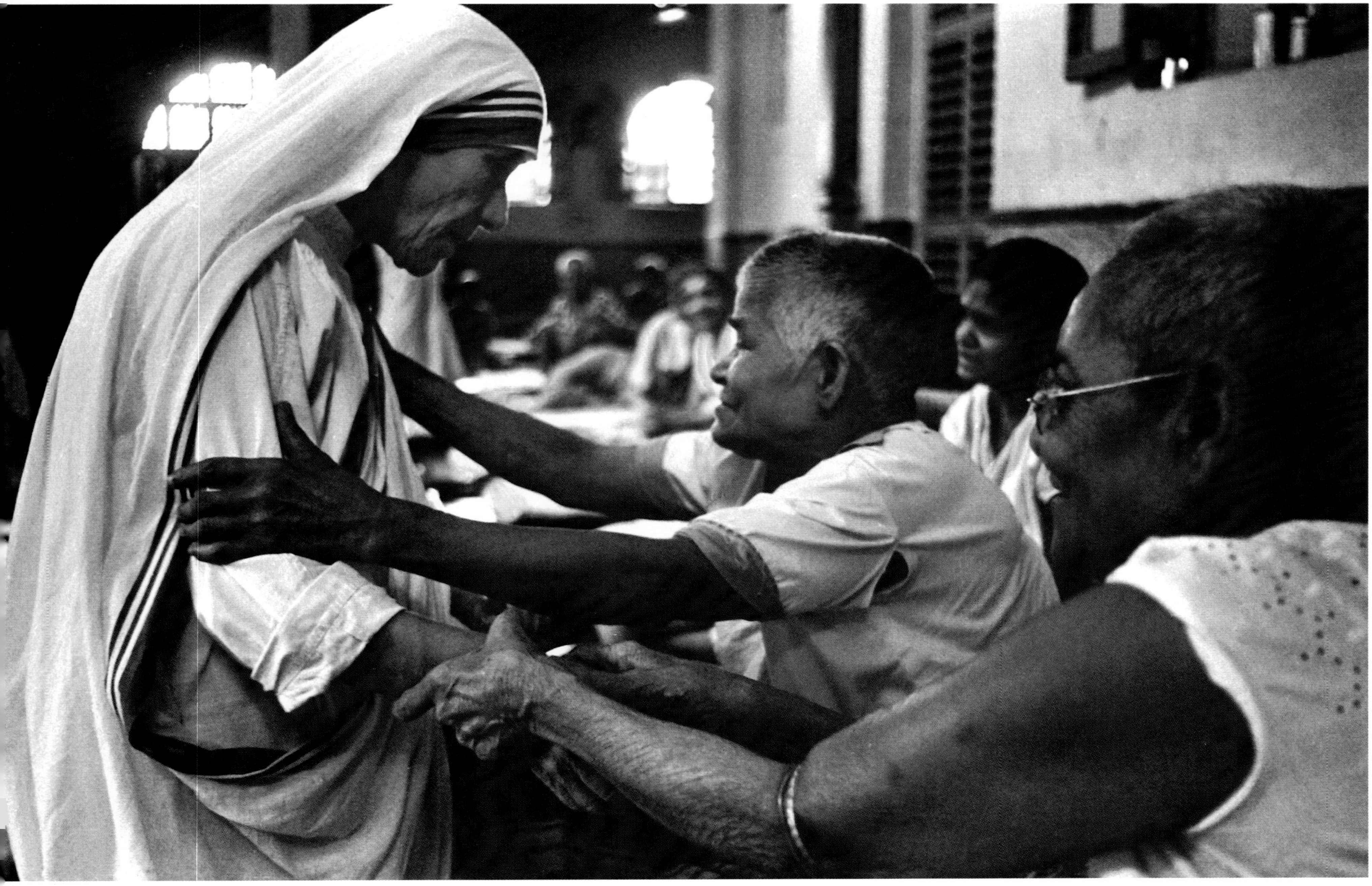

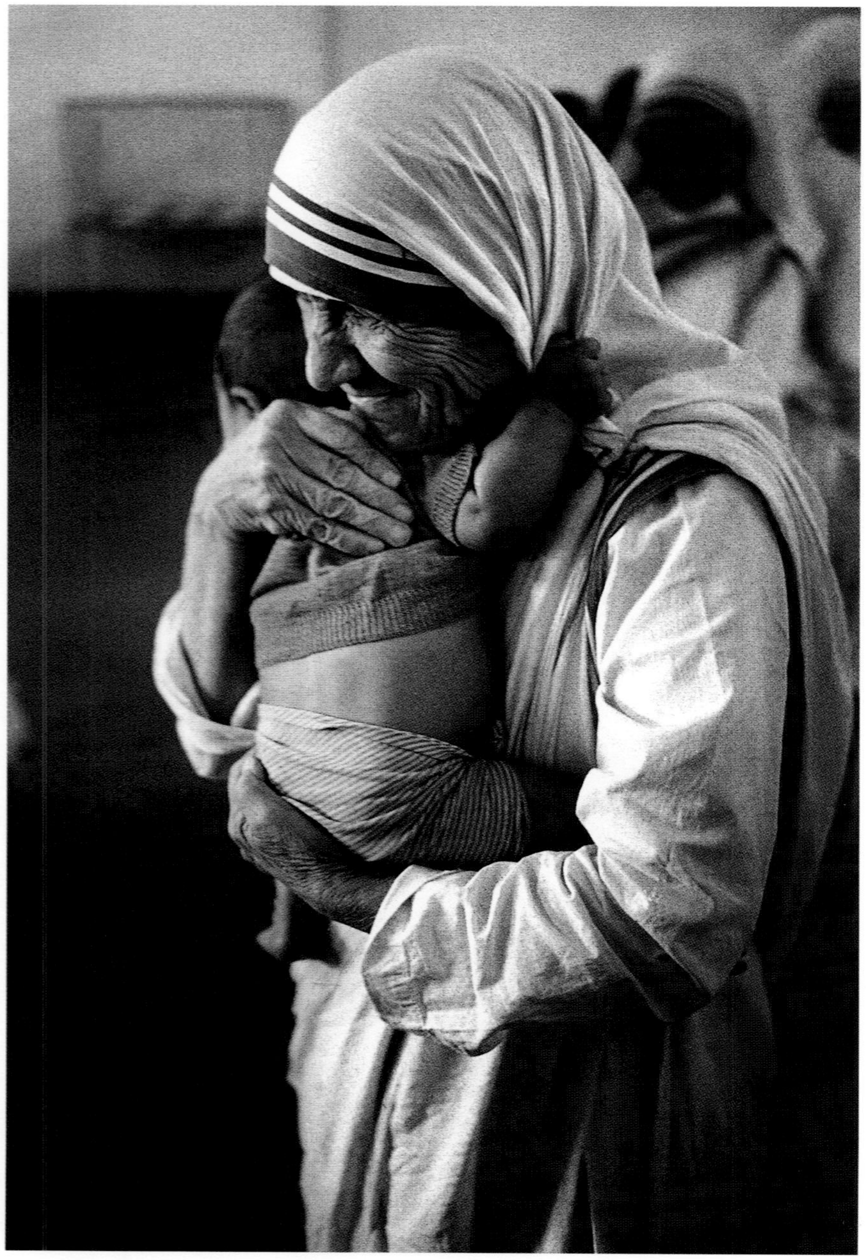

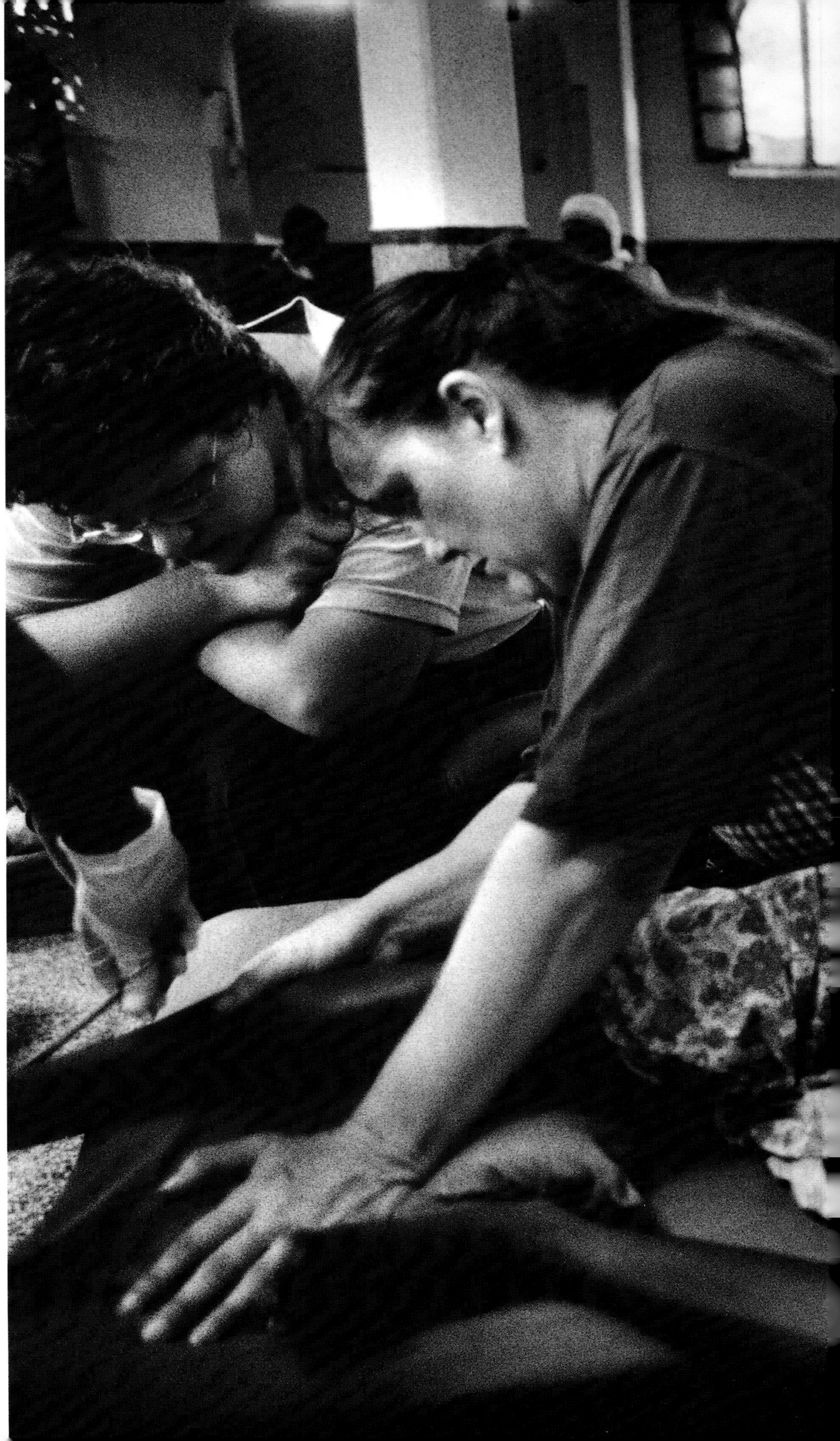

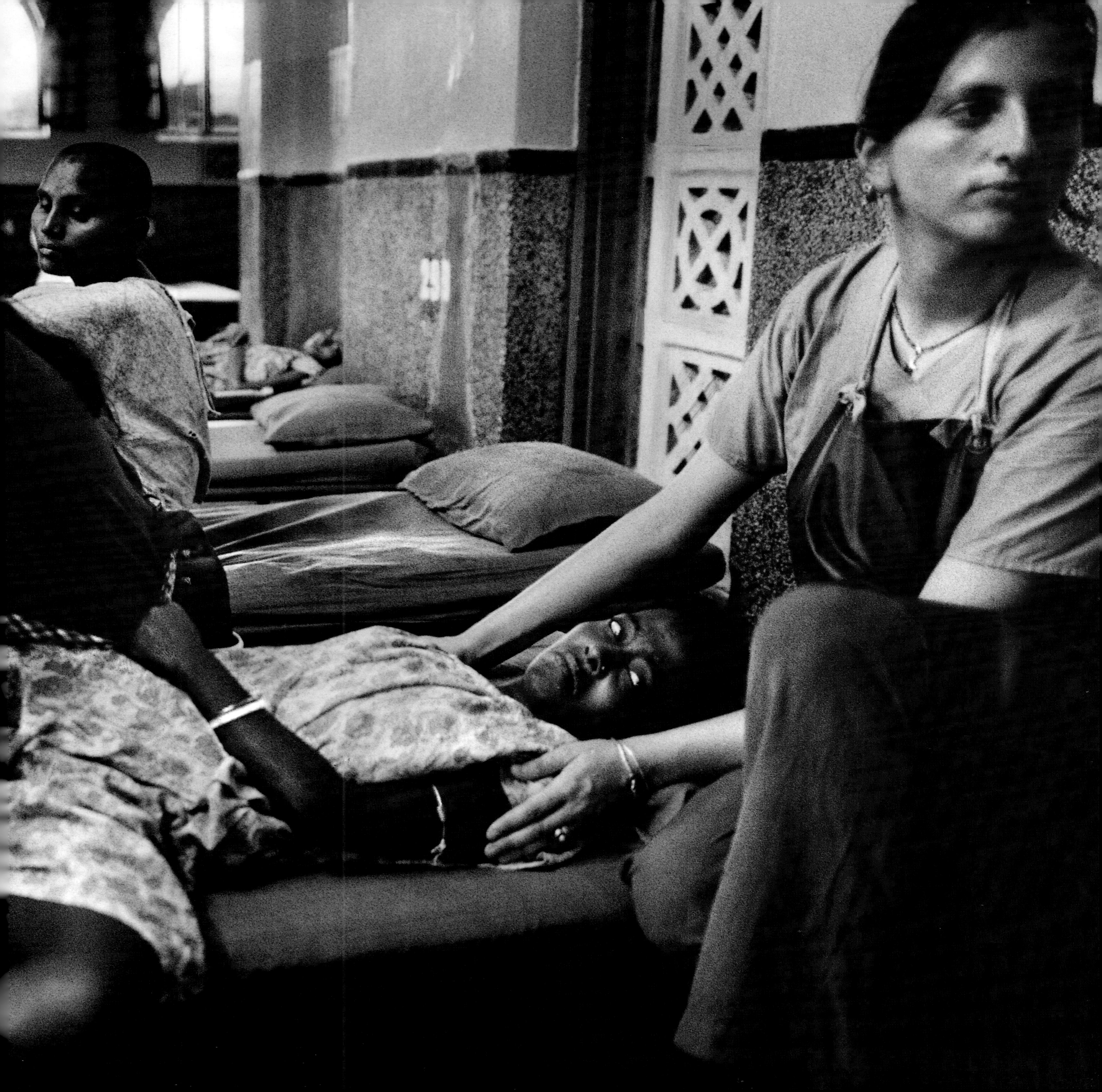

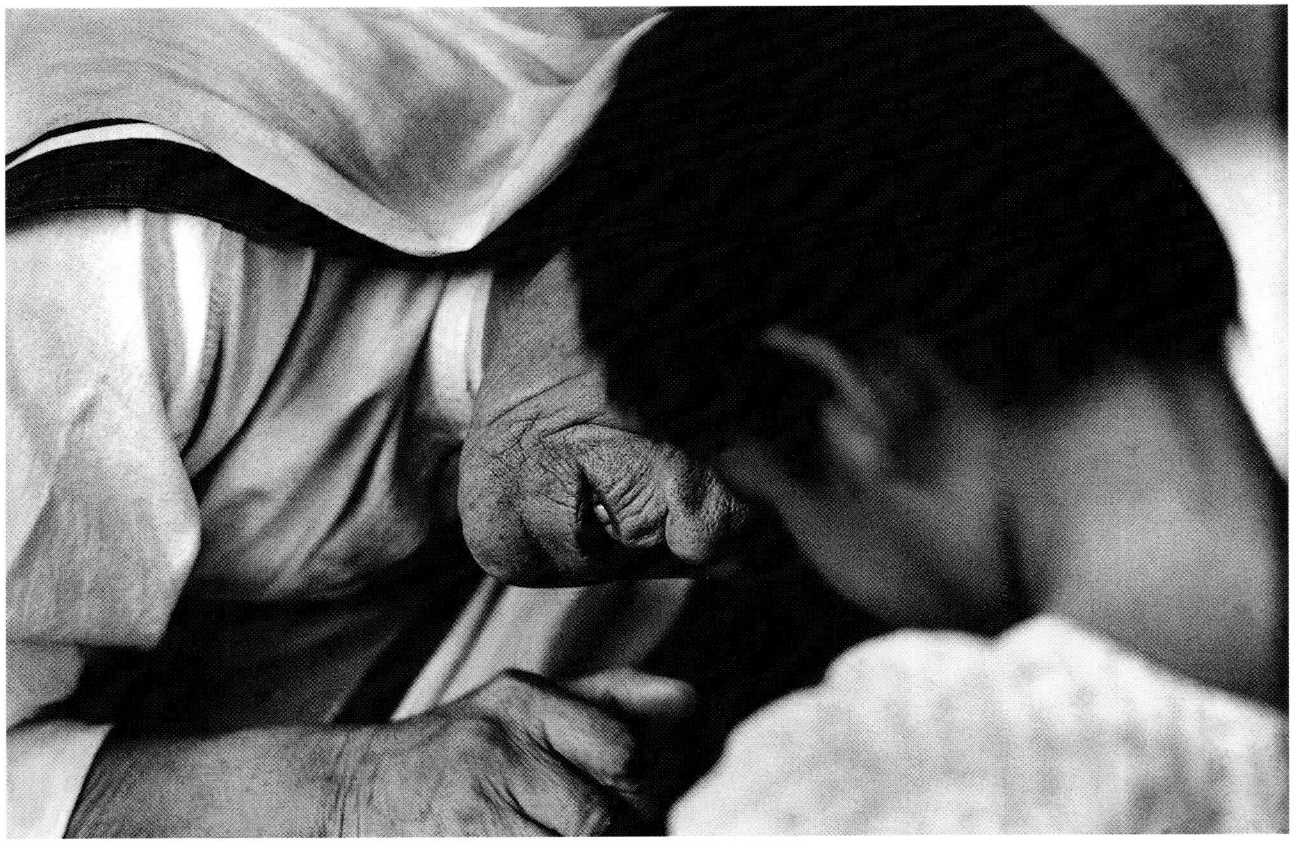

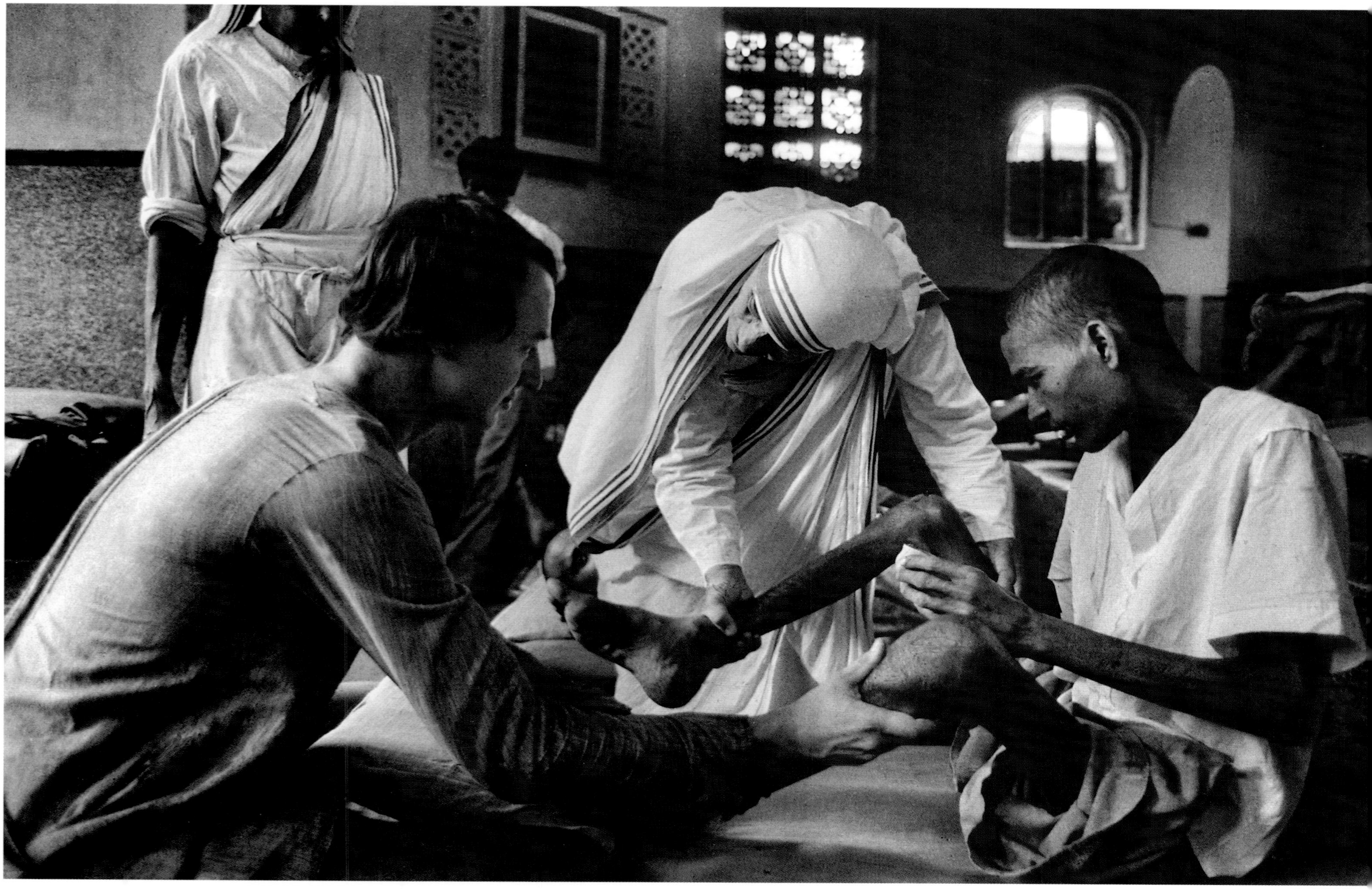

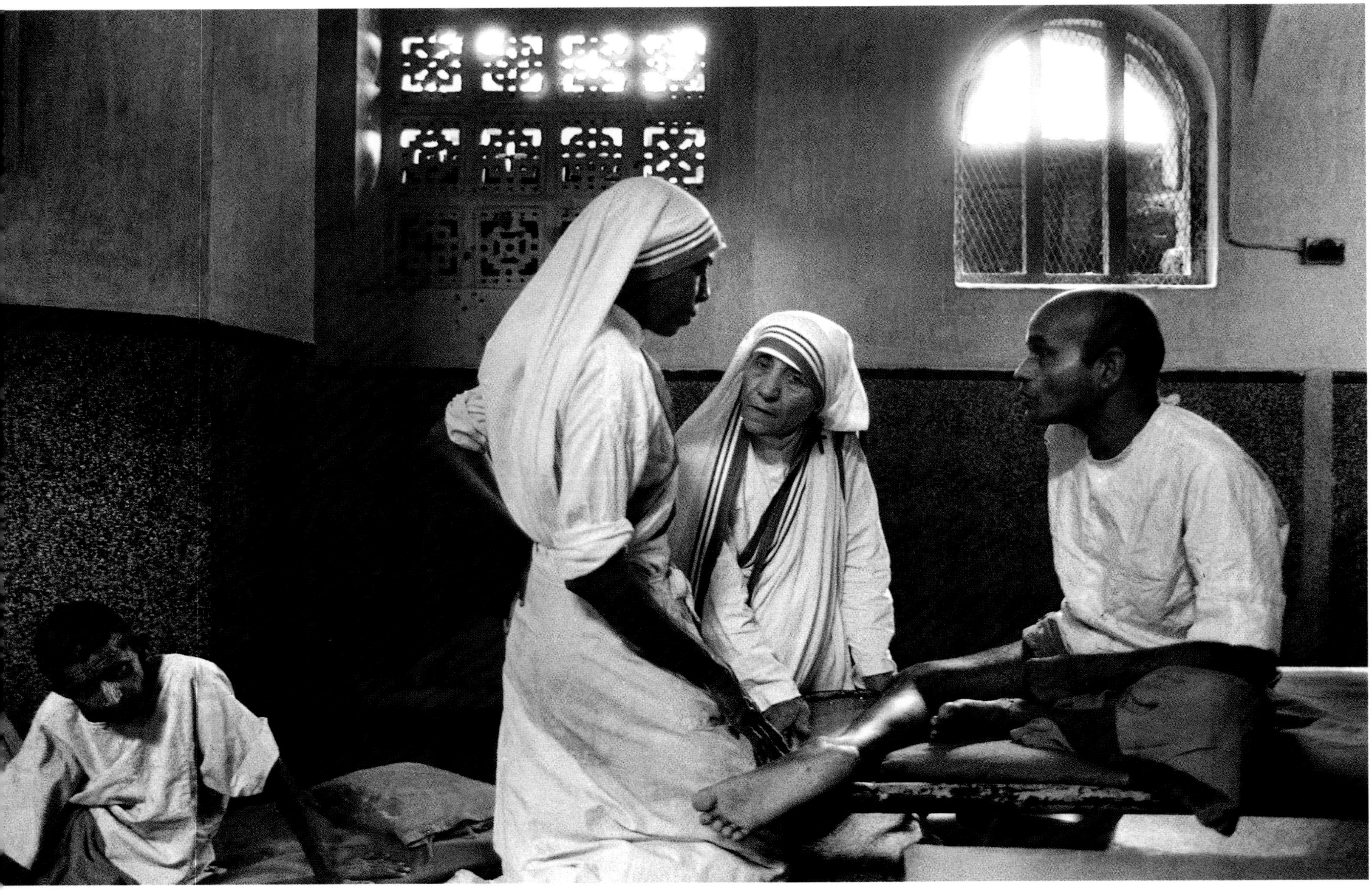

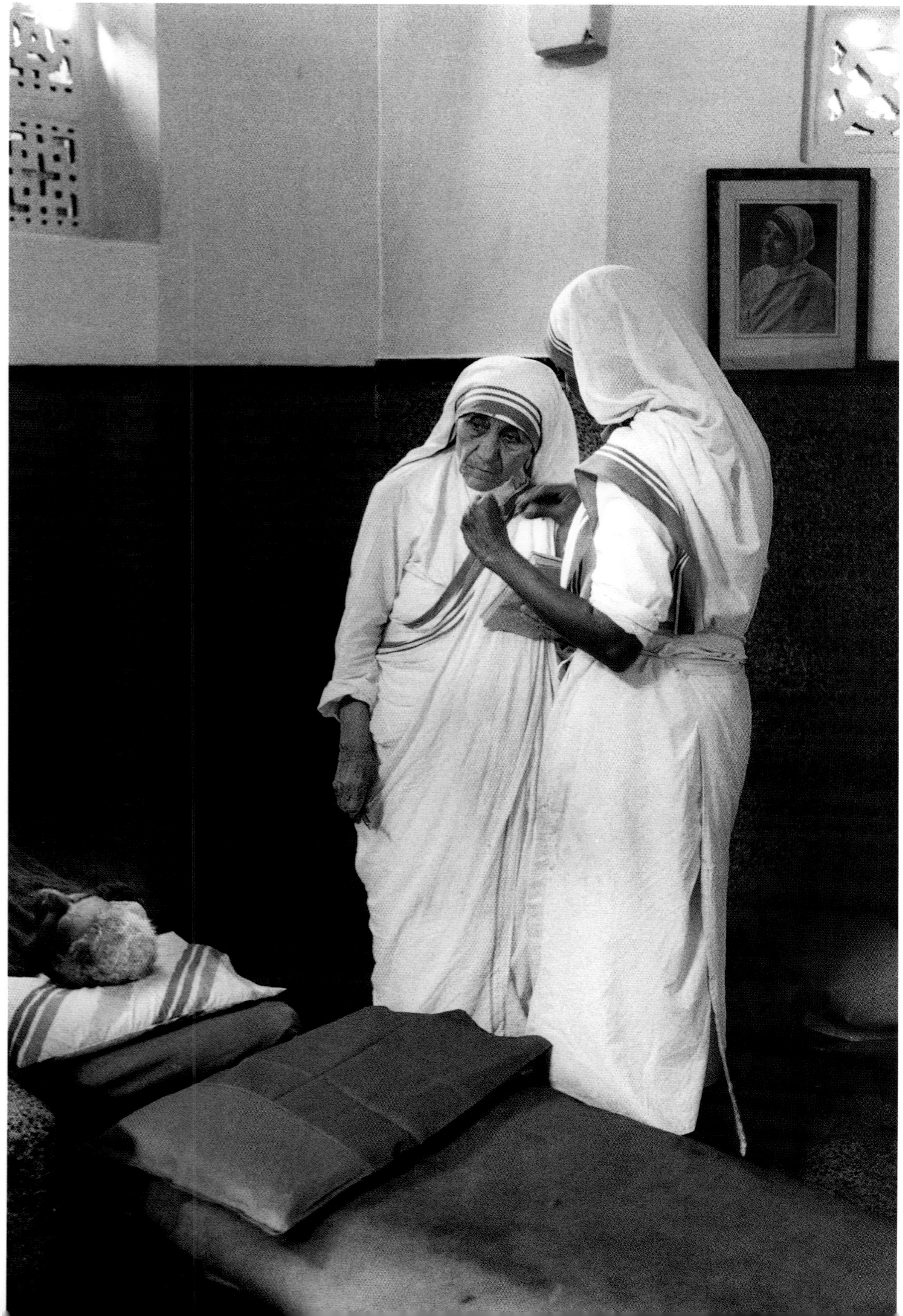

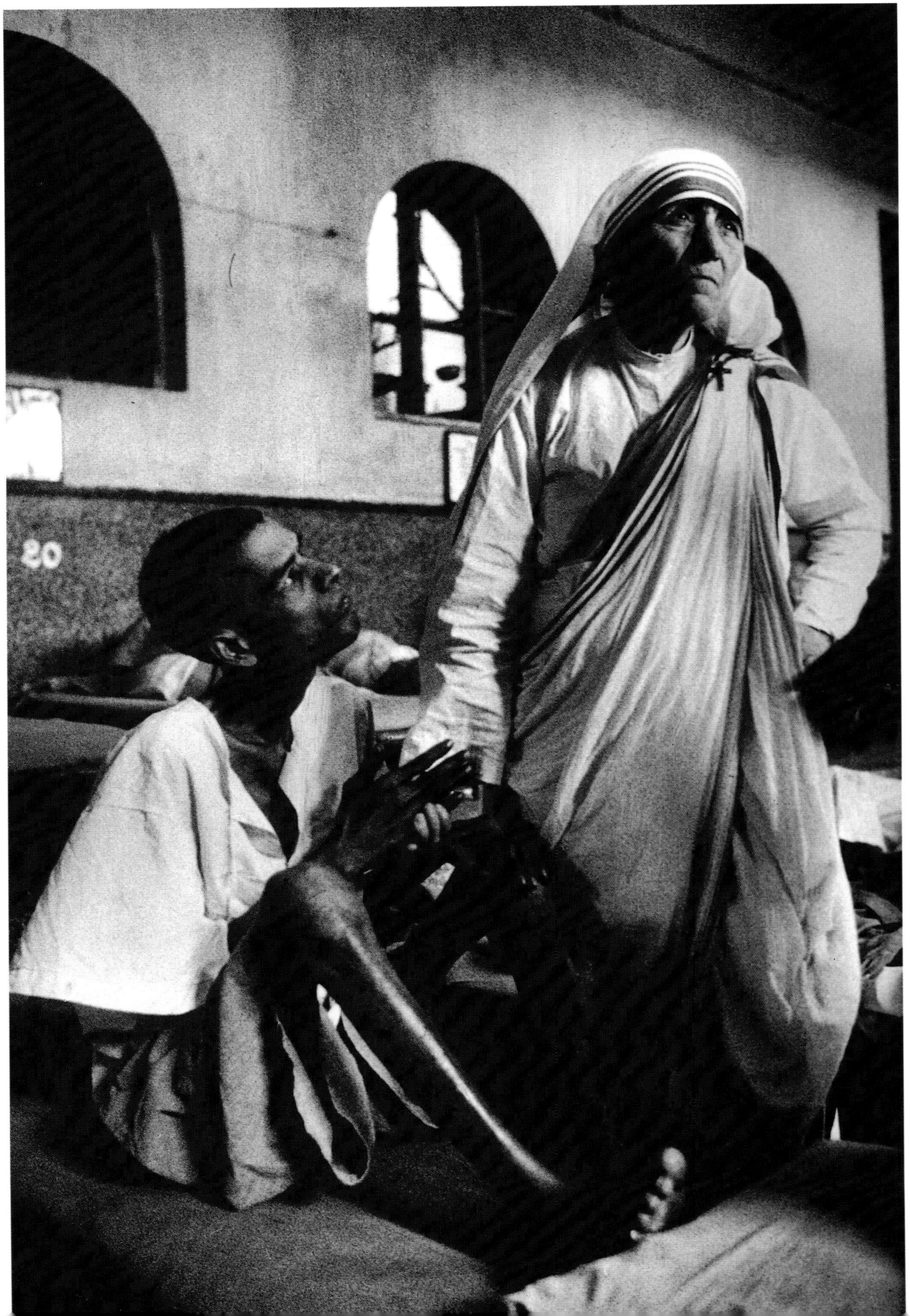
20

an intrusion: . . . and forgiveness

THERE WERE NO LIMITS TO FREEDOM, SO I THOUGHT.

After getting permission to take pictures in your Home (where all the sisters live) on a special day, it happened that I saw a sister making a confession. This picture, I did not want to miss. Not only would it portray the sanctity of a confession, it would also show that the nuns were humans after all, prone to err and willing to accept their mistakes.

A senior sister stopped me immediately. There was the question of my intrusion into the confessional and taking a picture of the sisters in one of their extremely private moments. The sister asked who had allowed me in. I said, "Mother."

Having been briefed about the incident, you summoned me for an explanation. "What were you doing in the sisters' area?" I quietly tried to explain to her that while taking pictures, I was neither a man nor a woman, I was just a photographer.

"I was only taking pictures of sisters making confession, a moment so human," I explained. She grasped my point of view and said, "All right."

The matter ended there.

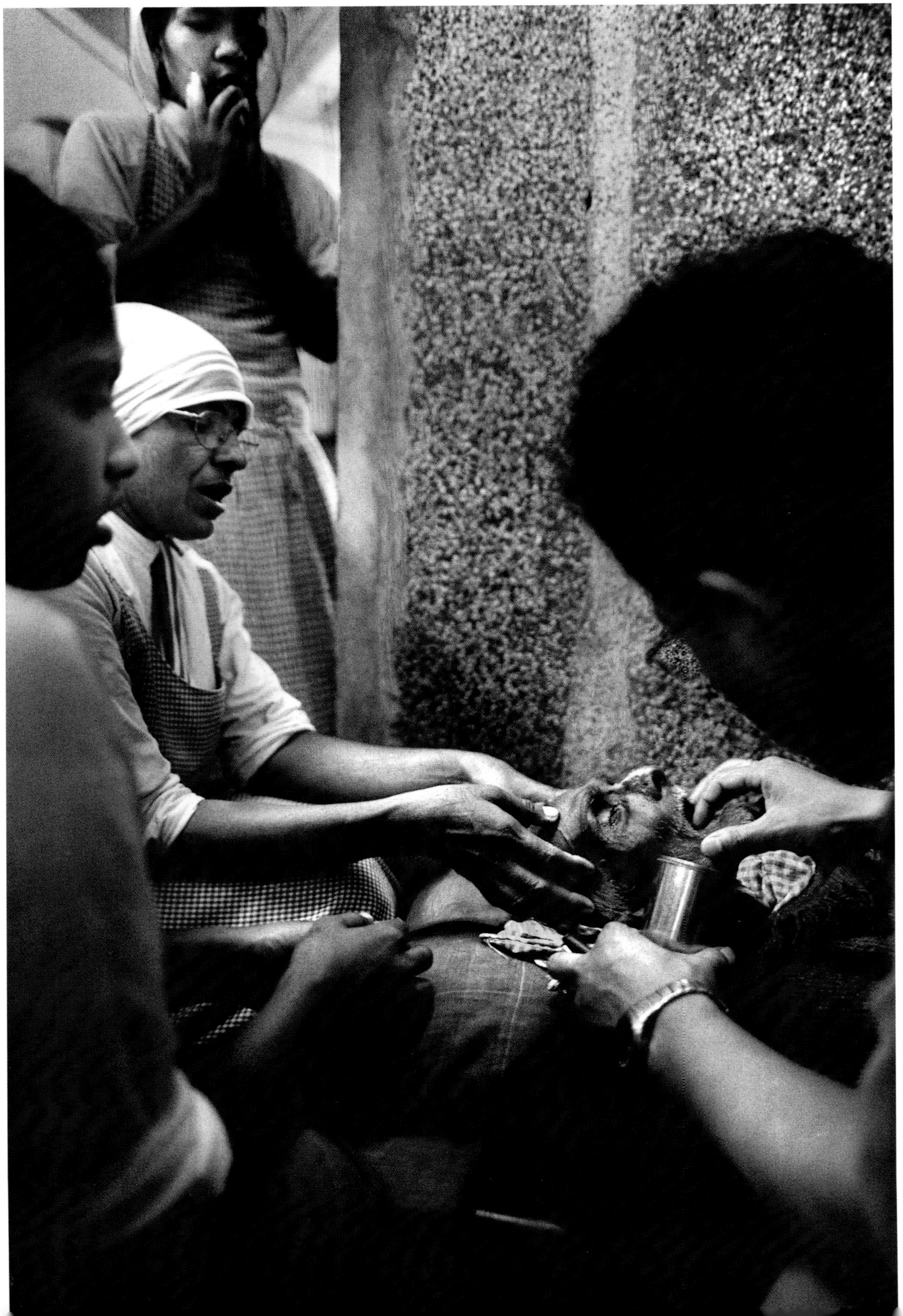

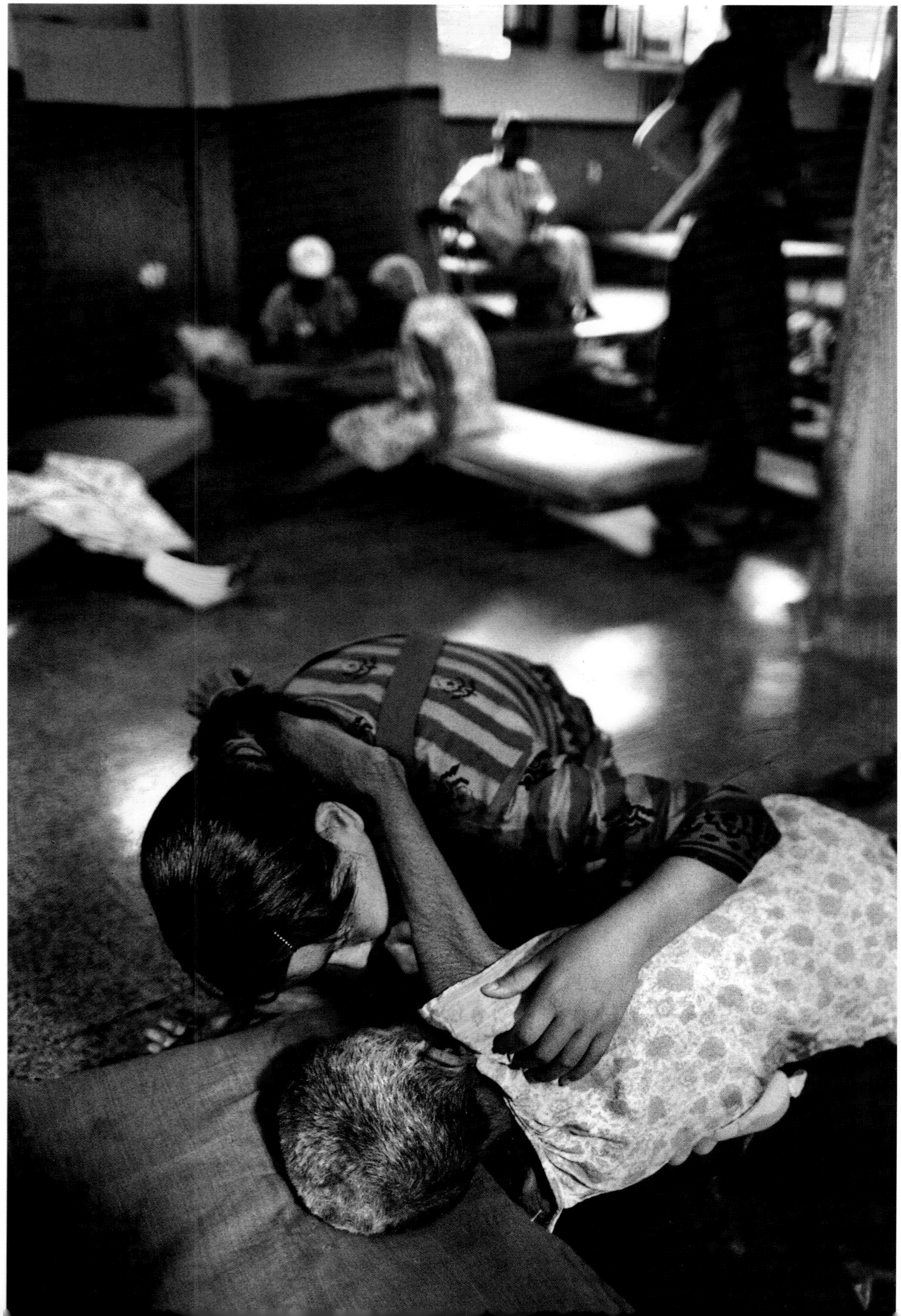

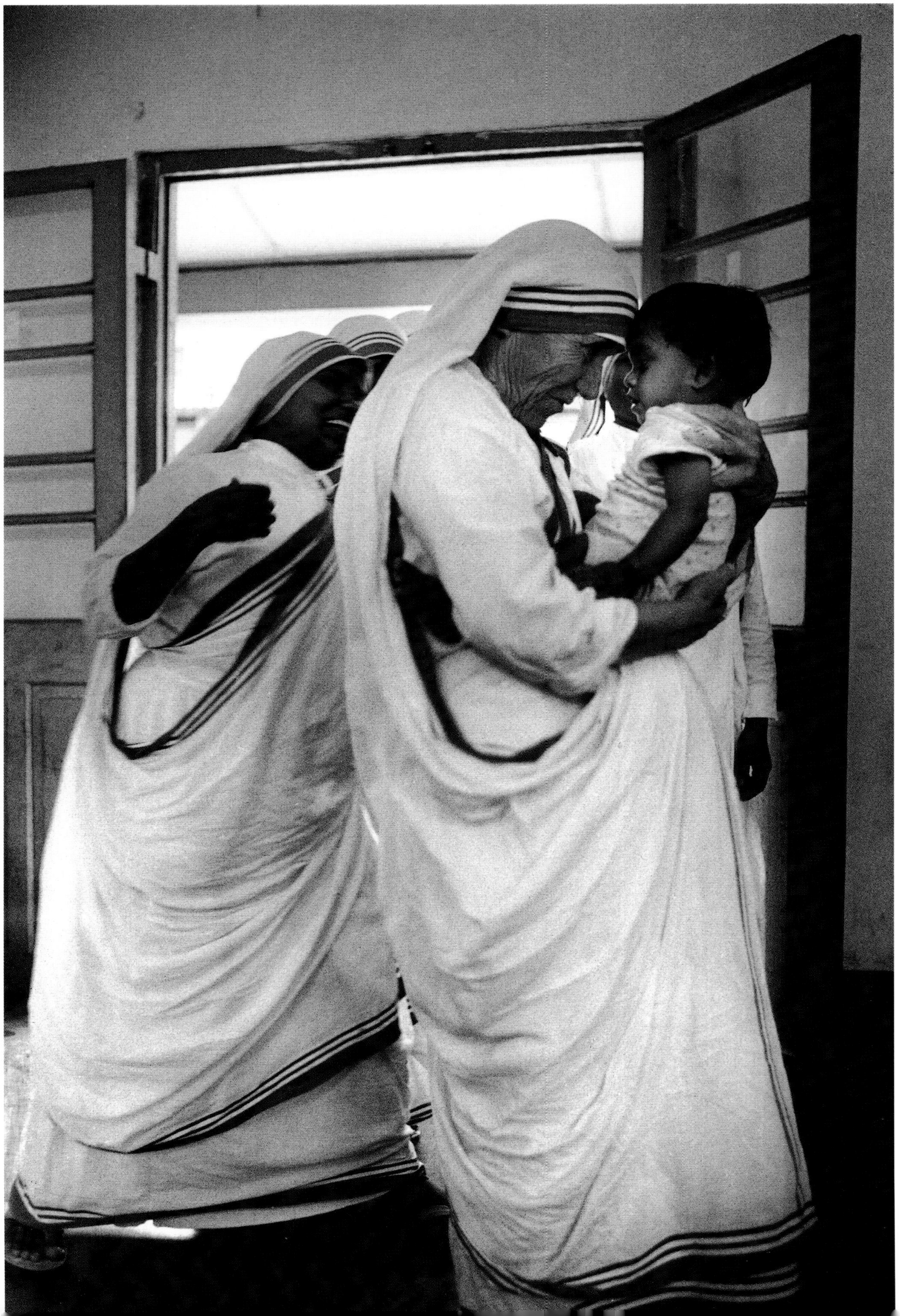

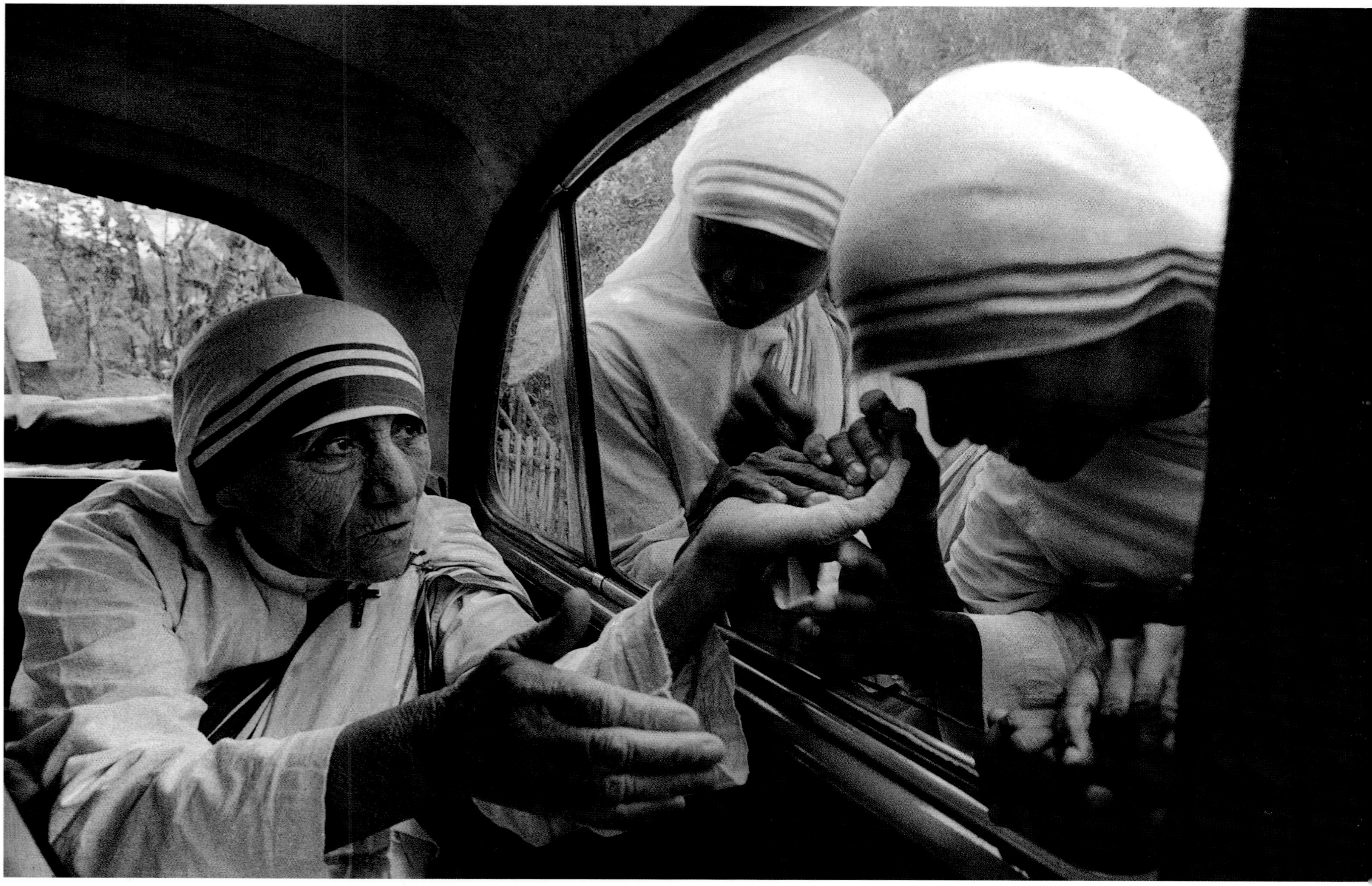

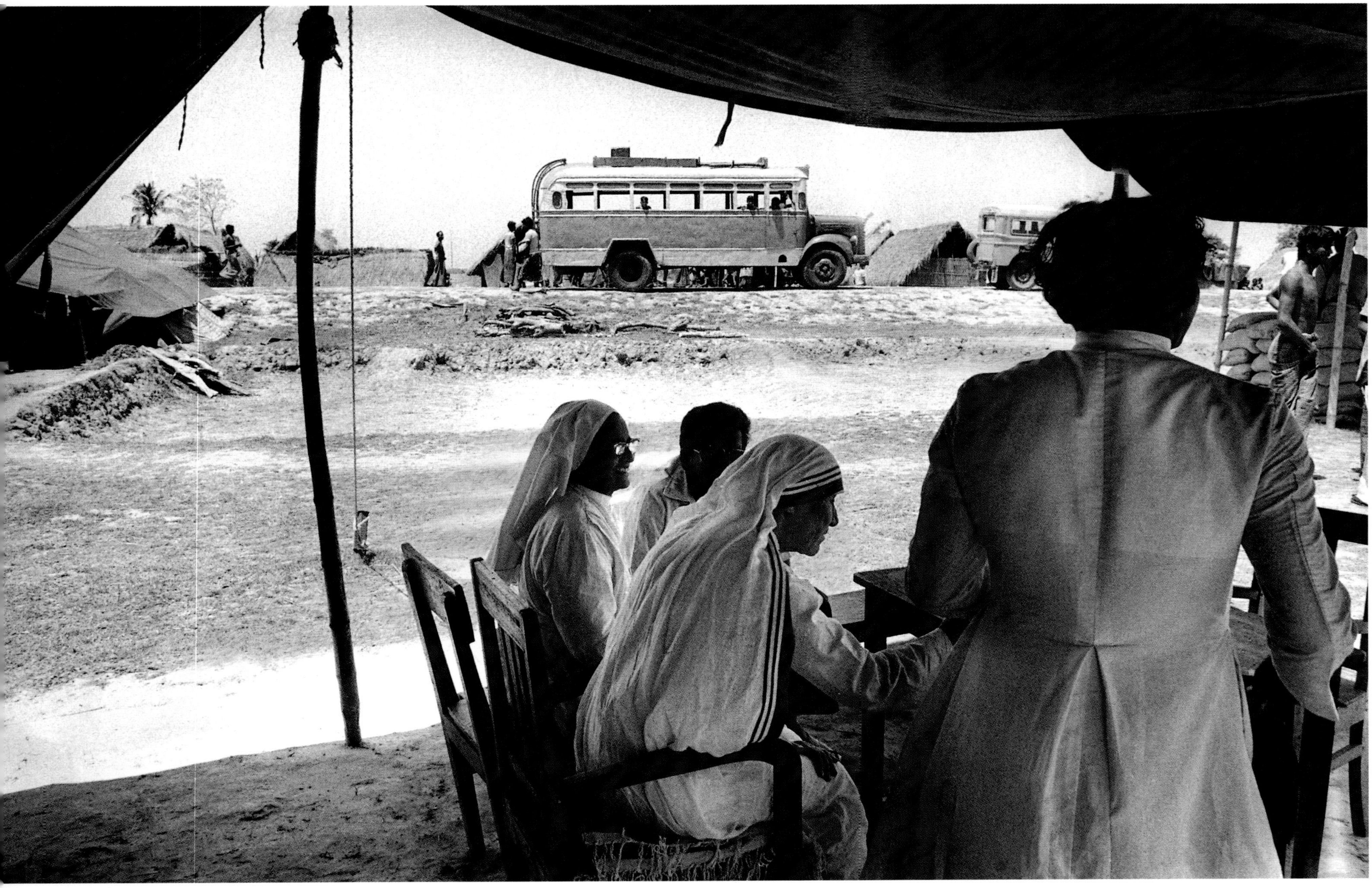

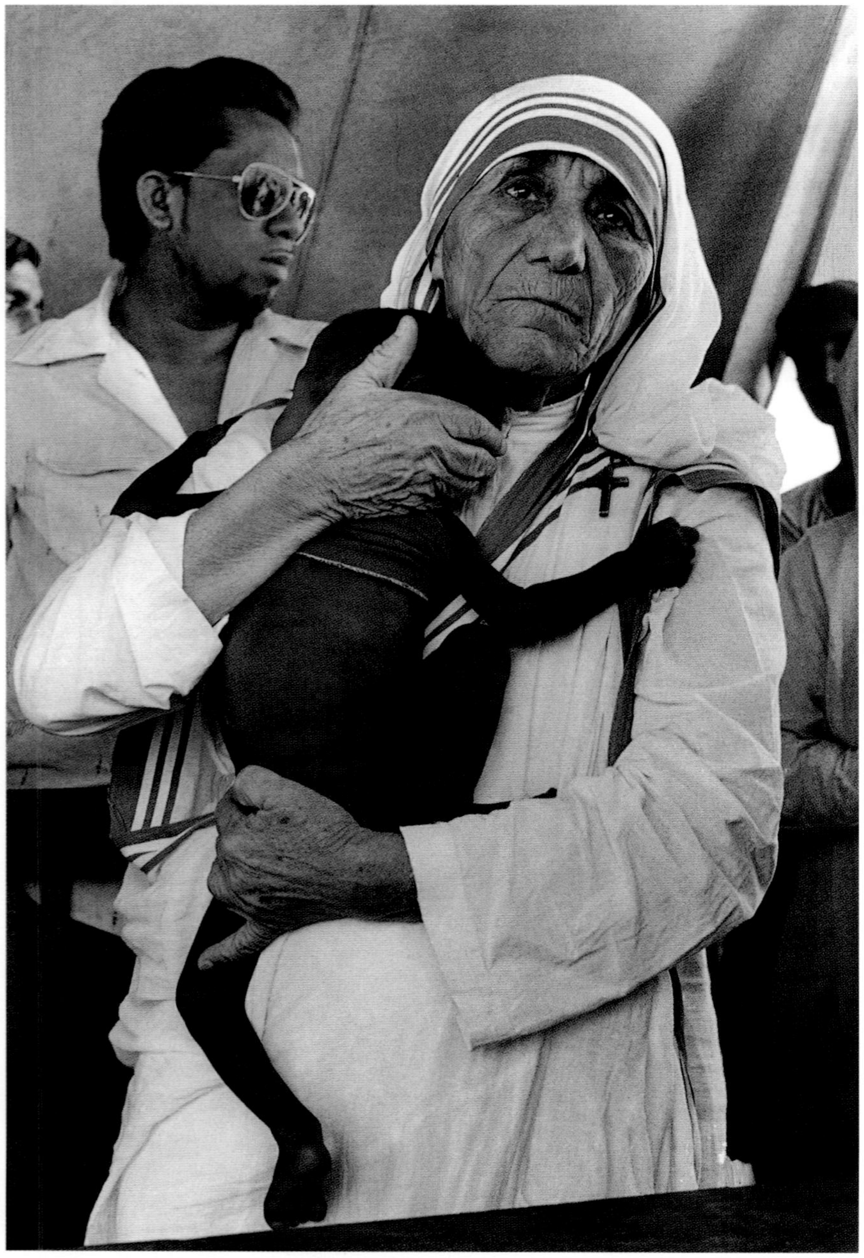

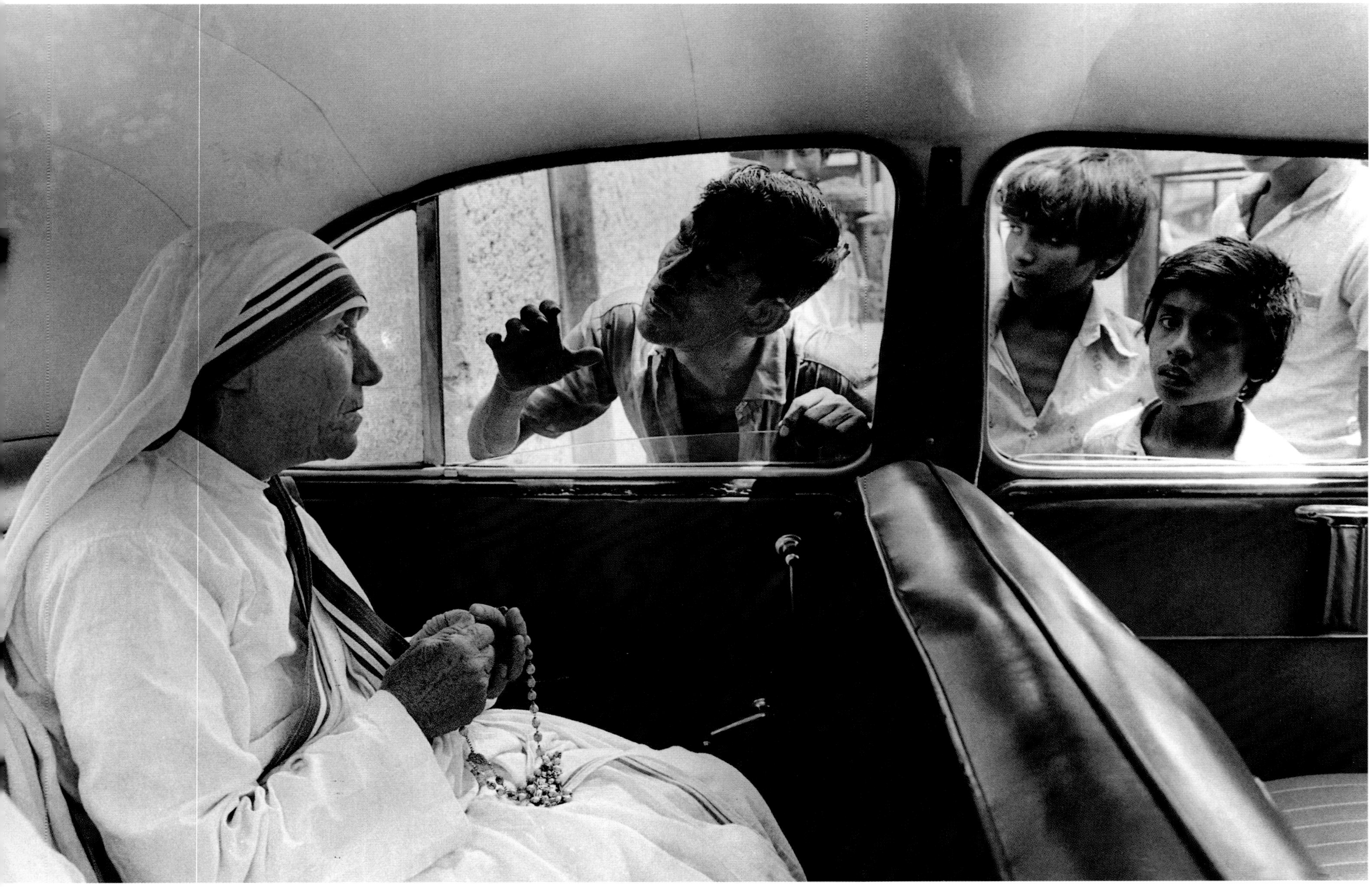

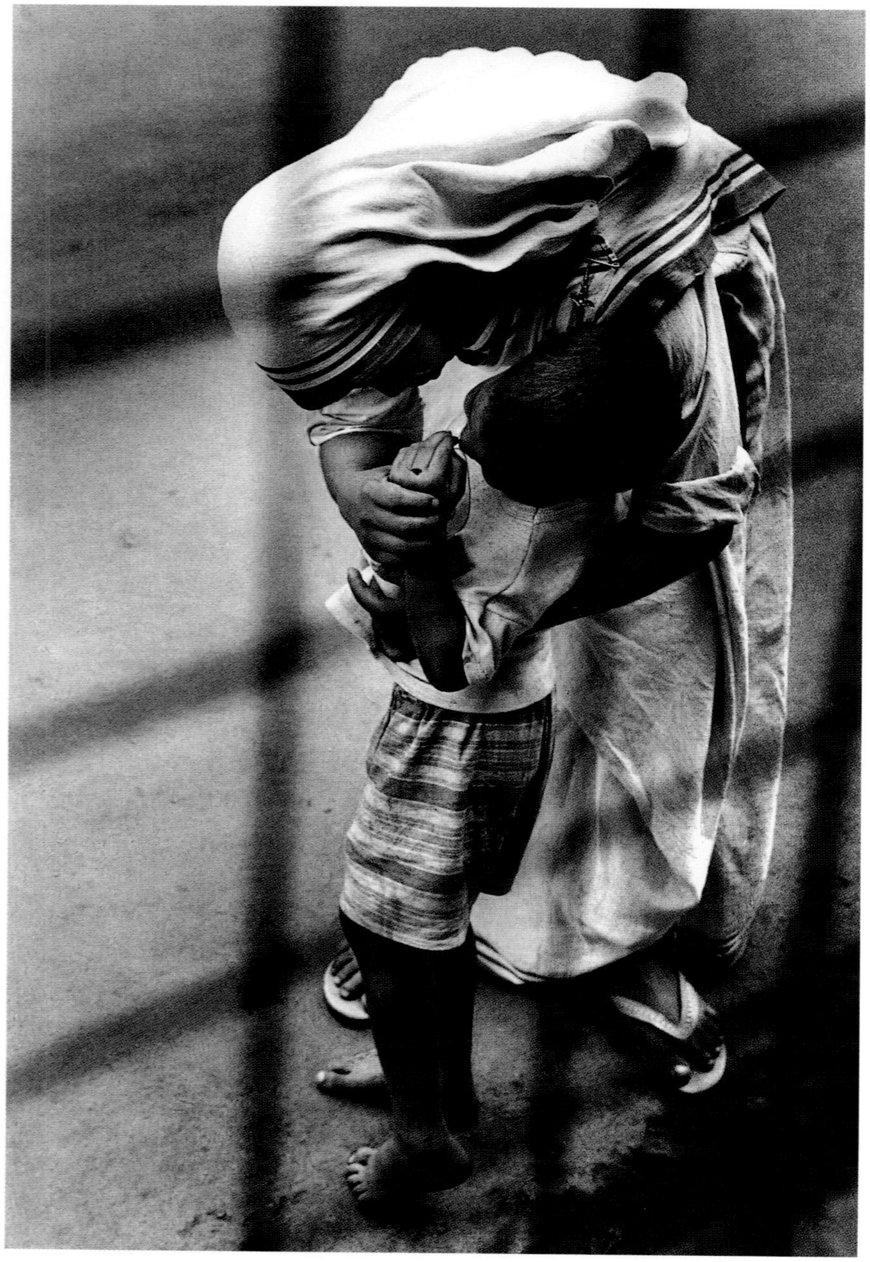

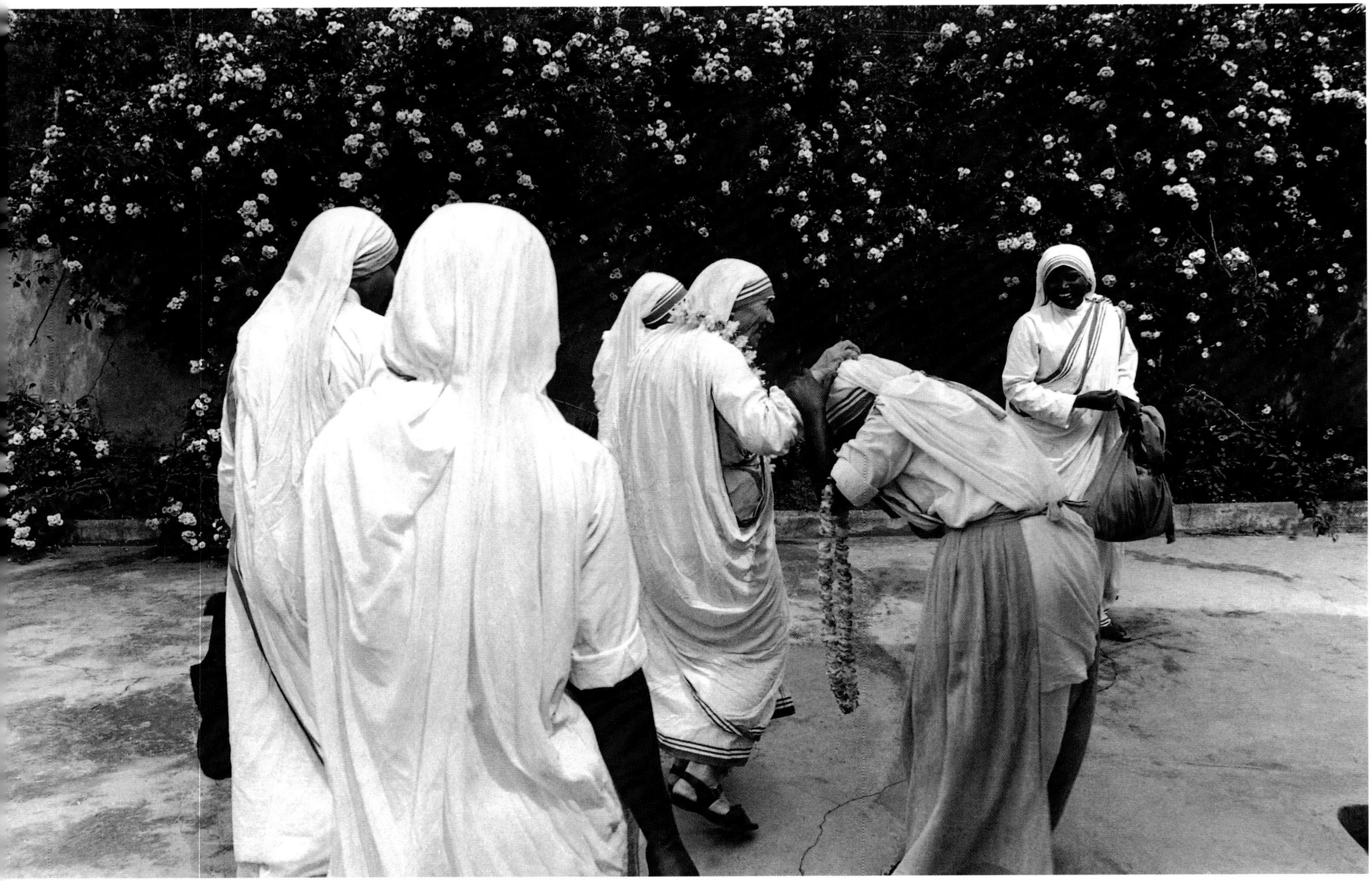

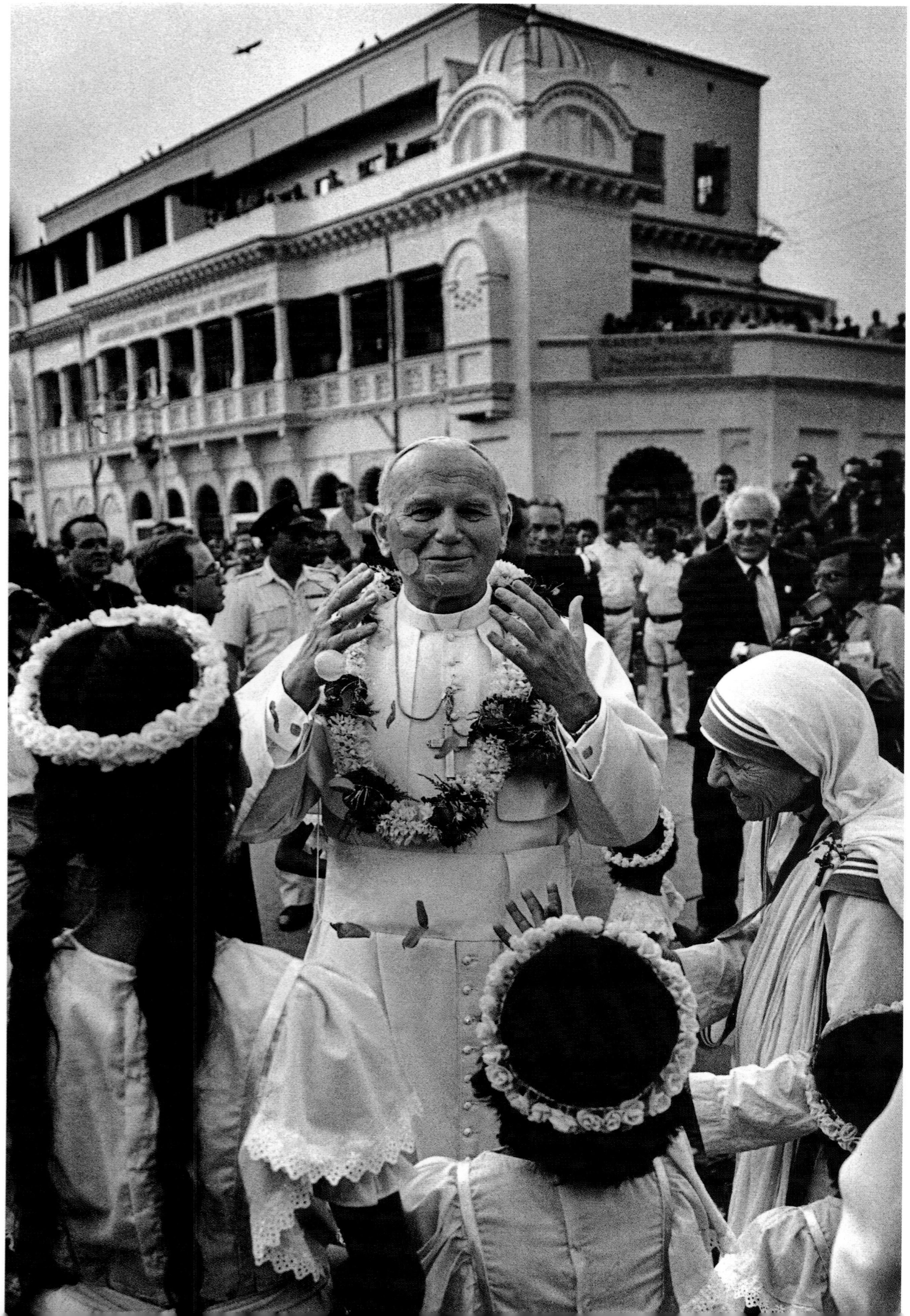

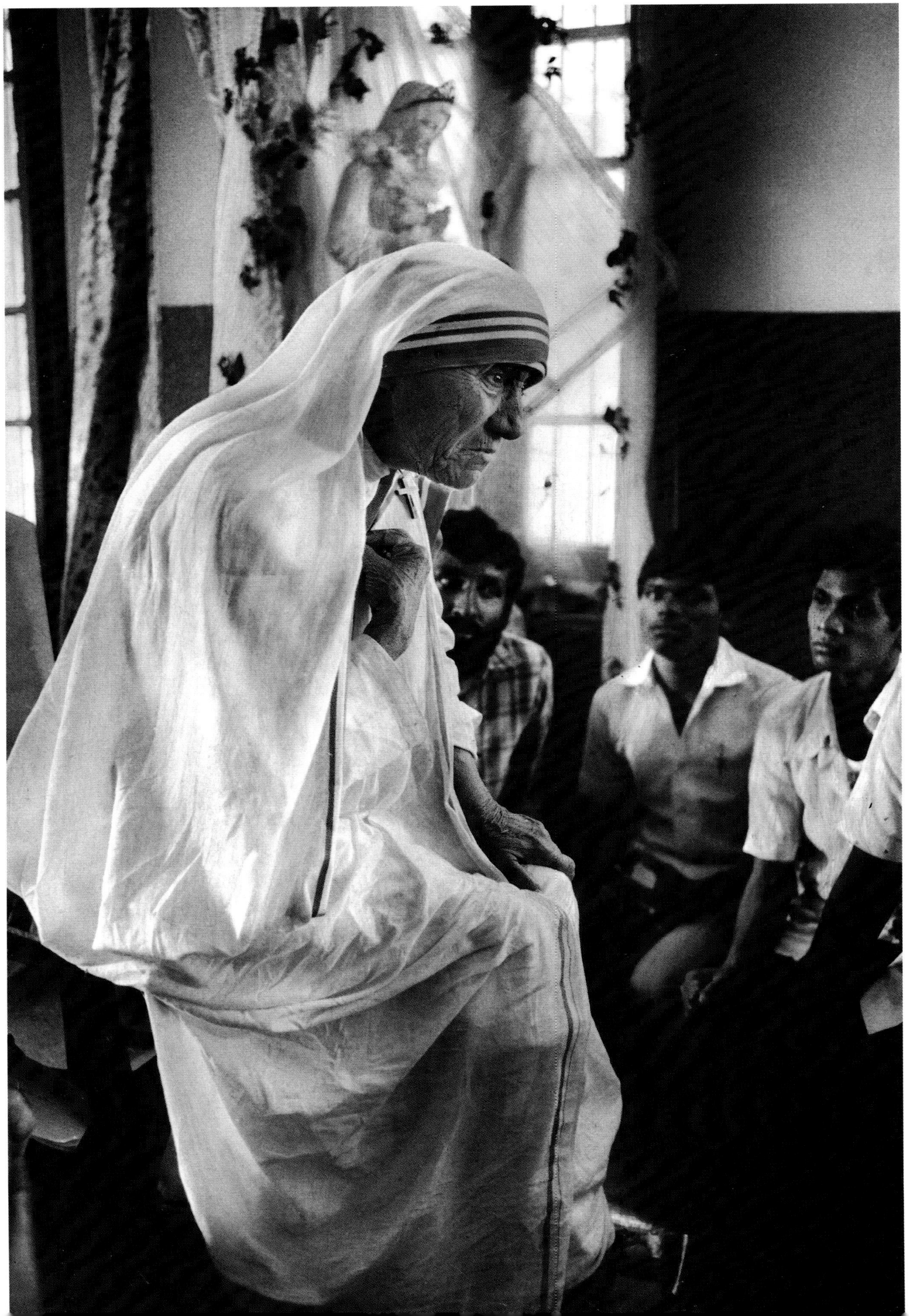

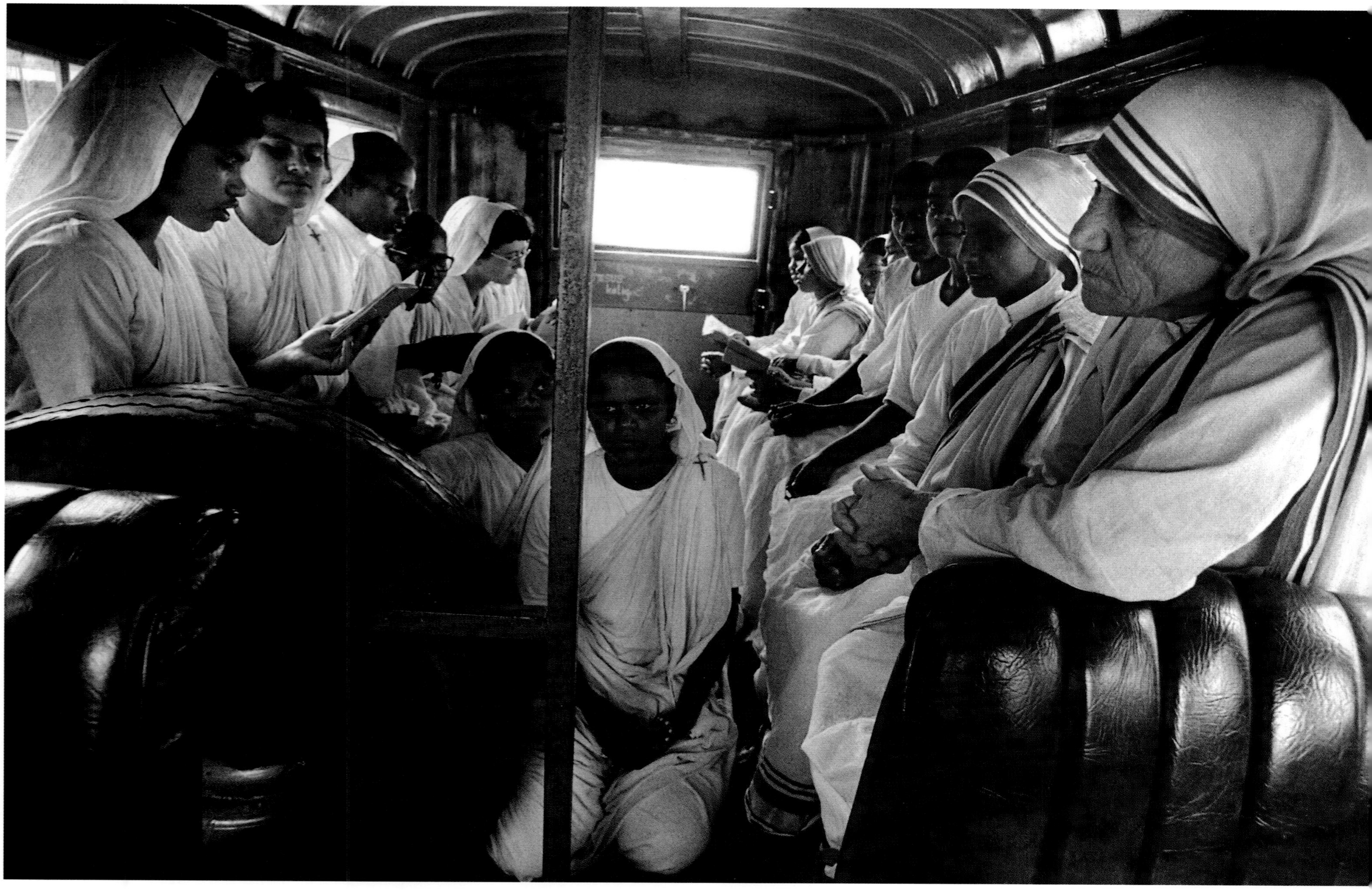

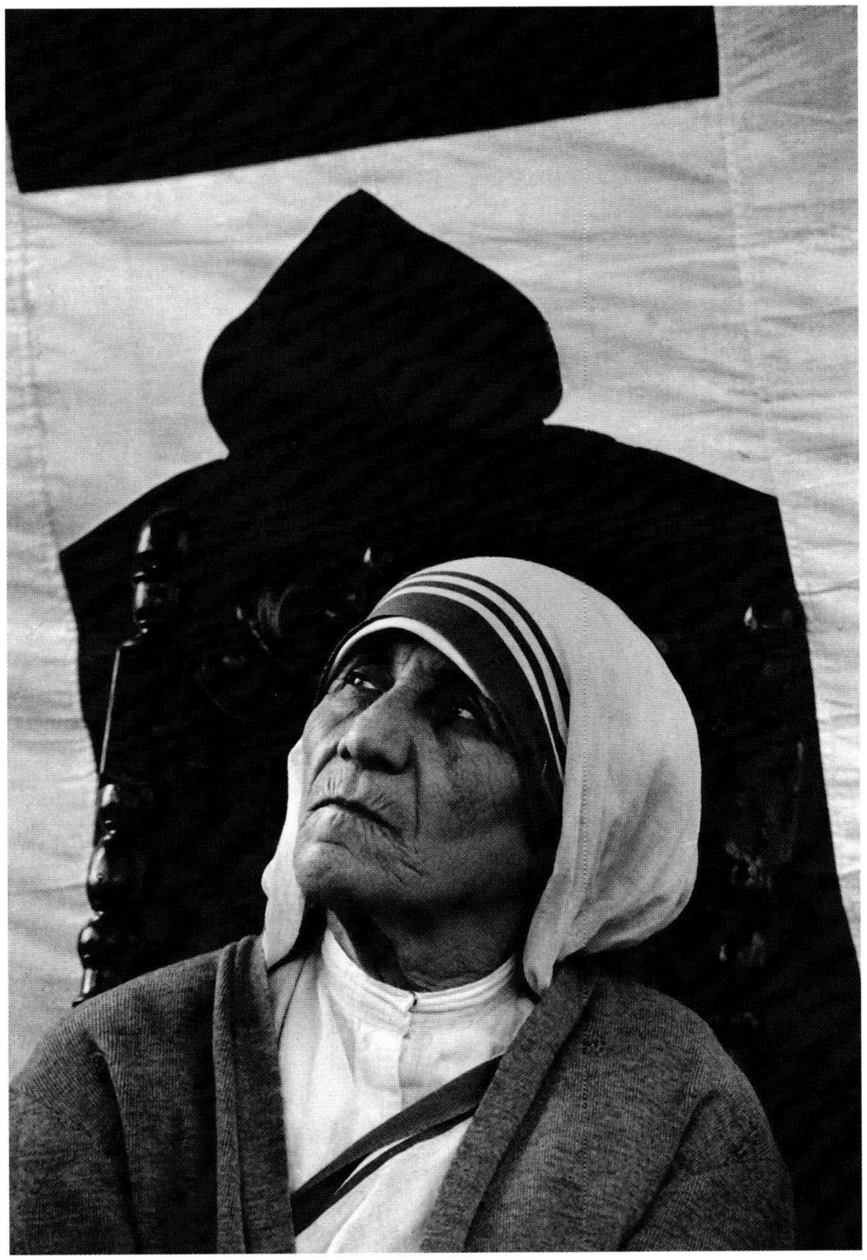

beatific radiance: all else is trivial

AS A PHOTOGRAPHER, I AM ALWAYS SEARCHING FOR MOMENTS CHARGED WITH THE ENERGY OF RARE EXPERIENCES.

It is this search that propels my inward and onward journey. This has been my unfinished quest.

There have been times when the moment left me completely mesmerized, disabling me, as it were, from taking pictures, from the core of my existence. I savor every element of such moments.

Mother, you were unwell at the time of which I now write, confined to bed and not allowed to meet visitors. Navin Chawla and I went to present a copy of our book *Faith and Compassion* to you, but were told by the sisters, that only if the doctors permitted would they wheel you out of confinement that morning.

We waited expectantly. We had several anxieties: our little questions about your appearance and your welfare, which now seem so trivial.

All these vanished the moment we saw you.

The days of sickness were, perhaps, the longest period during which none of us had intruded into your surroundings.

When you appeared, I was awed by what I saw: a tiny creature lit with beatific radiance. It appeared as if you had been bathed to purity, through a renewed and uninterrupted connection with the Divine. I use the word again and again, for there is no other word for it. You always radiated divine purity, but that morning it was as if it had been multiplied many times.

The light around you had enveloped me.

For me, this was a *Darshan* of "His" magnificence. The light was so captivating that my camera became inadequate for the moment.

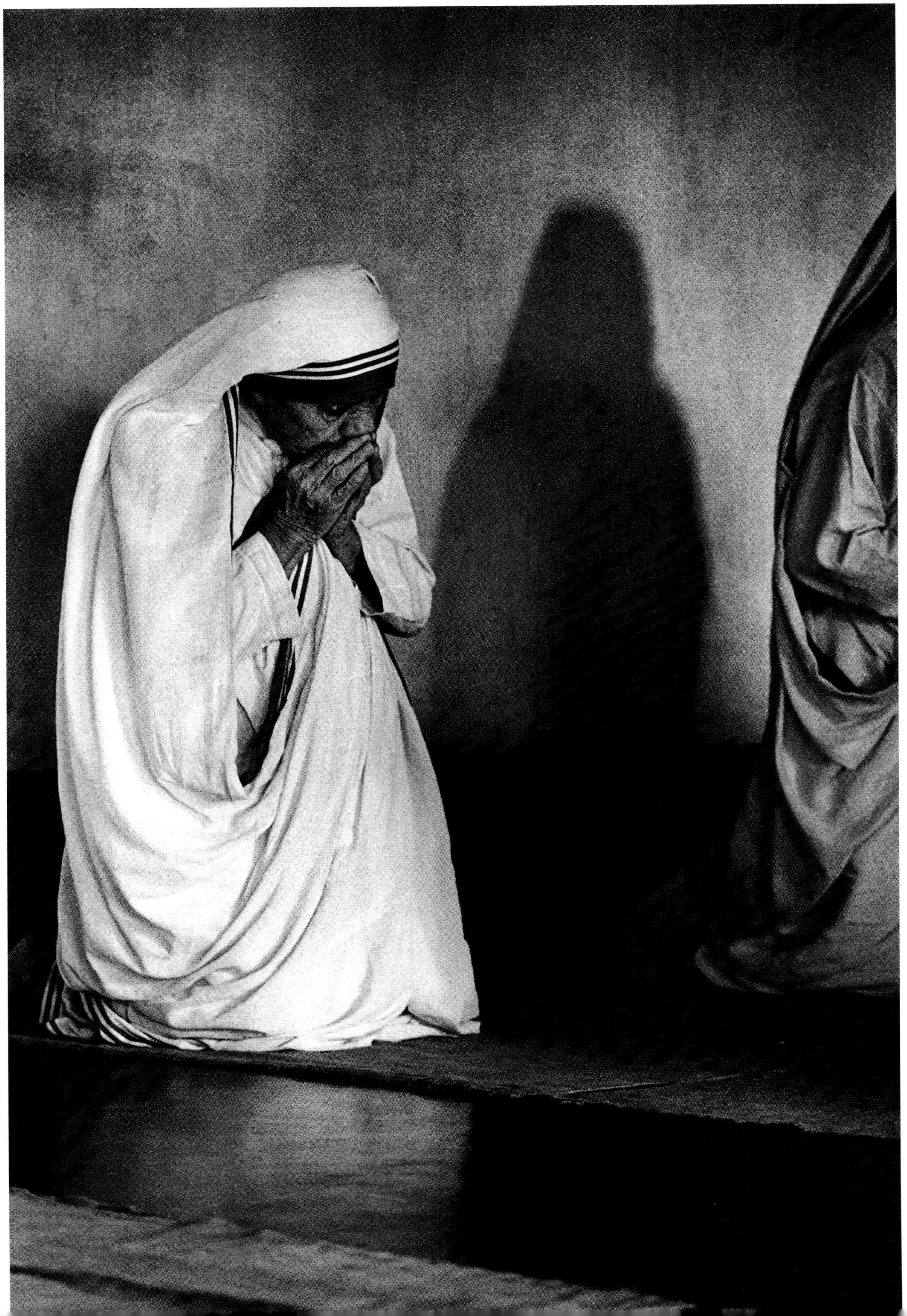

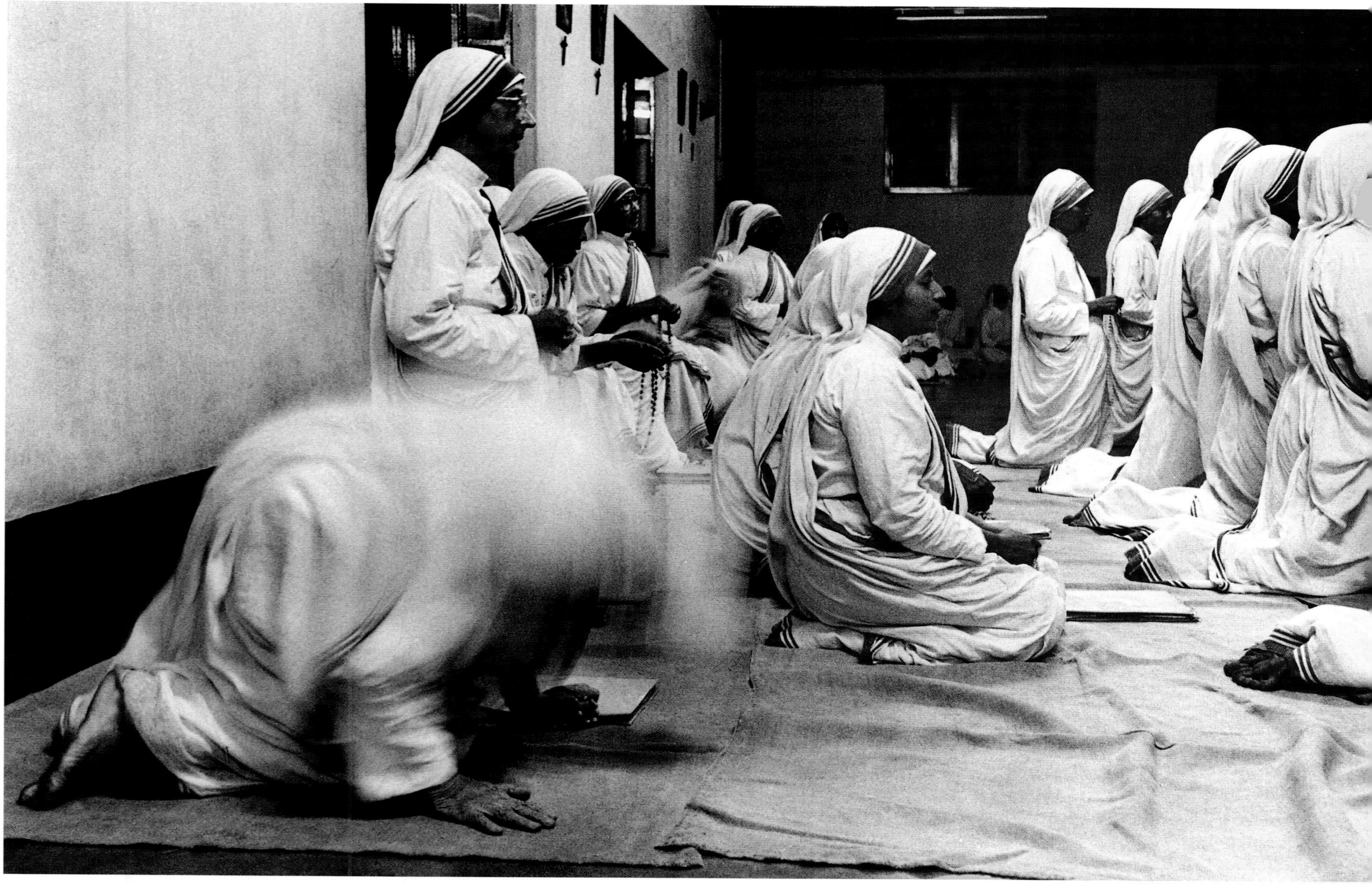

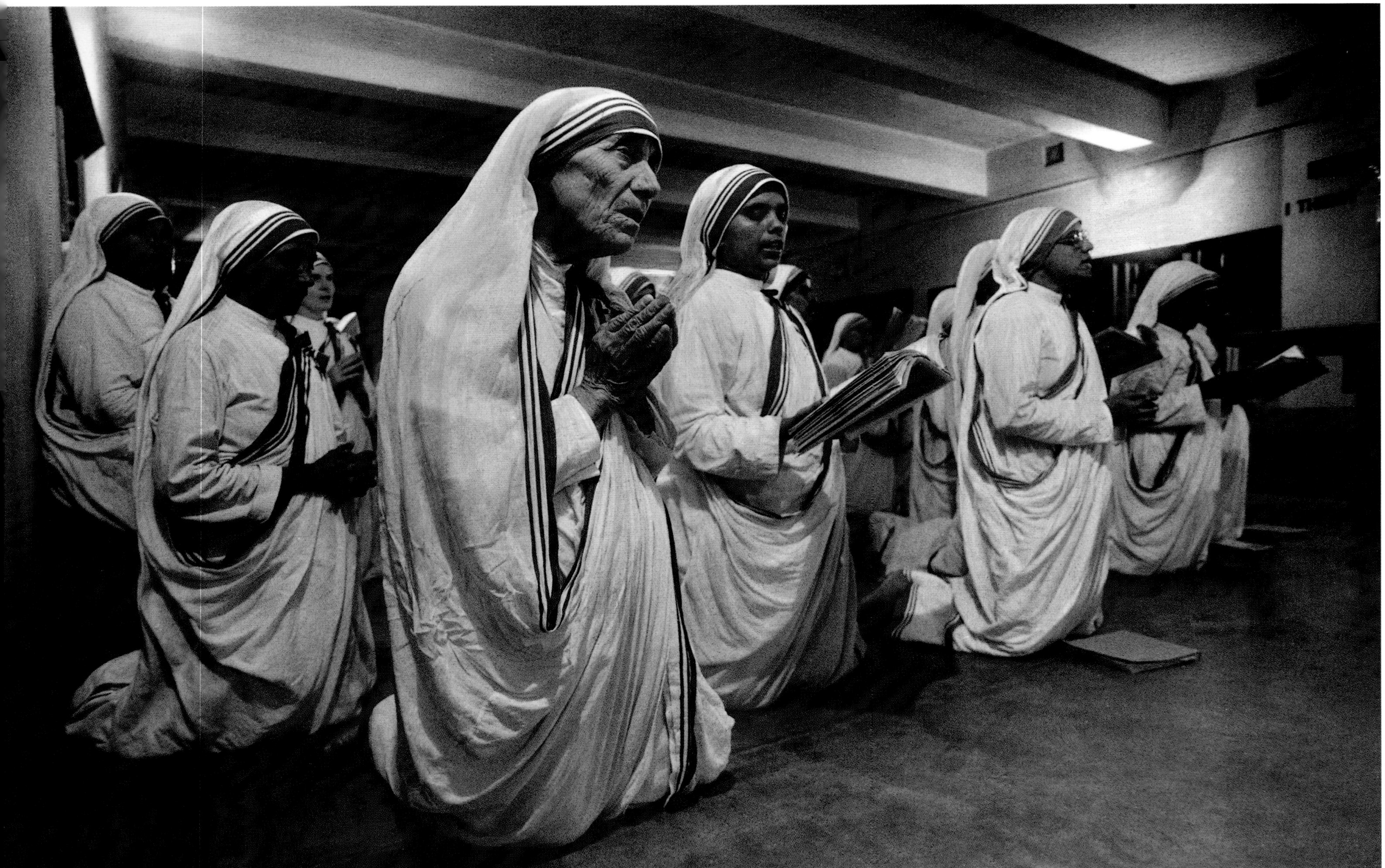

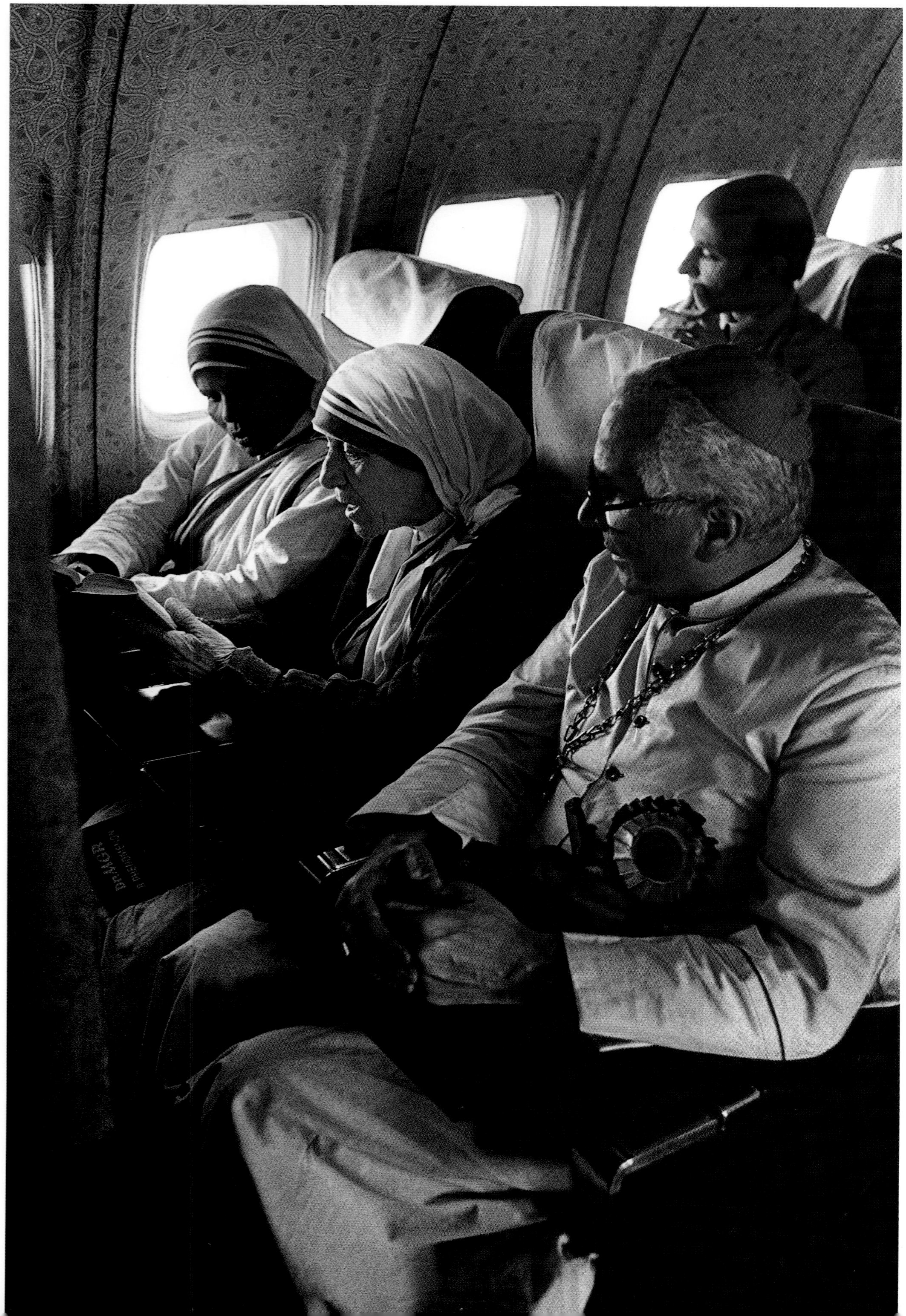

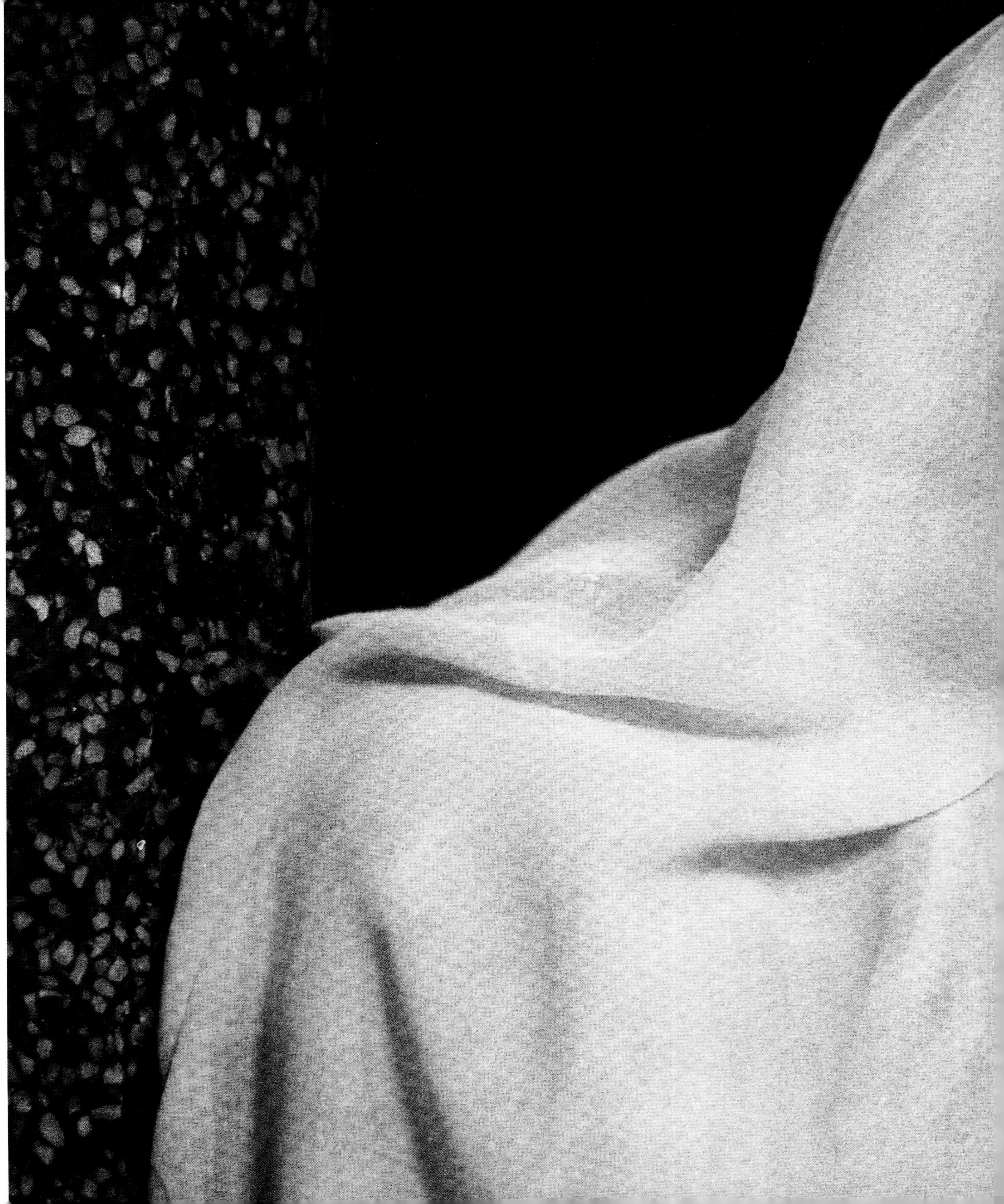

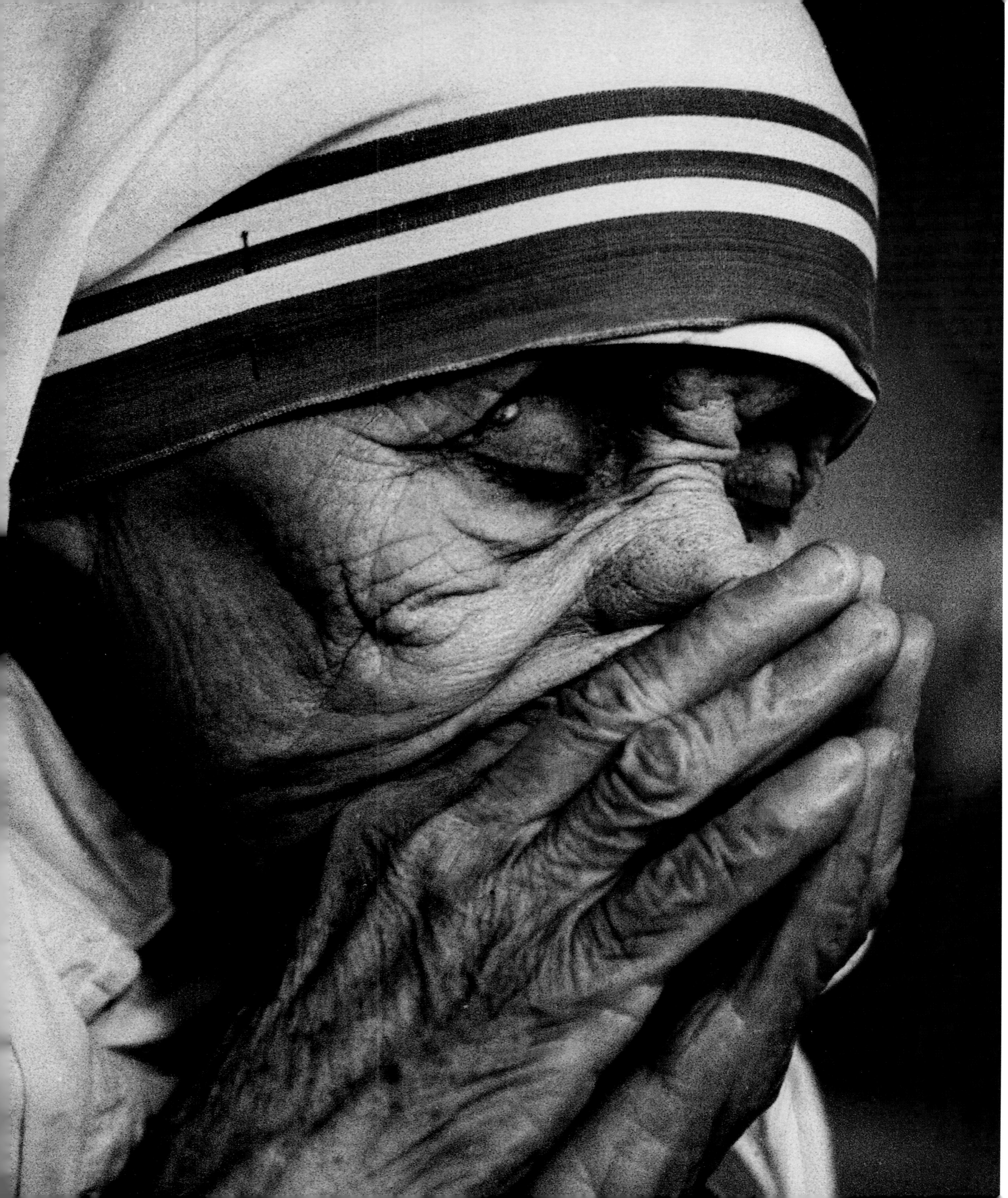

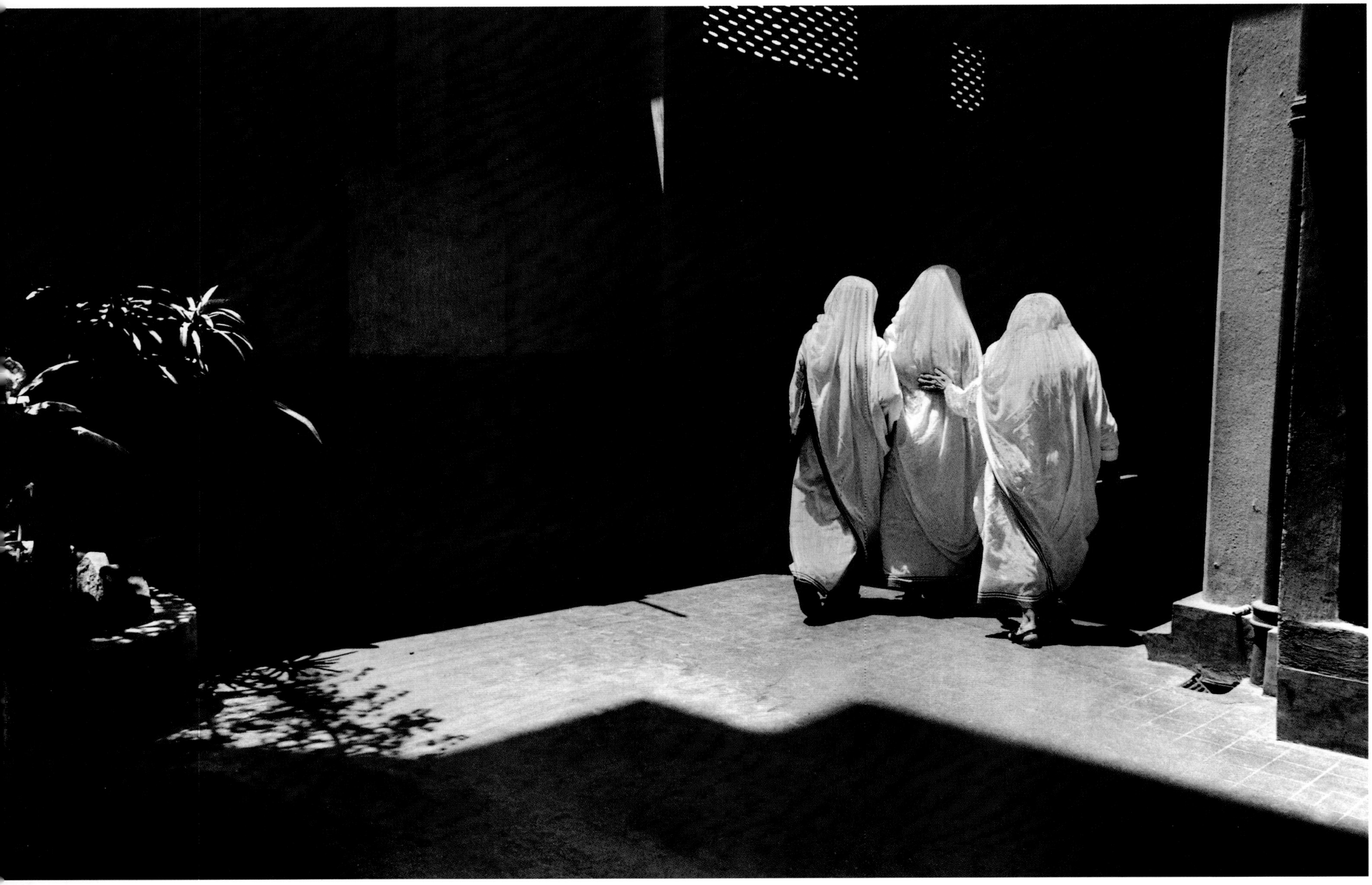

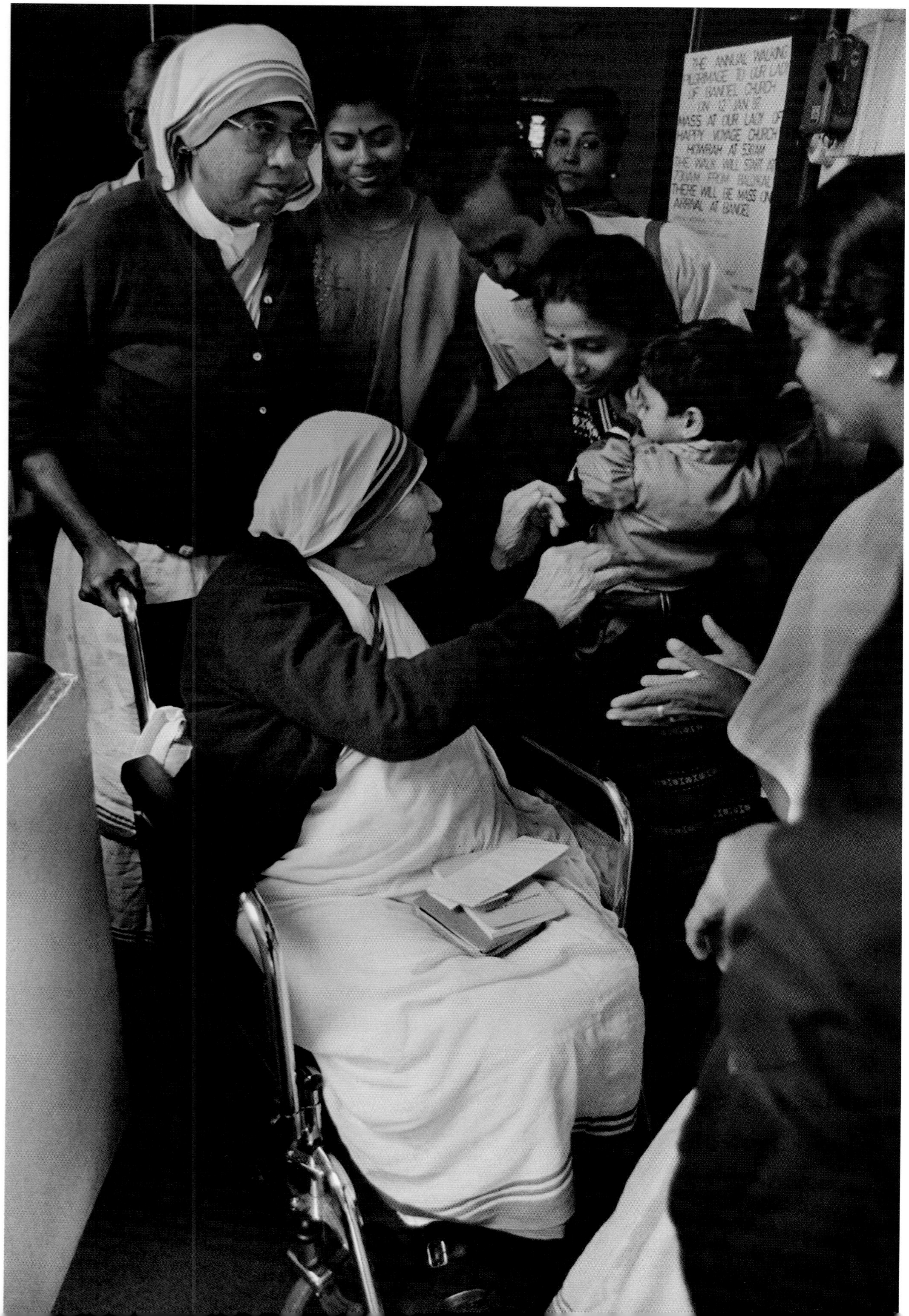
THE ANNUAL WALKING
OF BANDEL CHURCH
MASS AT OUR LADY OF
HAPPY VOYAGE CHURCH
THERE WILL BE MASS ON
ARRIVAL AT BANDEL

Agie—Guttadauro Mancinelli, Mother Teresa's niece at the funeral.

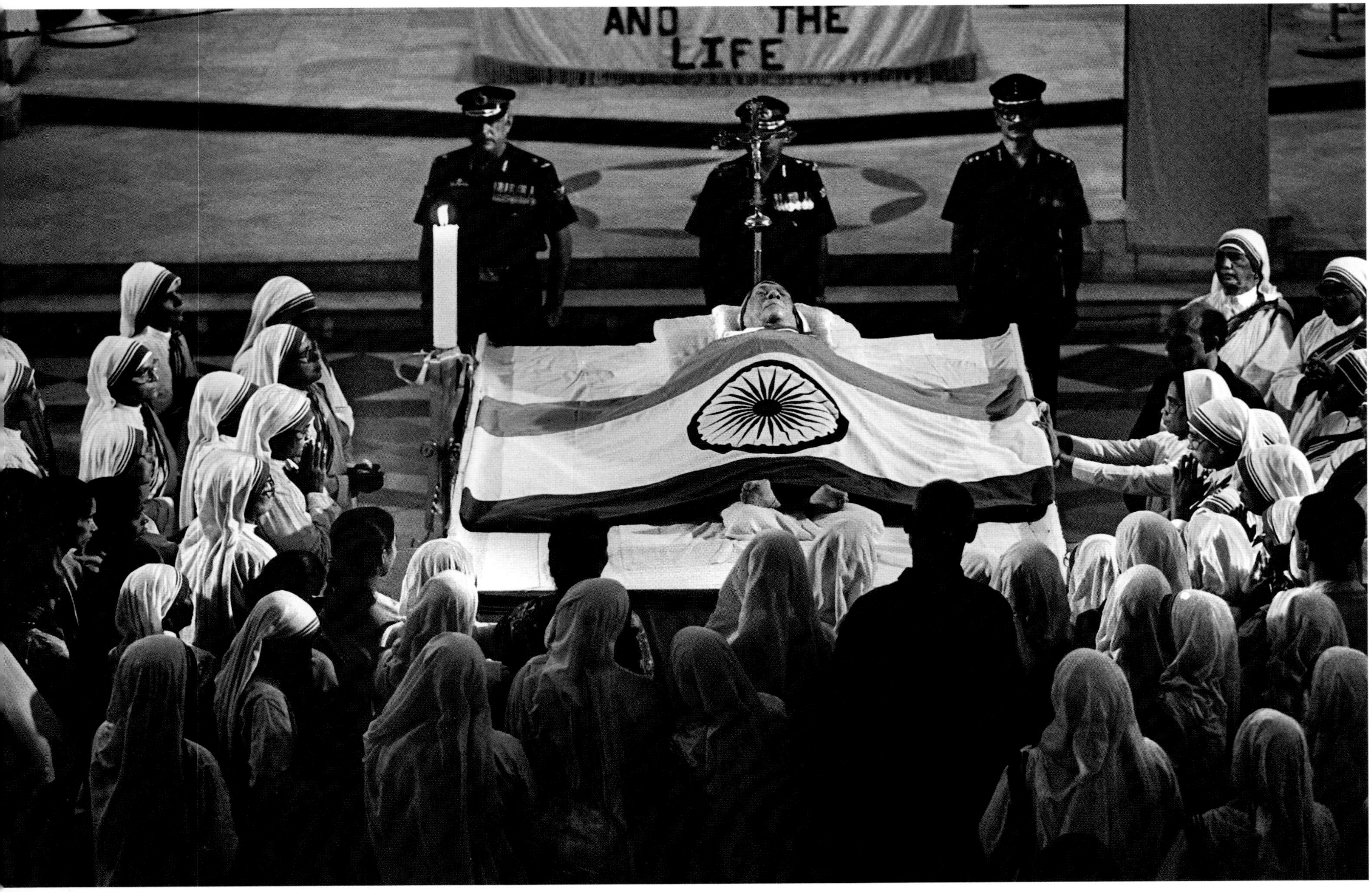

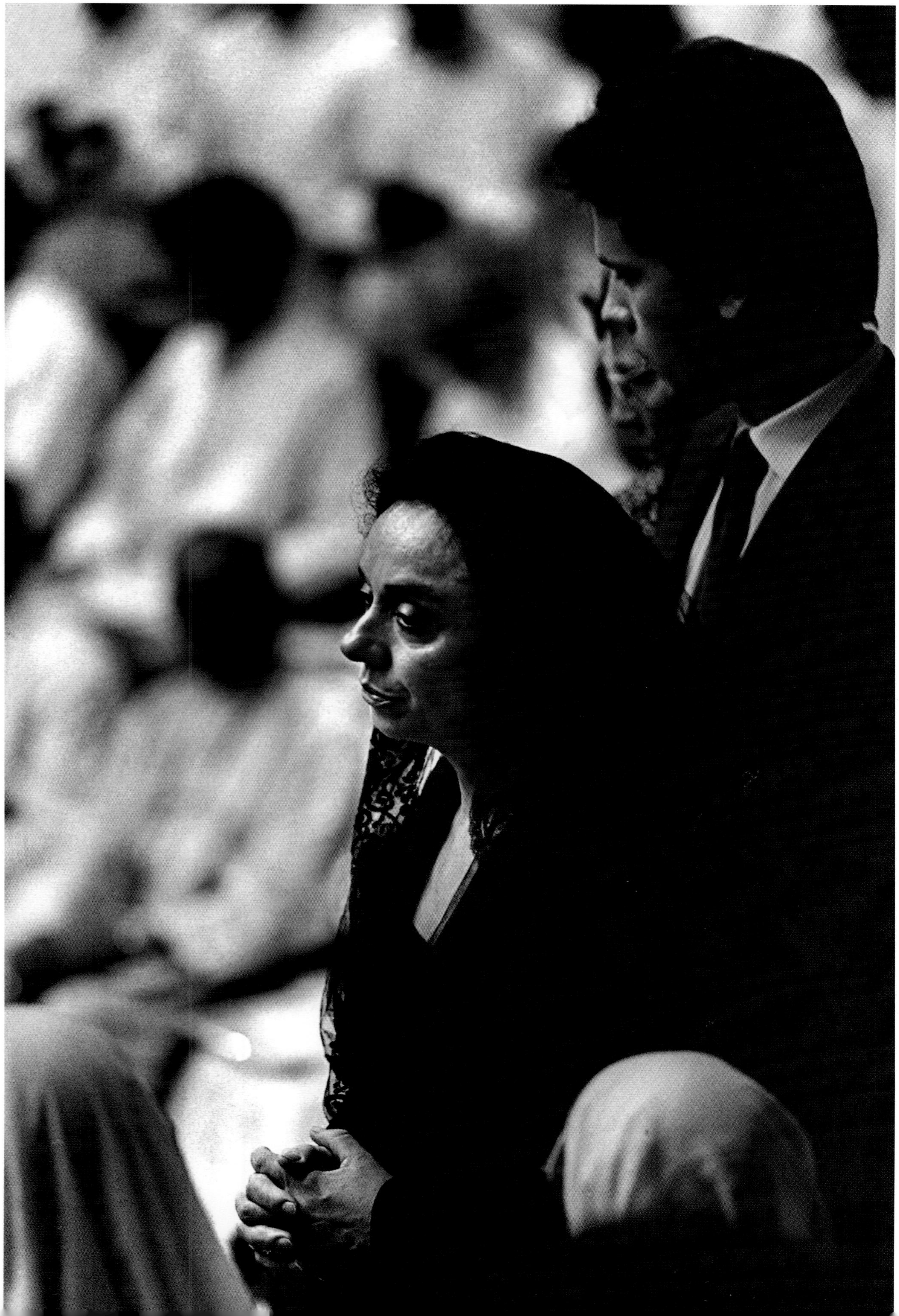

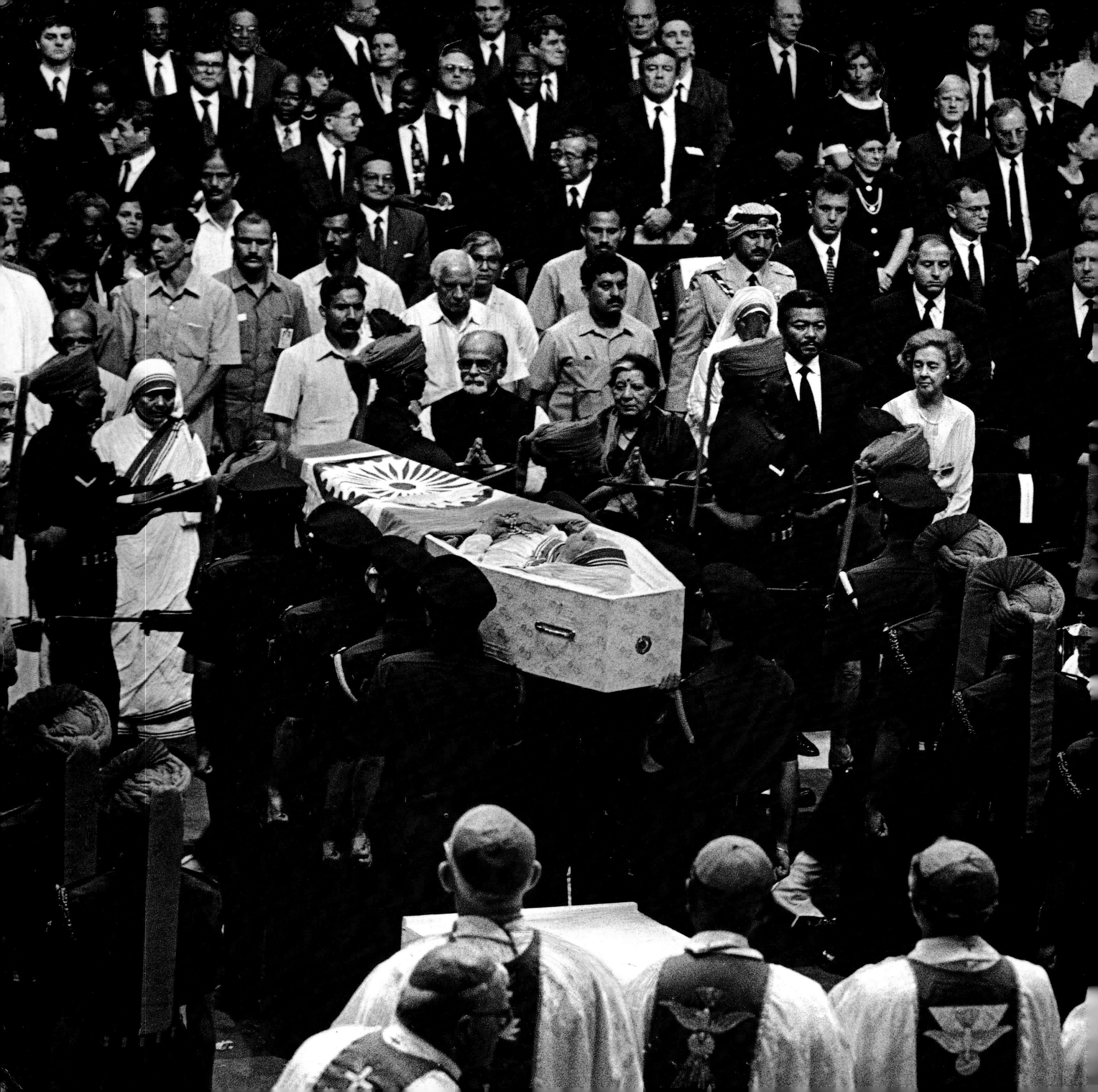

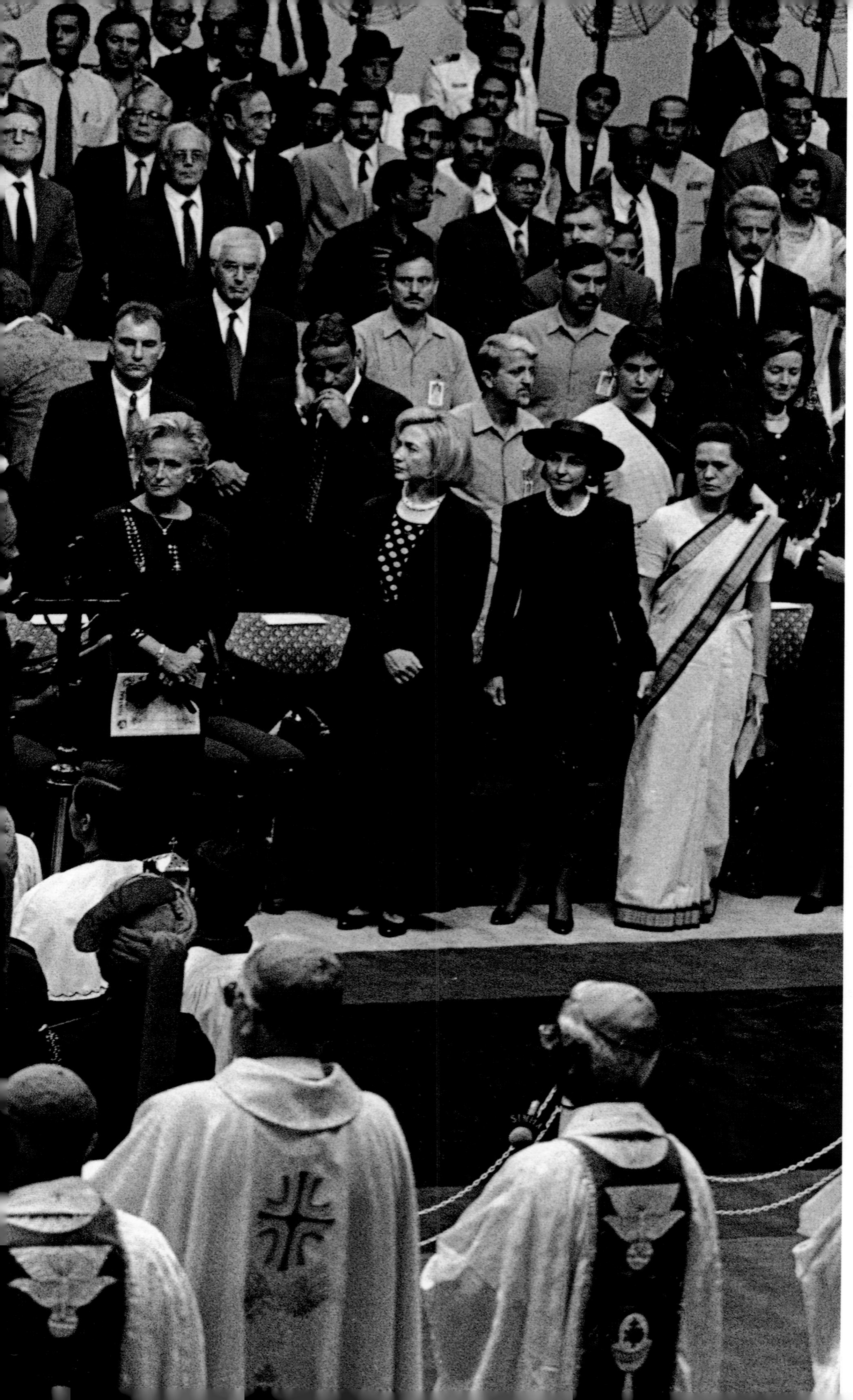

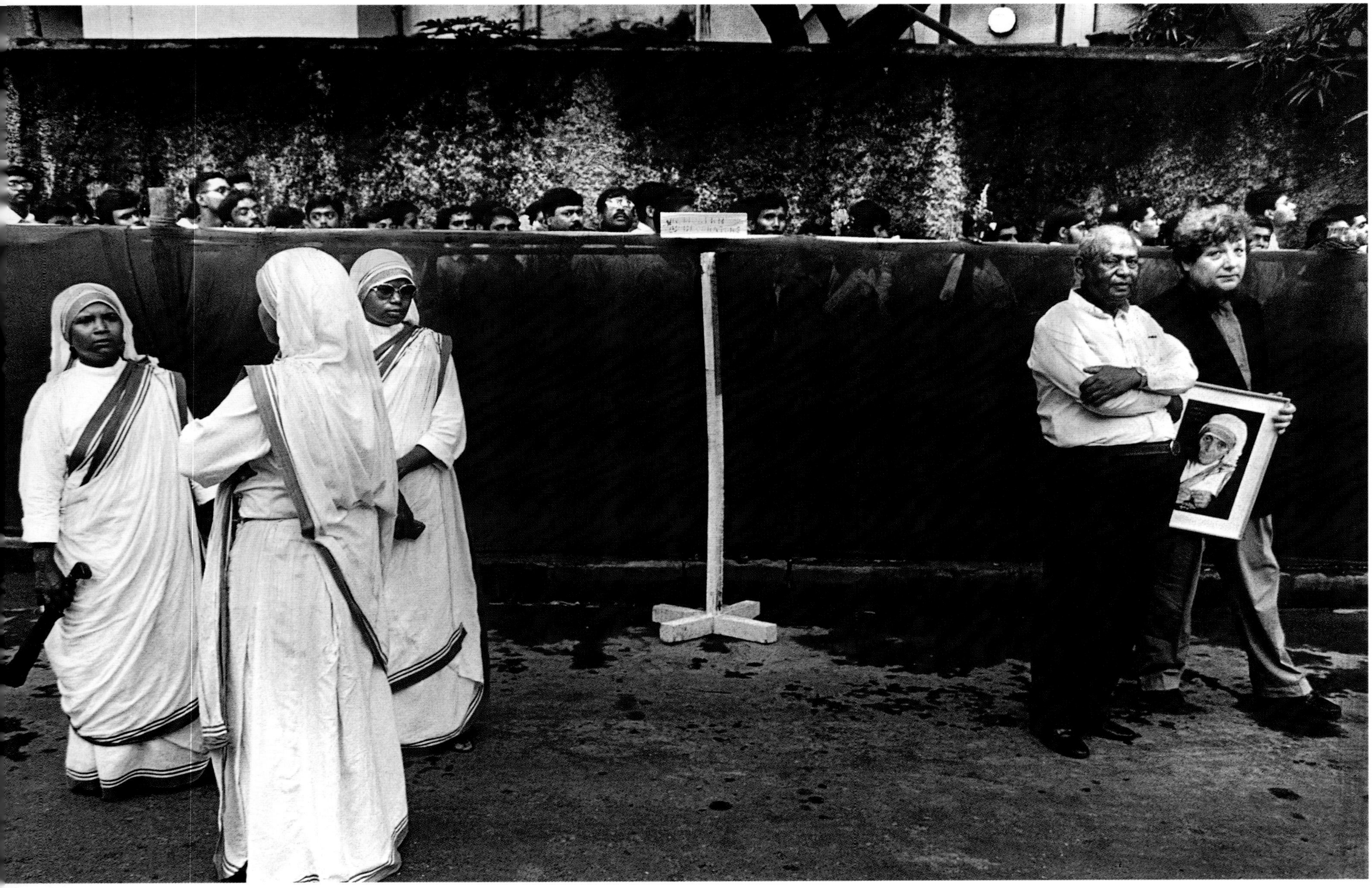

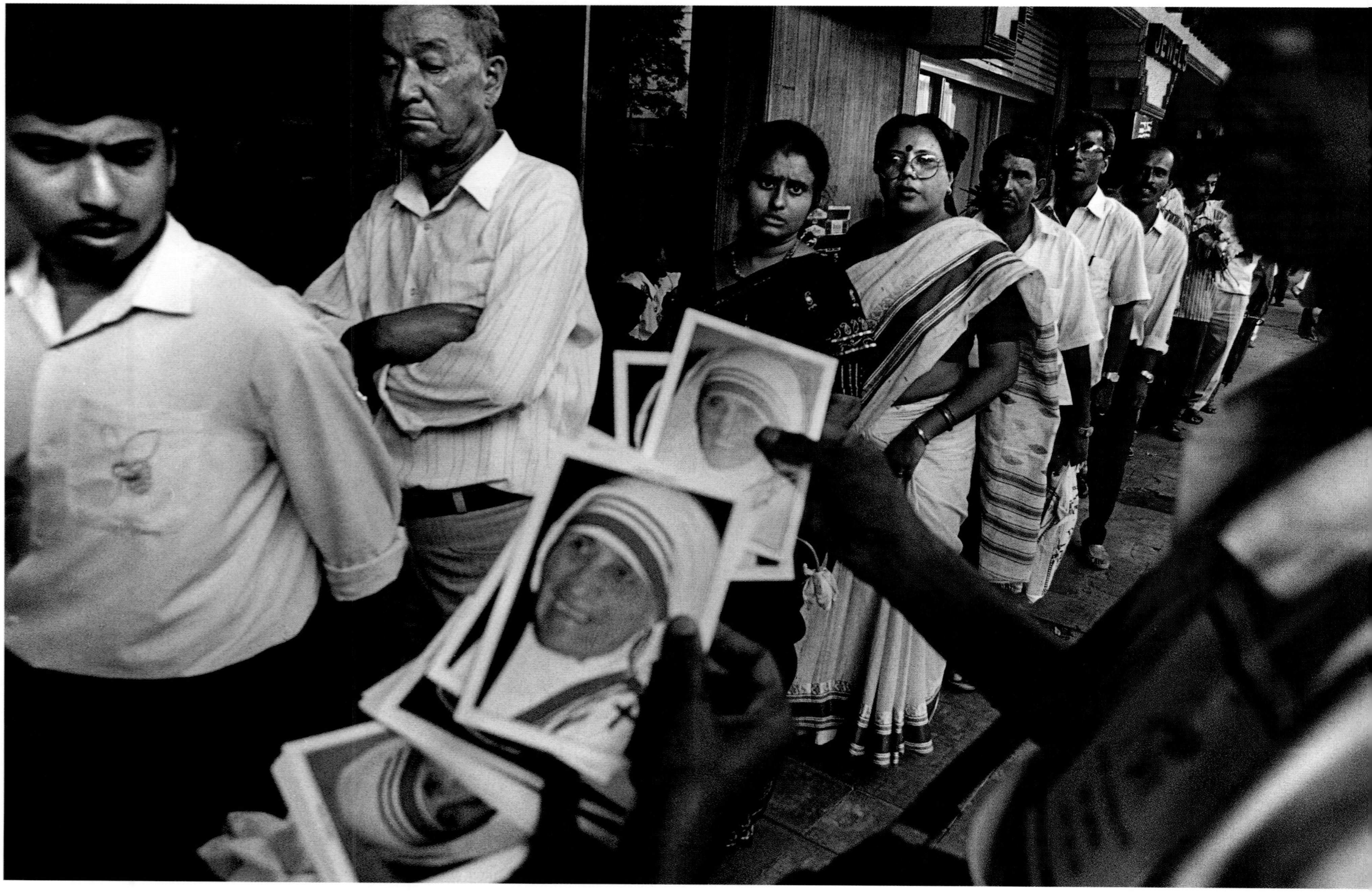

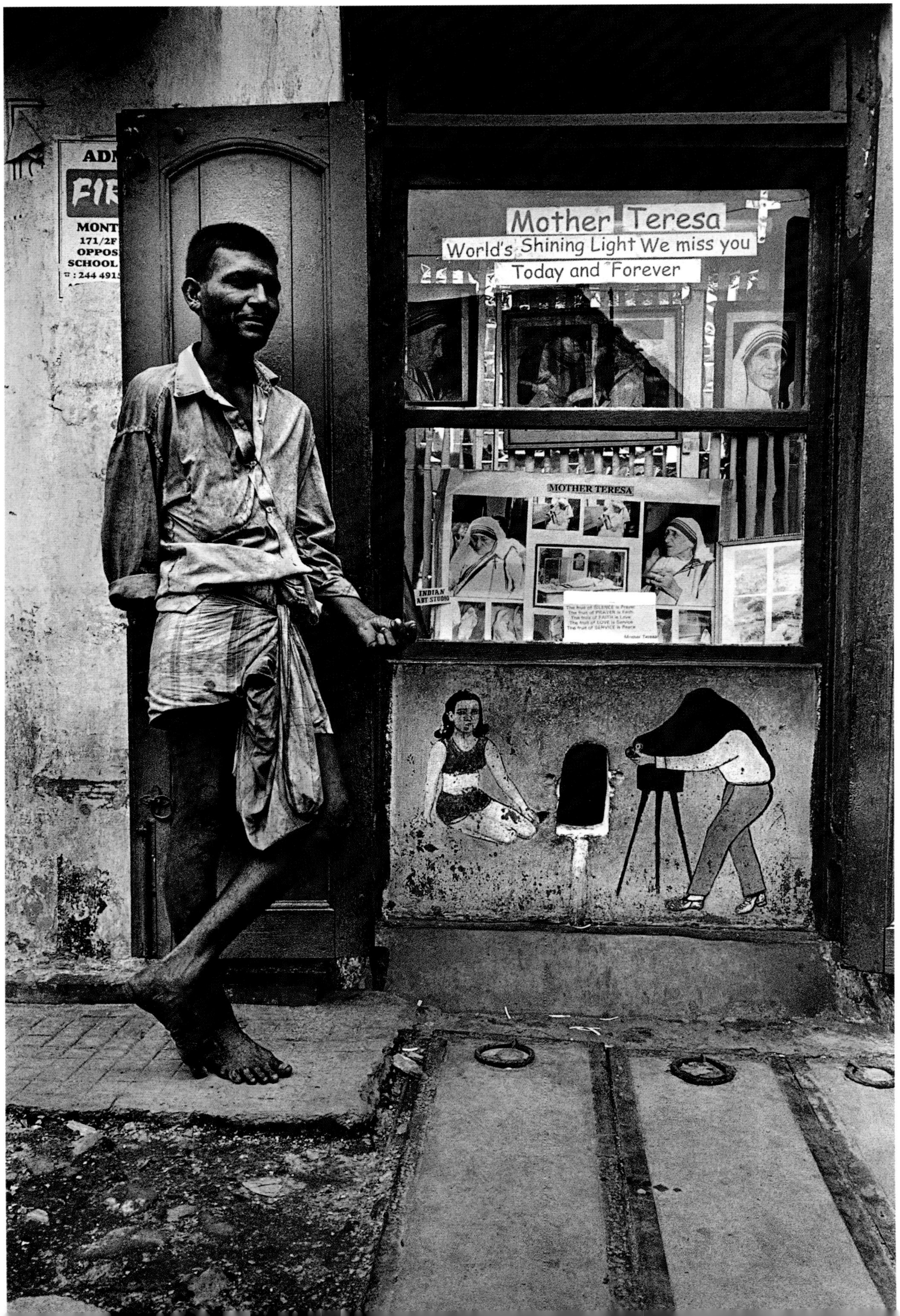
Mother Teresa
World's Shining Light We miss you
Today and Forever
MOTHER TERESA
INDIAN ART STUDIO

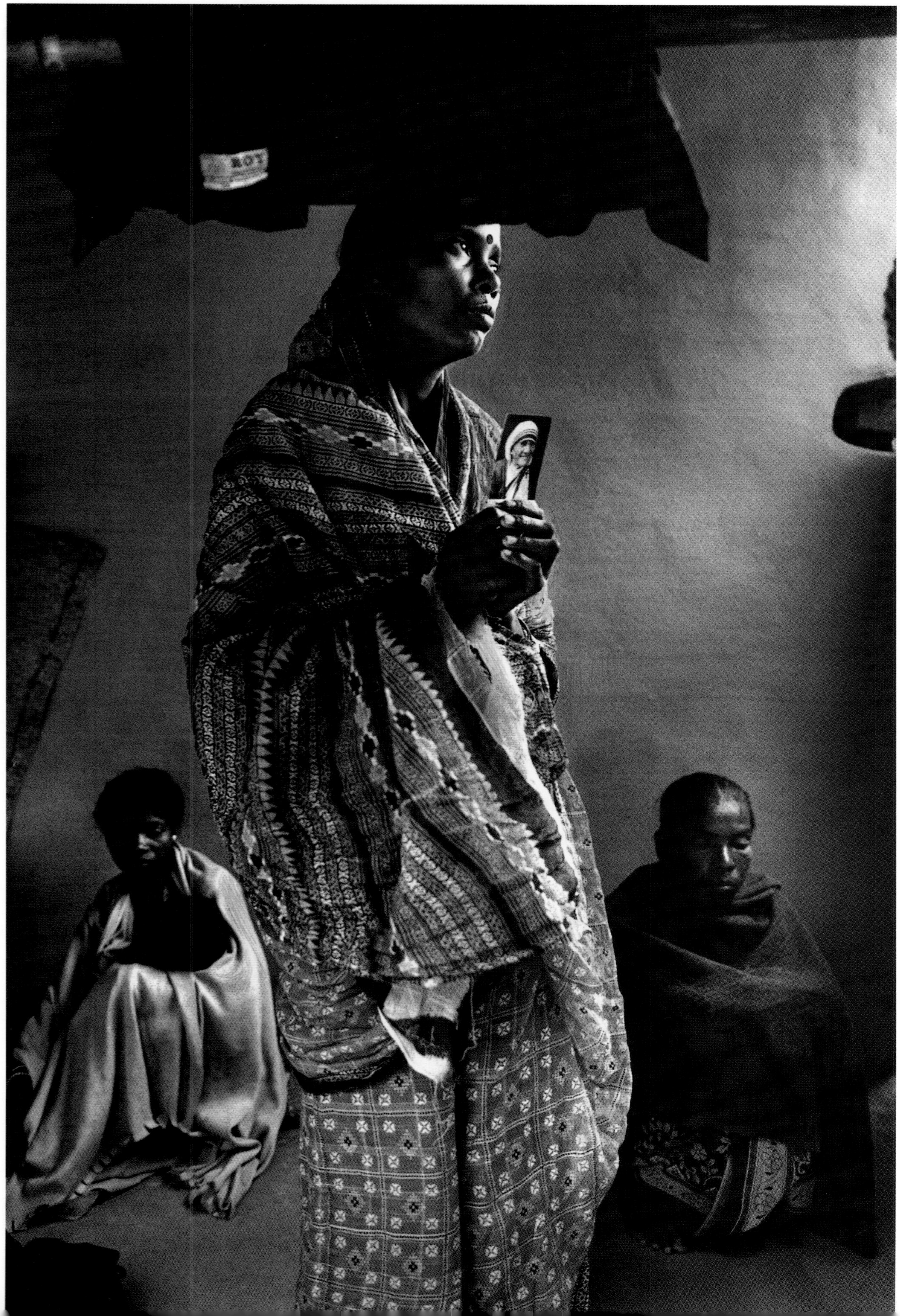

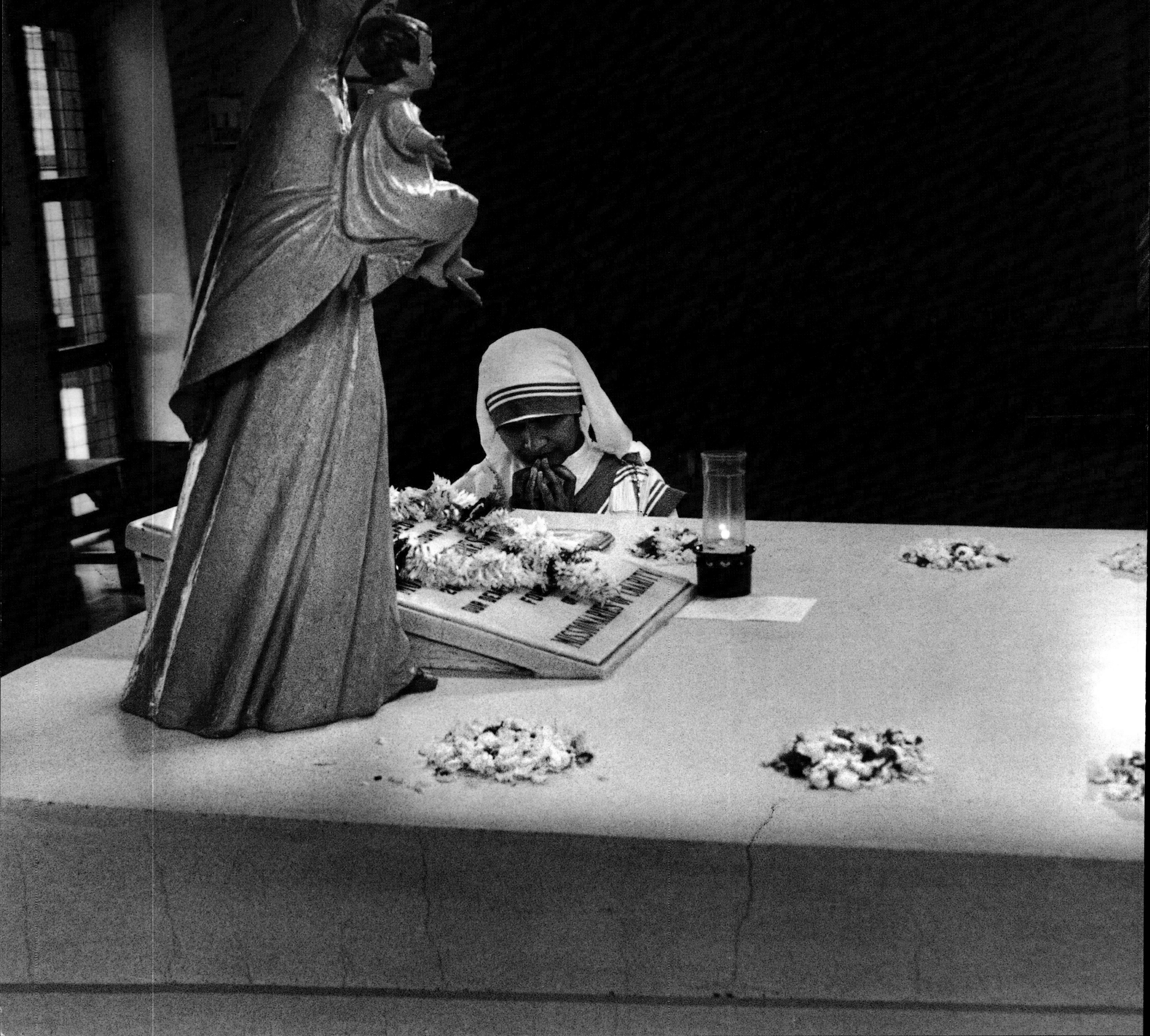

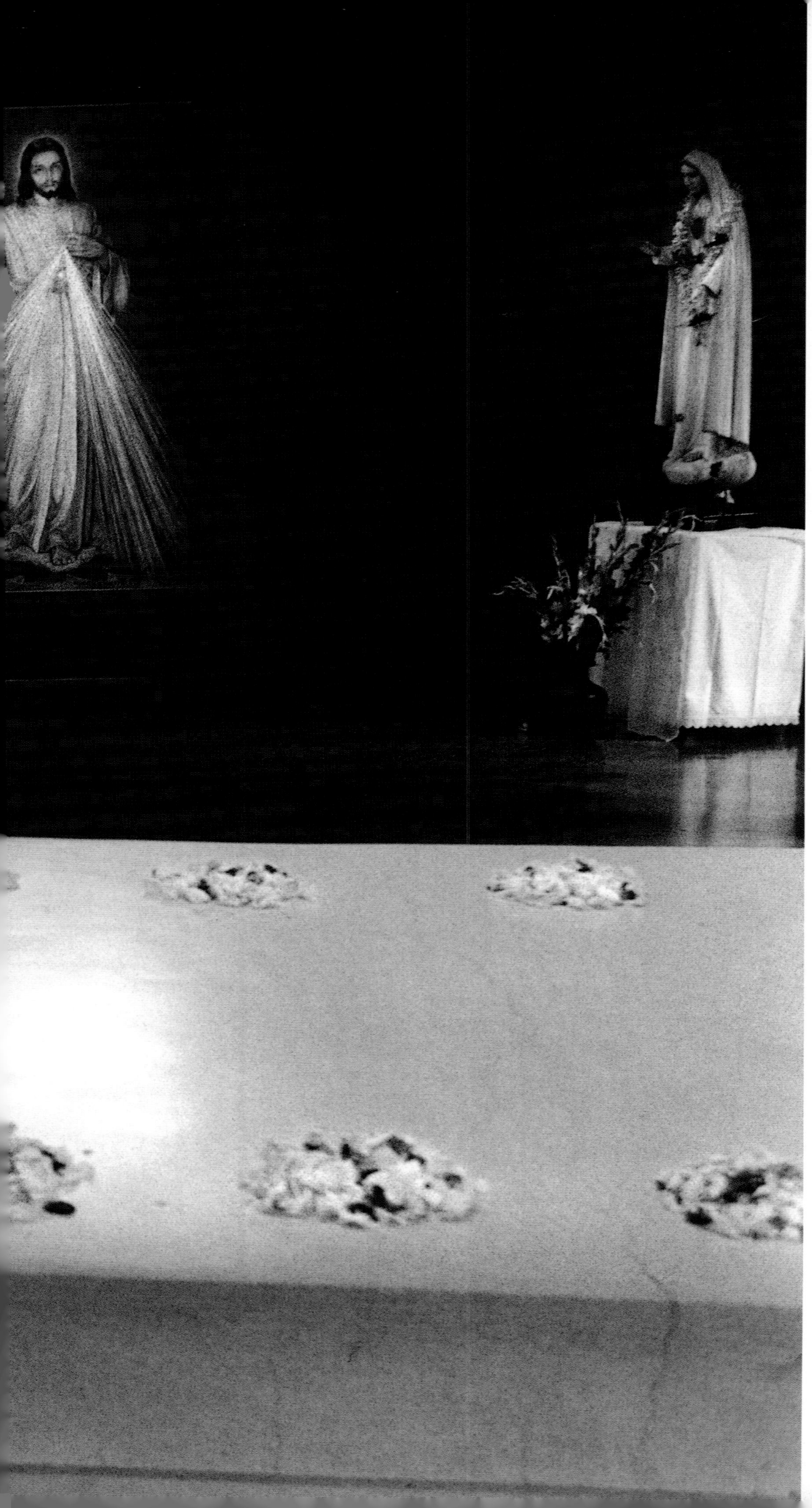

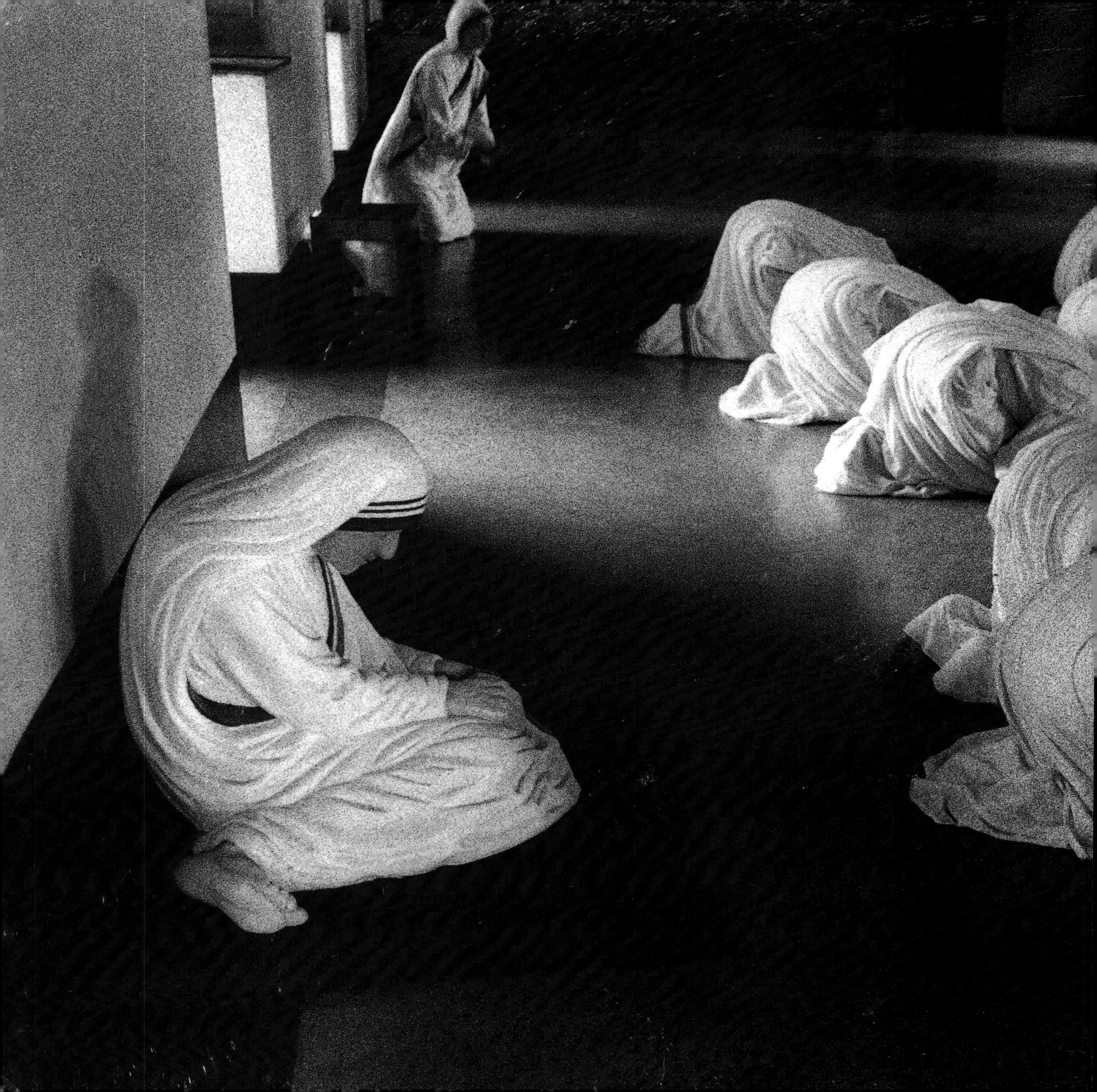

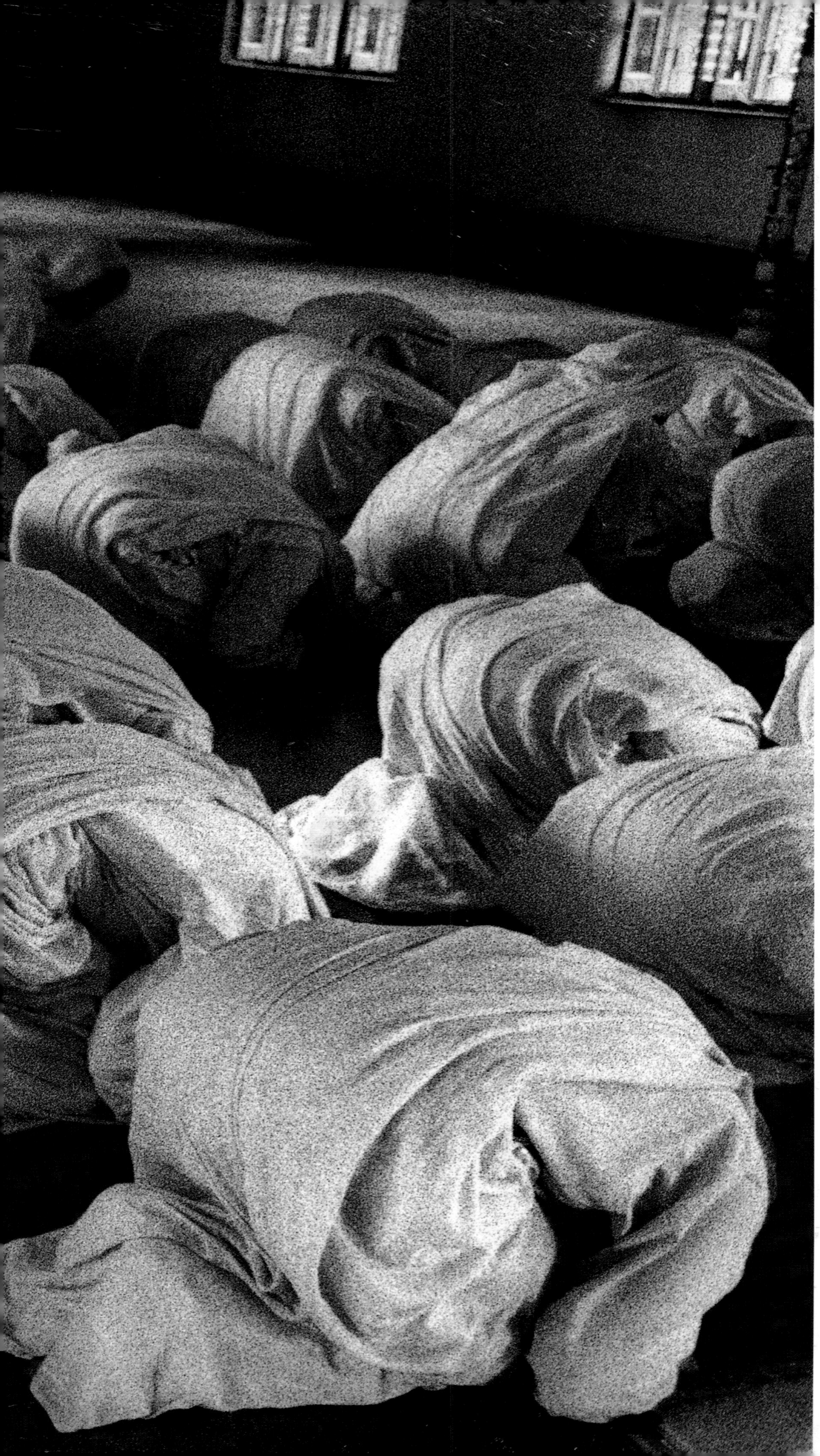

afterword

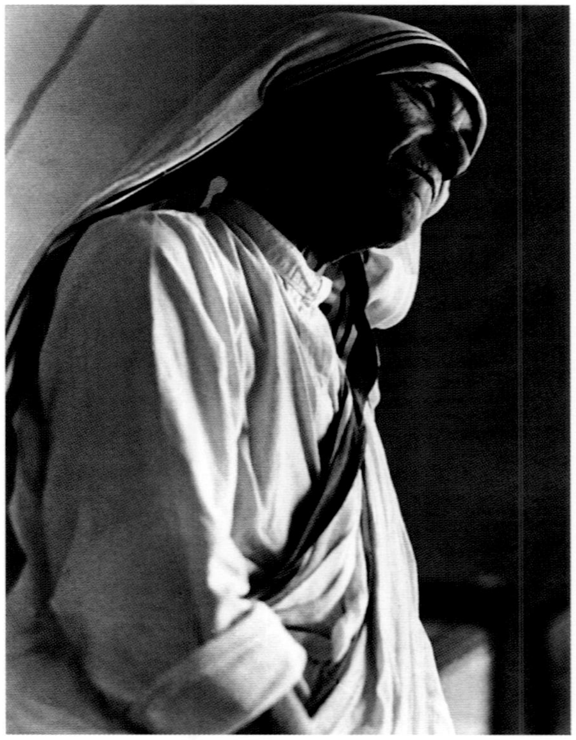

Saints, seers, and sages spend decades deciphering the higher purpose of an otherwise mundane life. Philosophers, men of learning and wisdom, expend their intellectual energies trying to decode the divine purpose behind the process of Creation. Most of their exertions are in vain. Seldom does anyone anywhere come so close to actually leading a life that reveals this divine purpose to ordinary mortals as the Blessed Mother Teresa did during her long years in the service of the poorest of the poor, not only in the slums of Kolkata but virtually all over the world.

Hers was an extraordinary life of selfless dedication.

That this extraordinary life emerged for someone born in everyday circumstances, who never developed pretensions to being extraordinary, leads you to only one conclusion: It is the divine hand that guides the course of events. How else does one explain the fact that Agnes Gonxha Bojaxhiu, born on August 26, 1910 to an Albanian merchant and his wife in faraway Skopje (now in Macedonia), develops an interest in overseas religious missions at the tender age of twelve, and decides that it is her vocation to serve the poor?

Her biographers tell us that young Gonxha (flower bud) was inspired to work in India by reports sent home by Jesuit missionaries in Bengal. At eighteen, she joined the Irish Sisters of Loreto and took the name Teresa in honor of the French saint Thérèse of Lisieux. (Saint Thérèse was renowned for her piety, goodness, and unflinching courage in the face of illness and early death.) After a brief period at Rathfarnham, where she learned English at the order's abbey, Sister Teresa sailed for India. She spent the next seventeen years as a teacher and then as principal of Kolkata's St. Mary's High School. It was on September 10, 1946, during a train journey up to Darjeeling, that she received a "call within a call" in which there was a divine directive for her to move to the slums. "The message was quite clear," she told colleagues. "I was to leave the convent and help the poor whilst living among them. It was an Order."

On both the occasions when she stepped out from her world to take up her vocation, there was a break from the existing order. Her family was a happy one, but there was an inner urge to devote herself to the service of God. It was explained to her that the life of a nun involves difficult choices, but that had been her choice.

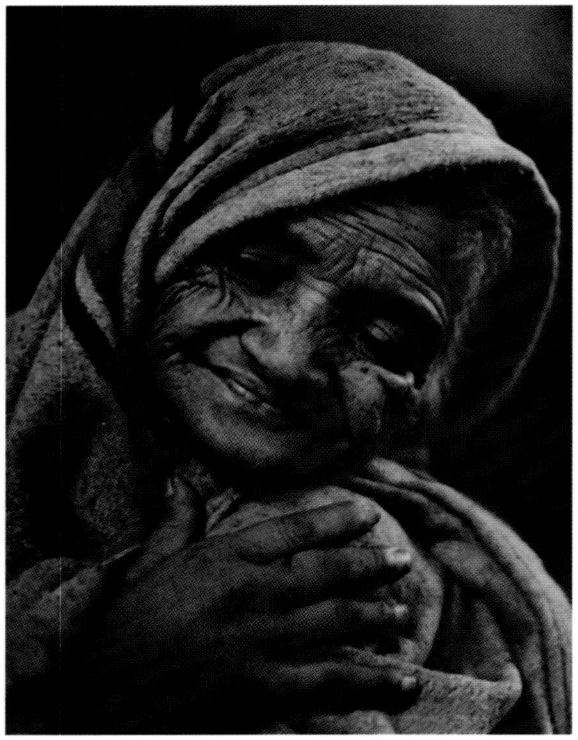

It was the second break from the established career path followed by nuns that actually established her as the different persona that continues to inspire and charm the world, even today. After all, her life as a nun, first as a schoolteacher and then as the principal of a prosperous school, did not offer her the opportunity to actually serve the poor. This life did not involve many sacrifices, and it was secluded, safe, and comfortable.

But the choice of her vocation in "caring for the poorest of the poor", and the location of her service in the hellish slums of Kolkata, actually made her a misfit. It is one thing to theoretically know that "God exists in every person" and quite another to actually bend down to lift a person in acute distress from the streets and nurse him or her with tender motherly care. Such a blending of words and deeds is a rare occurrence in our lifetime. In Mother's case, this went on for more than fifty years, day after day. This act has moved millions, and they have been inspired by her personal example to do at least one act of compassion. That this phenomenon took place in Kolkata—one of India's most densely populated cities—adds a different dimension. Let us not forget that the aggressive defenders of religious faith have always been suspicious of the motives of do-gooders. For them, it is unimportant if their coreligionists die in abject poverty or without care. But they dare not countenance a position where those practicing other faiths make inroads into the constituency of their beliefs. Mother took the first deserted "soul" she found on the streets of Kolkata to the temple at Kalighat. That's how the first home for the destitute and the dying was founded at Kalighat. Her acceptance by people of different faiths only ended up establishing the common bond with our Creator. There is a tendency to disparage Kolkata for its poverty and its lack of infrastructure. But the same Kolkata proved to be a very hospitable place for the Mother. Not only did the people of Kolkata sustain her efforts to help the poorest of the poor, but the flame lit by the Missionaries of Charity from here has been spreading its light all over the world. Today, there are more than forty-five hundred nuns and at least four hundred centers run by them all over the world. By modest estimates, the value of the property belonging to them in India alone is placed at over $75 million (£41 m).

There are overseas centers, like the one in New York, where the nuns are busy throughout the day simply acknowledging donations. There is no dearth of superlative writings about Mother's unparalleled efforts. There is hardly any human award or recognition that has not been conferred upon her. From the Nobel Peace Prize to the Bharat Ratna, she has received them all. Now comes the ultimate honor from the Church—her duly deserved beatification leading to sainthood. Every moment of her life and every nuance of her expression conveys her essential humility, the depth of her understanding, and the almost inexhaustible reserves of patience, love, and compassion that powered her missionary zeal. For believers, there is the concept that God is all pervasive. He is omnipresent. In her inimitable way, she saw this God all around her. "I see God in every human being. When I wash the leper's wounds, I feel I am nursing the Lord Himself. Is it not a beautiful experience?" she asked. It is this humility that made her stand tall and firm in a world that is populated by arrogance, and at a time when people depend on others to think for them. But then she not only had the character to strike out on an uncharted path, she also had the discipline, fortitude, and capacity to literally fight it out in the streets. She faced up to criticism with rancor. She would say, "If you are humble, nothing will touch you, neither praise nor disgrace, because you know what you are." Indeed, it would have been unusual if Mother had not had

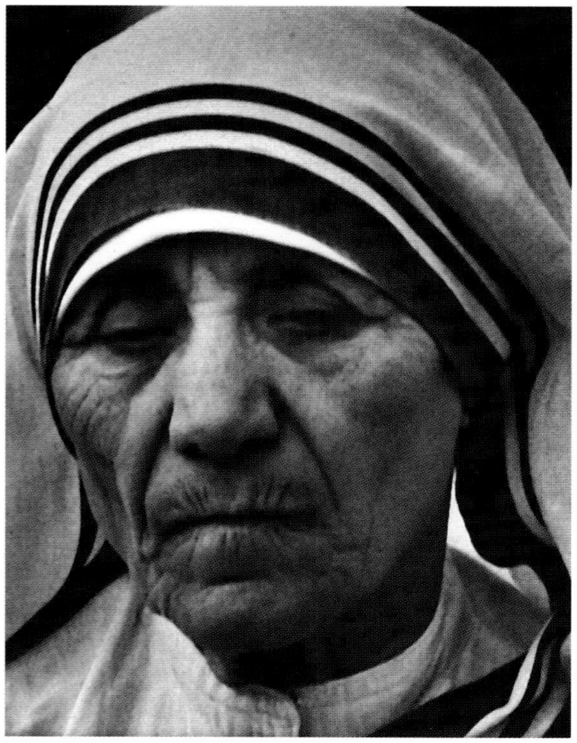

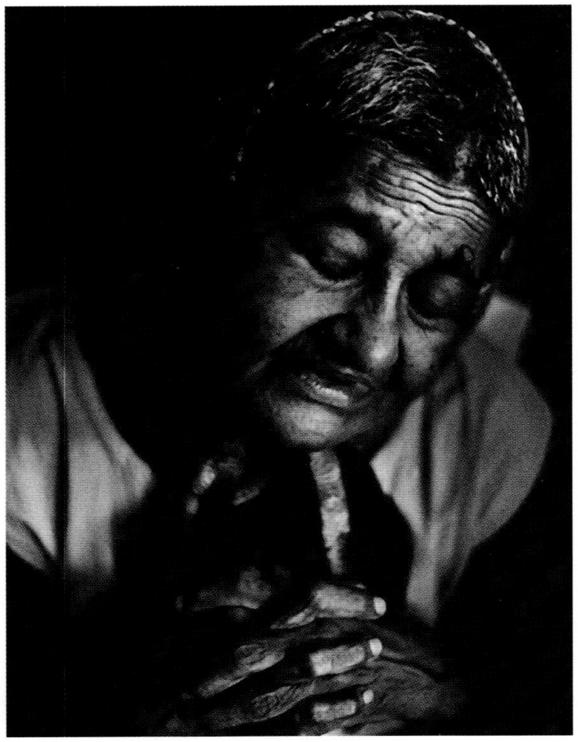

her share of critics. It is simply not human to accept someone so good. We all tend to look for faults in the "goodness" in others. Call it by whatever name you wish, this is a fact of life. There are those who say that she accumulated enormous wealth. There are others who argue that she defended the people who donated money to her cause. Then, there are others who also criticize her practices caring for the poor or running schools. But she had an entirely different perspective on all these mundane provocations. "It was all divine providence because, right from the very first, I didn't ask for money. It was all a gift. I wanted to serve the poor purely for the love of God. I wanted to give the poor what the rich get with money," she used to say.

Mother was equally aware of the fact that her effort to serve the poor was not adequate in the context of the magnitude of the problems of poverty and destitution. "We ourselves feel that what we are doing is just a drop in the ocean. But if that drop was not in the ocean, I think that ocean would be less because of that missing drop. For example, if we didn't have our schools in the slums, there would be none. They are just little primary schools where we teach the children to love and to be clean and so on—if we didn't have these little schools, those children, those thousands of children, would be left in the streets," she said. It is also argued that with the huge gifts Mother received, she could have built perfect institutions in terms of Medicare to address the needs of the dying.

But this sidesteps the core value of poverty that fired the zeal of the Missionaries of Charity. One of the vows for the nuns was, and remains, that of poverty. They make do with just two blue-bordered white cotton saris that are now their trademark uniform. The objective always has been to provide more and more dignity for more and more people, and not to provide high-class care for a limited few. The nuns' approach toward saving money and spending as little as required has to be seen in that context. Besides, as Mother herself clarified during her lifetime, they were just running a home for the poor, and not a hospital. Then again, those who stay at the home were the ones who had been turned down by the hospitals as cases that were beyond help.

Her life was shaped by her commitment to faith and compassion. Her faith in God was an abiding one and not limited by the confines of her religion: Christianity. In that sense, she was not the usual missionary fueled by a passion to have as many converts as possible. Her goal was not in numbers. But then she wanted all of us to come closer to Him. She firmly believed that "there is only one God and He is God to all; therefore, it is important that everyone is seen as equal before God. I've always said we should help a Hindu become a better Hindu, a Muslim become a better Muslim, a Catholic become a better Catholic." It was in the same spirit that she looked upon the nonbelieving communists. As she told a journalist from *Time* magazine: "When I went to China, one of the top officials asked me, 'What is a communist to you?' I said, 'A child of God.' Then on the next morning, the newspapers reported that Mother Teresa said communists are children of God. I was happy because after a long, long time the name God was printed in the papers in China." It was this essential faith that separated Mother from the run-of-the-mill social workers. "Faith is the gift of God. And our work, to be fruitful and to be all for God and beautiful, has to be built on faith. Faith in Christ who has said 'I was hungry, I was naked, I was sick, and I was homeless and He did that for me.' On these words of His, all our work is based," she observed. Devoured as we are by the daily complexities of our existential struggle, it is difficult for us to comprehend the direct simplicity of such overwhelming faith.

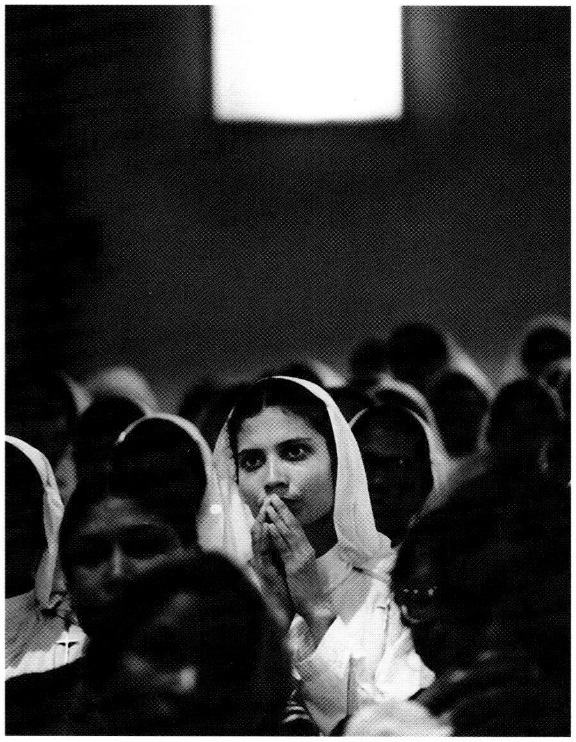

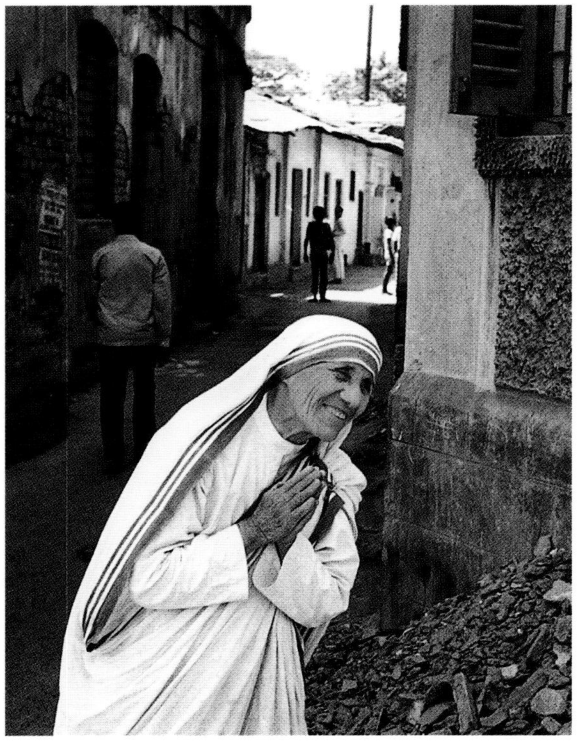

But then, this is not the only zone of our spiritual inability. For us, poverty is just limited to material poverty. For her, there was another more serious dimension to impoverishment that affected the world's rich. She observed, "In the developed countries, there is a poverty of intimacy of spirit, of loneliness, of lack of love. There is no greater sickness today than that one." In her mission to tackle poverty, she is believed to have taught the concept of "touching others" to Princess Diana, the other global icon with whom she shared a special relationship, almost like that of a loving mother with a vulnerable daughter. She also pointed out that we had a lot to learn from the poor. She said, "The poor give us much more than we give them. They are such strong people, living day-to-day with no food, and they never curse, never complain. We don't have to give them pity or sympathy. We have so much to learn from them." That's how Mother Teresa was able to touch the larger world beyond the realm of physical proximity, one of the simple concepts she enunciated. She counseled: "It is not how much we do, but how much love we put in the doing. It is not how much we give, but how much love we put in the giving." In the same spirit, she advised against greed: "The more you have, the more you are occupied, the less you give. But the less you have the more free you are. Poverty for us is a freedom. It is not a mortification, a penance. It is joyful freedom. There is no television here, no this, no that. But we are perfectly happy." A love for the poor and prayers for God were her two most important tools. She explained that the world is not only hungry for bread, but hungry for love, hungry to be wanted, and hungry to be appreciated. And, she added, "If we pray, we will believe. If we believe, we will love. If we love, we will serve."

In fact, for Mother, prayer was also the vehicle for her direct communication with God. It was with these tools that she was able to instill the same sense of patience and service among the nuns who chose to join her order. That her order could attract forty-five hundred sisters is essentially a tribute to the intrinsic merit of her simple path—service to the poor and prayer. That she could persuade these women to give up their homes and step into a world of poverty and service with no rewards, in the accepted sense of the term, reveals the magnetism of her personality. Her motto in serving the poor was very simple: "Let's do something beautiful for God." Then, all her life she went on to demonstrate that doing something beautiful for God is very simple. You just have to believe that actions speak louder than words. You do not have to articulate complex philosophies conveyed via complex vocabularies for that purpose. When her first biographer, Malcolm Muggeridge, asked her with mock incredulity, "You mean that the road to faith and the road to God is via our fellow human beings?" she replied, "Because we cannot see Christ, we cannot express our love to Him. But our neighbors we can always see, and we can do for them what—if we saw Him—we would like to do for Christ . . . in the slums, in the broken body, in the children, we see Christ and we touch Him." All of us could be doing something beautiful for God if only we had the ability to find our God in such a simple way.

glow of His glory: a spiritual energy that never dimmed

Mother, we first met in the early 1970s when you were less known to the world outside. But you, who left us the other day, were the same simple, loving spirit engaged in selflessness. Mother, you never fluctuated as a human being nor dimmed as a spiritual energy. You taught me that humanness and spirituality are indistinguishable. And today, I am the more blessed, for in you I learned that the glow of His glory never diminishes.

acknowledgments

Inderjit Badhwar, Dr. Savyasaachi, Anil Sharma, Jane Perkins, Kalidas, Rajinder Singh, Tushar Chakravarty, Paromita Desarkar, Chandan Ahuja, Amit Chaudan, Brenda McSweeny, and my wife Gurmeet Rai

★

All the sisters of the Missionaries of Charity

Saint Mother
Each time I met her
She restored me to myself . . .

This book is dedicated to
THAT LIGHT
The light of spiritual energy and compassion
That never dimmed or fluctuated

Raghu Rai

Project Manager, English-language edition:
Céline Moulard

Jacket design, English-language edition:
Michael J. Walsh Jr.

Design Coordinator, English-language edition:
Rita Jules

Production Coordinator, English-language edition:
Kaija Markoe

Library of Congress Control Number: 2004110005

Published in 2005 by Harry N. Abrams, Incorporated, New York.

Printed and bound in France
10 9 8 7 6 5 4 3 2 1

HARRY N. ABRAMS, INC.
100 FIFTH AVENUE
NEW YORK, N.Y. 10011
WWW.ABRAMSBOOKS.COM

ABRAMS IS A SUBSIDIARY OF
LA MARTINIÈRE GROUPE